THE GERMAN CABARET
LEGACY IN AMERICAN
POPULAR MUSIC

ALSO BY WILLIAM FARINA
AND FROM MCFARLAND

---

*Eliot Asinof and the Truth of the Game:
A Critical Study of the Baseball Writings* (2012)

*Chrétien de Troyes and the Dawn
of Arthurian Romance* (2010)

*Perpetua of Carthage: Portrait of a
Third-Century Martyr* (2009)

*Ulysses S. Grant, 1861–1864: His Rise
from Obscurity to Military Greatness* (2007)

*De Vere as Shakespeare: An Oxfordian
Reading of the Canon* (2006)

THE GERMAN CABARET LEGACY IN AMERICAN POPULAR MUSIC

William Farina

McFarland & Company, Inc., Publishers
Jefferson, North Carolina, and London

LIBRARY OF CONGRESS CATALOGUING-IN-PUBLICATION DATA

Farina, William, 1955–
　　The German cabaret legacy in American popular music /
William Farina.
　　　　p.　　cm.
　　Includes bibliographical references and index.

　　ISBN 978-0-7864-6863-8
　　softcover : acid free paper ∞

　　1. Popular music — United States — History and criticism.
　　2. Music — Germany — 20th century — History and criticism.
　　3. Music — United States — German influences.　I. Title.
ML3477.F36　2013
781.640943'0973 — dc23　　　　　　　　　　2012049983

BRITISH LIBRARY CATALOGUING DATA ARE AVAILABLE

On the cover: Louis Armstrong and Marlene Dietrich at the Riviera
Hotel in Las Vegas, Nevada on February 19, 1962 (Associated Press)

Manufactured in the United States of America

*McFarland & Company, Inc., Publishers
　Box 611, Jefferson, North Carolina 28640
　　www.mcfarlandpub.com*

To the German and Jewish American
communities of the Upper Midwest

Acknowledgments

Thanks to Marion Buckley, my patient partner in life, for helping to keep me on the right track. Once again thanks to Phillip and Kathleen Farina for lending me books and encouragement. Thanks to Nancy Seeger for reading portions of my draft manuscript and making useful suggestions. Thanks again to Jerome Bloom for pointing me in productive directions. Thanks to the staff at the Sherman and Ruth Weiss Community Library in Hayward, Wisconsin, for your consistently enthusiastic professionalism. Special thanks to all of the working writers and performers who shared their valuable insights and comments, especially Kevin McMullin, Randy Wydra, Eva Apelqvist, Jill Hoffman, Marlene Hogue, and Stewart Figa.

Table of Contents

Introduction

"Cabaret was an ephemeral art, and its material remains are widely scattered."— Peter Jelavich[1]

During the summer of 2011, a gala theatrical event for Duluth, Minnesota, was yet another revival run of the now classic 1966 American musical *Cabaret*. Not only is this landmark in the history of stage and cinema becoming more contemporary with each passing decade, its popular appeal seems to be widening as well. The location is also noteworthy, not being Broadway or Hollywood or Chicago, but rather, *Duluth*, a comparatively small Midwestern city not normally noted for offerings of risqué entertainment.[2] Nevertheless, audiences flocked to the sold-out Spirit of the North Theatre at Fitger's Inn and Brewhouse to experience an art form pioneered in Weimar Germany during the late 1920s and early 1930s. No doubt few were even aware of these distant stylistic origins, despite the story making repeated, overt references to *Nationalsozialist* political ascendancy during that particular time and place. What audiences certainly would have appreciated was the brilliant, off-beat, and subversive appeal of the cabaret musical style, as updated by and filtered through the songwriting genius of John Kander and Fred Ebb.

The Duluth production was not an isolated occurrence. Less than a century after the *Kabarett* style first startled and delighted German nightclub patrons with an innovative, audacious blend of foreign borrowings and domestic topicality, it has since become a world-wide phenomenon.[3] Students of music history may recall that when modern cabaret first appeared in Weimar Germany during the 1920s, no one had ever before seen anything quite like it. The singing style had itself originated in the Paris nightclubs of Montmartre during the 19th century *Belle Époque*. The distinctive German version, however, emerging in the humiliating aftermath of World War I, was a strange amalgamation of French *chanson réaliste* ("realistic song"), American jazz, burlesque dance, standup comedy, outlandish vaudeville, and provocateur performance art, all laced with a heavy (and sometimes lethal) dose of sharp-edged,

1

socio-political commentary. Love songs were plentiful as well, but often unconventional. By the time Kurt Weill's *Die Dreigroschenoper* ("The Threepenny Opera") became a smash sensation in 1928, German *Kabarett* had progressed from being a hybrid mutation of Jazz Age models into perhaps the most revolutionary new form of music drama since Richard Wagner's *Gesamtkunstwerk* ("art encompassing all of the arts"). From street level, cabaret seemed to be the true music of the future, and possibly the first exponent of "world" or "cross-over" music taking its initial cue from the American vernacular.

By the mid–1930s, however, the glory days of German cabaret had been forcibly suppressed by the rising Nazi regime, which declared it a breeding ground for *entartete Musik* ("degenerate music"). Some three decades later, after another World War had been fought and when McCarthyism began to subside in the U.S., a successful English-language revival of *The Threepenny Opera* resulted in countless popular recordings of "Mack the Knife." *Threepenny* also won an unlikely Tony Award for Weill's widow and long-time muse Lotte Lenya, who would later sign on as a key cast member for the original Broadway production of *Cabaret*. Thus the updated musical legacy of Weimar made its indelible impression on the young up-and-coming American songwriting team of Kander and Ebb, both of whose families were German-Jewish in ancestry but whose forebears escaped to the New World before the horrors of early 20th century Europe took hold. Back in 1933, however, most German cabaret artists had to run for their lives. One was a still relatively young (but by then notorious) Marlene Dietrich, both an early, outspoken critic of Adolf Hitler and bona fide movie celebrity, thanks to her unapologetic, femme fatale persona so memorably introduced in the 1930 Josef von Sternberg masterpiece *Der Blaue Engel* ("The Blue Angel"). Two decades later, Dietrich the Hollywood film diva played a significant role inventing modern day Las Vegas while providing inspiration for a whole new generation of English-language songwriters such as Lennon-McCartney and Bacharach-David.

If German cabaret in its original incarnation was stamped out overnight, its powerful resurgence during the latter half of the 20th century was even more dramatic and defiant. Nevertheless, the worldwide popularity of the genre remains curiously un-remarked upon to date. Any cursory survey of contemporary American popular music will reveal the staggering, quantitative influence of Weimar cabaret's cultural legacy. After the revival of *The Threepenny Opera* cleaned up on Broadway for nearly seven years, Kander and Ebb picked up the ball and continued the tradition with a string of provocative musicals over the next four decades that, to varying degrees, all paid homage to this unique aesthetic. Within the sphere of musical theater alone, their work has created a huge ripple effect. Concurrent with this trend, the posthumous reputation of Kurt Weill has enjoyed continuous and growing veneration, beginning with jazz musicians, and extending into the realm of 1960s and 1970s pop music. Thanks to performers like Bob Dylan — an admirer of Lotte Lenya since his Greenwich Village days — topical themes have found a permanent place in American song lyrics (see Chapter 18). By the early 1970s, even African American soul music had caught the spirit of serious social consciousness. A massive Motown hit such as Marvin Gaye's *What's Going On* (1971) owes much to that which preceded it in terms of its scaled-back, atmospheric production combined with a running commentary on the times — a musical approach pioneered during the 1920s by many now forgotten German artists. Today, the successful transcontinental careers of Ute Lemper and Max Raabe are difficult to imagine without *Kabarett* models of the past. In the final analysis — and this will be underscored herein — the cabaret ethos represents a long continuum. What may be perceived as French or German in origins can actually be traced to earlier times; what later found full flower in the U.S. has now turned into a worldwide phenomenon.

A Microcosm of the World

As in this author's previous book projects, this study represents somewhat of a personal journey. Shortly after a recent job relocation to remote northwestern Wisconsin (with Duluth as the nearest urban center), all misconceptions of the area were quickly swept aside. Despite an undeserved reputation as a backwater, Duluth in fact is home to a thriving community theater scene, among many other regional attractions. Closer inspection revealed that, in addition to being the birthplace of Robert Zimmerman (aka Bob Dylan), Duluth has a long established German-Jewish community that, among other charitable activities, is a vigorous supporter of the performing arts.[4] This local heritage constantly manifests itself in small ways. One of the downtown entertainment district restaurants, Zeitgeist, is named after a German coinage translating roughly as "spirit of the times." This word first found widespread usage in Berlin during the Roaring Twenties, a time in which modern *Kabarett* was first being invented and popularized.[5] Duluth's continuing enthusiasm for German *Kleinkunst* ("miniature art forms") can still be seen in other popular local attractions, such as the annual "Cabaret" fundraiser for the Duluth Festival Opera, Le Cirque Rouge Cabaret and Burlesque Show at the Teatro Zuccone, and the Vocal Jazz Cabaret at the Clyde Iron Works, to name just a few.[6]

In the larger scheme of things, contemporary Duluth has become a microcosm of world performance art. This fascinating localized aspect inexorably leads to broader, more universal topics of interest; moreover, the cabaret "zeitgeist" appears more topically relevant than ever. This study will not be about the music from a mere technical standpoint or strict literary examination of song content. Not being a musician and, at best, musically semi-literate (i.e., barely able to read a hymnal), it would be well beyond the personal expertise of this writer to attempt such analysis. Instead, this study shall be written from the viewpoint of an enthusiastic fan and amateur historian. In any event, this project seeks a wider readership than working musicians or musicologists. Anyone during the late 20th century not touched by cabaret music was simply not listening, for it permeates our entire sphere of entertainment. This is not to say that we always knew where the style came from, or even necessarily thought of it as a style. On the other hand, it was certainly there, it affected our society, and therefore should be written about. Above all, emphasis will be placed upon raising reader appreciation for this important form of expression which appears more relevant than ever in today's unstable world.

The author's first personal exposure to this kind of music came as a child listening to Bobby Darin's 1959 hit recording of "Mack the Knife"—a catchy, likeable song even if one has no idea what the translated words mean (see Chapter 4).[7] As a budding pre-teen lover of rock 'n' roll, however, there was no missing the excitement and danger in Darin's performance. Thus many baby boomers first came into contact with cabaret, unknowingly and indirectly through AM radio hit parade. Half a century later, this book project came to fruition, originally as homage to the incomparable Duke Ellington — whose compositional work defines 20th century American music — then as a tribute to the late Fred Ebb — whose song lyrics rank among the very best of those produced by any Broadway songsmith.[8] Finally, Ellington and Ebb led straightaway to *entartete Musik* and cabaret. In effect, more recent creative teams such as Kander and Ebb achieved prominence by re-popularizing a foreign performance style originally influenced by American jazz composers such as Ellington.

Debatable Definitions

In more recent years some highly accomplished American scholars have attempted to define the *Kabarett* style and identify various widespread misconceptions attached to its legacy. Peter Jelavich of John Hopkins University provides a list of essential characteristics that, nevertheless, might also describe many forms of American counterculture entertainment. These main features include (1) a small venue and stage with audiences seated at tables and having direct eye contact with performers, (2) short five to 10-minute performances including songs, skits, monologues, dances, pantomimes, puppet shows, and films, (3) satire or parody on sex, commerce, culture, or politics, (4) acts presented by professional performers and writers, and (5) performances presided over by a *conférencier* (today commonly referred to as a master of ceremonies or emcee).[9] This seemingly specific, common-sense definition, however, runs into trouble the moment one takes a closer look at either past or present incarnations. For example, it could well describe any contemporary club culture at home or abroad. One could argue that the important role of *conférencier* might as easily apply to a modern-day hip-hop emcee as to the 19th century French models upon which its German counterpart was later based. In fact, even cabaret's emphasis on shortness of performance time length — usually considered its most distinctive trait — breaks down once we consider the more lengthy, more elaborate, and thematically-connected Berlin revues of the late 1920s designed for larger theaters and serving as a crucial springboard for the career of Marlene Dietrich.[10] Jelavich wisely concludes by qualifying: "...pure cabaret was rare, and when it miraculously appeared, it was short-lived."[11]

Alan Lareau of the University of Wisconsin has perceptively noted that no matter how hard one attempts to pinpoint the distinctive hallmarks of cabaret, good exceptions to the rule can always seemingly be identified:

> Cabaret is a theatrical form using a mixture of small forms; the term is derived from a divided serving plate or hors d'oeuvres tray, offering a little bit of something for everybody. Accordingly, a cabaret program is a series of individual numbers, including dances, poems, songs, comic monologues, impersonations, sketches, and one-acts. Traditionally, these shows take place in a small theater or pub, with the audience seated at tables, eating and drinking during the performance — yet there are many instances of cabarets with traditional theater seating. Satire, which critiques reality by contrasting it with a norm or ideal to usually humorous effect, is indeed a popular tool in many cabarets, but cabaret need not necessarily be satirical. Nor must satire be progressive or leftist, as is often assumed in these portrayals.[12]

What gets many commentators into analytical trouble on this topic are attempts to define the *Kabarett* style too narrowly — or to define it all. To try and characterize "pure" cabaret as, say, Trude Hesterberg's Wild Stage, or the Kadeko, or Dietrich's *The Blue Angel*, or Weill's *The Threepenny Opera*, is perhaps to assay the wrong question. Ultimately, one cannot precisely define cabaret, but therein certainly lies its wide appeal and special greatness. One may well argue that the true timelessness and durability of cabaret are to be found in its inherent resistance to any particular rigid definition, despite certain generic features obvious to most audiences. Better questions to ask, it would seem, are how distinctive traits of this older art form have affected modern popular culture, and whether these will continue to do so in the future.

Both Jelavich and Lareau usefully remind us that most non-specialist perceptions of cabaret have been shaped by images not representing cabaret in the strict historical sense. In regard to artists such as Dietrich and her big screen portrayal of Lola Lola, or Liza Minnelli's portrayal of Sally Bowles, or even the famed songwriting team of Weill and Brecht, Jelavich proclaims: "None of these figures, however, corresponded to cabaret as it was understood at that time." Noting for example that Bertolt Brecht only made one documented appearance in a Berlin cabaret, Jelavich observes that Brecht eventually secured his permanent reputation as a poet-playwright and not as a live stage performer. Then he acknowledges another, perhaps more important side of the same coin: "Although these figures cannot be equated with cabaret, it would not be wrong to link them with cabaret's environment." By the end of his opening remarks, Jelavich discerningly concludes:

> Finally, it can be said that although Brecht and Weill did not write for cabaret, they were part of a wider culture of satirical, mildly critical, often cynical songwriting which found its best expression on cabaret stages. Lola Lola, Sally Bowles, and Brecht and Weill were, in short, on the boundaries of cabaret. And those boundaries were very fluid.[13]

"Boundaries" is the key word here, for that is what cabaret is all about, as we shall see throughout this study. The music dramas of Weill and the film performances of Dietrich, though neither really representative of *Kabarett* in its authentic original form, were nonetheless the two main vehicles by which distinctive elements of German cabaret eventually reached deep into the international consciousness. Lareau, though assigning a more disciplined descriptor to *Kabarett* (epitomized by the Berlin literary cabarets of the early 1920s), admits that the serious opera work of Weill, Dietrich's film performance in *The Blue Angel*, and even 1920s German pop tunes, have all come to represent cabaret in the popular imagination, even for Germans.[14] Specialists now more or less agree that terms such as the French-derived "cabaret" and German *Kabarett* today have separate meanings, whereas at the time these were used interchangeably. Nowadays (at least in Germany), "cabaret" tends to mean strip show while *Kabarett* represents the pure and more literary art form that found full expression during the Weimar era of 1919–1933.[15]

And yet there are still many good counterarguments. Sternberg's provincially set Blue Angel performances on film are fairly faithful re-creations of the German *Tingel Tangel* (see Chapter 1), a direct 19th century precursor of *Kabarett*. Sternberg had also carefully assembled a stellar team of veteran performers with unimpeachable *Kabarett* credentials. If *The Blue Angel* was not true cabaret, then it certainly was designed to fool people into believing that it was. The same might also easily be said for Weill and Brecht's *Threepenny Opera*, whose original 1928 cast, besides Lotte Lenya, featured a number of established cabaret performers, several of whom would go on to appear in the masterwork 1931 film version by G.W. Pabst. Once again, it seems that one cannot separate alleged pure *Kabarett* from the popular film and stage works helping to shape its public perception. Nor is it easy to distinguish *Kabarett* from its approximate American counterpart, exemplified by the Cotton Club of New York City — the same venue in which Duke Ellington first made a national name for himself. At a glance, the main difference with home-grown American cabaret would seem to be an understandable submersion or restraint of political combativeness on the part of African Americans in pre–Civil Rights era entertainment. Then again, politics are nowhere to be found in the low-brow *Tingel Tangel* universe of the Blue Angel.

Themes and Attitudes

Perhaps the best way to understand the cabaret style is to return to the notion of boundaries. When asked what qualities he associated with cabaret, Kevin McMullin, a respected and highly knowledgeable working musician in northwest Wisconsin, first evoked the visual image of smoky nightclub atmosphere patronized by clientele representing a diverse cross-section of society. As for musical style, cabaret to him suggested what he described as "borderland" music of ambiguity, including a generous use of major-minor key combinations. Pointing to recordings by Dietrich, he suggested her artistic greatness resided not in mere technical singing skills (which, by her own admission, were quite modest), but rather in a confident delivery that never seemed to desert her over the course of half a century. To be sure, whenever Dietrich walked on to a stage, she owned it; this innate quality was captured on film by some very good movie directors on more than one occasion. If there was ever a performer who occupied the "borderland" of respectability, it was Marlene Dietrich.

Kevin also highlighted another one of cabaret's distinctive associations, namely, its perceived (and very real) Jewish ethnicity. Although Marlene Dietrich was not Jewish, many if not most cabaret stars in Weimar were, and all of them without exception, along with most anyone associated with them, eventually suffered grievously for it at the hands of the Nazis. The reasons for this obvious connection are manifold, including a traditional Jewish identification with African American music, from which in turn cabaret took some of its original inspiration. Both generously utilized Old Testament themes and imagery as an oppressed, disdained minority living within and apart from mainstream society (see Chapter 2). There was also the indisputable fact that many of the best musicians in central Europe during this era were Jewish, the same period in which cabaret first took off with mainstream popularity. The improvisational ethos of Yiddish Klezmer, as well as its energetic, uninhibited exuberance, had well prepared many of these artists for similar musical values inherent in American jazz.[16] As Cole Porter, a non–Jewish American song-writing genius, once famously quipped to Richard Rodgers (in the form of a mock threat), "I'll write good Jewish tunes"— a sly reference to most of his creative competitors in both America and Europe. Indeed, it is impossible to discuss the origins and vast influence of cabaret without a detailed analysis of its many distinctive ethnic inflections, both Jewish and African American.

Most commentary on the historical development of cabaret music has tended to gloss over prevalent themes and attitudes typically found within the songs themselves. This is unfortunate because "attitude" may be cabaret's most singular, enduring trait. Among scholars, Weimar historian Peter Gay of Yale University has made a good attempt at summarizing the qualities that made all art created from this period, including cabaret, so enthralling and fresh: "The excitement that characterized Weimar culture stemmed in part from exuberant creativity and experimentation; but much of it was anxiety, fear, a rising sense of doom.... Weimar culture was the creation of outsiders, propelled by history into the inside, for a short, dizzying, fragile moment."[17] Gay succinctly notes that "The exile holds an honored place in the history of Western civilization."[18] Thus a good part of continuing interest in the origins of *Kabarett* has to do with our knowledge that these artists lived in a very stressful time and place, and most would eventually be forced to make a personal choice between exile or death. These features recall McMullin's portrait of cabaret as "borderland" music — songs ambiguous both in musical keys and lyrical meaning, created by artists who, more often than not, came from the margins of society. These same artists somehow managed to briefly find a wide audience, usually by venturing into the margins or boundaries of style noted by Professor Jelavich, before their own society turned violently against them.

In studying the recurring themes and attitudes of cabaret, one must realize that the music's staying power and irrepressible energy was fed by the catastrophic political events playing out all around it. In listening to recordings from the period or, for that matter, later interpretations of the same songs, it is difficult to miss a sheer sense of joy and spiritual release in the performances. This quality is even more remarkable given that cabaret has never held itself out as religious or sacred in character, despite having spiritual roots in the Expressionist movement of the early 20th century (see Chapter 9). Like its sacred counterpart, cabaret music often displays great emotional gravitas and depth while generally ignoring institutionalized religion, except occasionally to criticize it as an instrument of political mischief. In both genres, topical music and lyrics are often used to reassure frightened or nervous listeners that they are not alone in their controversial attitudes or beliefs, as well as to provide incentive for social interaction. Such is the joy of all good music, including cabaret.

Cabaret song lyrics are frequently stereotyped as strictly agitprop or politically liberal in content. Scholars have taken issue with this narrow characterization, noting that political themes in fact represented a fairly small sampling of total song output.[19] Modern listeners tend to forget that unrestrained political commentary in 1920s Germany, even after the official lifting of censorship, could be a very risky and life-threatening proposition. As most people know, the Nazis were committing murder long before attaining full power; on the other hand, as many others do not seem to realize, life in Germany after the Great War was precarious for just about everyone in every way. Street violence was commonplace and easily provoked. Given such a volatile environment, it is impressive that many songs did in fact venture strong political content. Performers were often brave, if not fearless. In the case of those who were committed Marxists (of which there were a significant number), outside observers might well view them either as deliberately suicidal or incredibly foolish (see Chapter 7). Above all, prevalent *Kabarett* themes should be properly viewed as boundless and unpredictable rather than narrowly restricted to any single or small group of topics. For enthusiastic audiences, cabaret's overriding mantra was one of surprise and delight.

Of all the non-political subject matter found within the songs, arguably the most prevalent was the theme of illusion, unsurprising given that Weimar audiences and performers were living in an unstable and dangerous society. Most patrons were paying to escape from reality, not be reminded of it. Illusion itself was occasionally offered explicitly to audiences as a commodity for sale (see Chapter 12). In between the escapism, however, if a talented artist or group of artists were involved and decided to take risks, then remarkable moments of social and political exegesis could transpire, however briefly. Not only would politicians be the target of stinging barbs but sometimes the voters who elected them as well. Intentional insults aimed at the audience were not unusual, and it is remarkable how often these were taken in seemingly good cheer.[20] Other targets included mindless consumerism, unbridled greed, physical vanity, intellectual pretense, and every other human folly, foible and vice that could be catalogued. No one was safe from the satire of cabaret, not even the performers.

And then of course there was sex — usually lots of it. Authentic cabaret sometimes meant little more than striptease, and still does, many would say. On a somewhat higher plane, the persona of femme fatale or vamp was *de rigueur* for many female performers, and songs were accordingly tailored to fit this desired image.[21] Love and physical attraction tended to be portrayed as fleeting things. Unfaithfulness was normal and monogamy non-existent. Alternative sexuality in all of its variations was often explored matter-of-factly and sometimes embraced. Add a deliberate overlay of levity, buffoonery, and hi-jinks, and one begins to get a picture of typical cabaret "love" songs. Closely attaching to this newly open sexual freedom were women's rights, thus overtly linking sex and politics, not for the first or last time in history, but never more emphatically than in Weimar.[22] In *Tamerlan*, a highly effective, disturbing song written by Rudolf Nelson and Kurt Tucholsky (both Jews, the latter writing under an alias, not an unusual occurrence either), a sympathetic *chanteuse* admits being physically attracted to a powerful Hitler-like dictator. Is this song intended to be ironic or not? One could debate the question endlessly, as no doubt the authors intended. From this work, one should get a good sense of how ambiguous and fluid boundaries can become in the cabaret worldview, especially with respect to matters of love. And (lest we forget) in cabaret, the boy and girl *never* live happily ever after.

Cabaret and the Classical Tradition

Another way to better appreciate how different German *Kabarett* was from its predecessors (and many of its successors as well) is to contrast it with other contemporary styles, many of which enjoyed significant popularity during the same time period. Exhibit A in this regard are the late Romantic operatic works of Richard Wagner. By the early 20th century, Wagner's grandiose, original style had achieved undisputed dominance inside the world of classical music, spilling over notably into the popular realm. Wagner was, after all, Hitler's favorite composer. Wagnerian Romanticism also found its way into Hollywood as newly exiled Jewish composers brought their own version of lush, large-scale orchestral works to the American big screen. Safe to say that very few attentive listeners have failed to be seduced by Wagner's overwhelming art at one time or another; many, however (including this one), have had some second thoughts after the seduction. Brilliant, thrilling technical innovation is certainly there, but mature emotional content is a questionable proposition at best. To find this latter quality, listeners must turn to other sources, and one of these is cabaret.

It should be added that cabaret artists were not the only ones at the time rebelling against the homogeneity of the Wagnerian aesthetic (see Chapter 1). Within the classical repertory, the most prominent dissidents against 19th century Romanticism were members of the Second Viennese School, led by the formidable Arnold Schoenberg. The problem with the new compositional language of 12-tone was that it could never reach a wide audience, at least not in the near future. Simultaneously, in America, an exciting melting pot of utterly original forms was beginning to reach deep into the popular consciousness. Some of these included jazz, blues, gospel, country, folk, and Broadway musicals — all propelled by the new technological mediums of film, sound, and radio. As fabulous as all of these were, however, they had little to do (at least initially) with the adult complexity or international outlook of *Kabarett*. It was left to the performing artists of Weimar to incorporate these and other diverse elements into a completely new sensibility that would quickly rebound back to America and beyond, even as it seemed to be extinguished by outraged fascist authorities.

Historical Overview

For those readers needing a quick refresher on historical context, the trajectory of the Weimar Republic can be briefly summarized. After Germany's devastating defeat in World War I (1914–1918), the Kaiser fled into exile and the oppressive terms of the Versailles or Paris Peace Treaty (1919) were imposed on the loser by its vindictive former foes. Following a failed (and violently suppressed) Marxist takeover in 1919, Germany sank into a prolonged period of widespread chaos and near anarchy, subsiding only somewhat with the stabilization of the German mark in 1924 and the election of war hero Field Marshal Paul von Hindenburg as Weimar president in 1925. Thanks mainly to economic prosperity throughout the Western world during the late 1920s, Germany enjoyed a brief respite of comparative calm and prosperity.

Then in late 1929 came double disaster. First, Hindenburg's most trustworthy and able minister, Nobel Peace Prize winner Gustav Stresemann, died suddenly of a heart attack; then, catastrophically, the American stock market crashed and its ripple effect hit Germany harder than any European nation because of its heavy dependence on U.S. capital. By the early 1930s, Adolf Hitler's Nazi party — before then widely viewed as marginal crackpots and outliers — began to achieve startling electoral gains with firm promises to swiftly rectify the country's deepening economic woes, in tandem with venomous oaths to root out all traitors and non-conformists.

In 1933 came the end. With the moderate center of German public opinion badly fragmented, the Nazis had swept away all opposition in recent elections, and proceeded to convert the republic into a dictatorship. An ailing, senile Hindenburg was soon forced to resign, appointing Hitler as new German Chancellor.[23] A mere 12 years later (by 1945), countless millions across the globe had been killed and large swaths of the civilized world lay in ruins.

Organization

While informed scholarly writings on the origins of cabaret are plentiful, commentary on its vast influence during the post–War War II period are surprisingly scarce. After laying out the beginnings of German *Kabarett* in Part I, the second half of this study traces its steady, rapid progress in American popular culture throughout the latter half of the 20th century. Obviously, these latter-day observations will be more subjective, given lack of specialized critical opinion to date. Non-translated German-language commentary on *Kabarett*, which is rich and extensive, has not been consulted. This is obviously a limitation; however, evidence in the public domain is there for all to see and hear regardless of language. As will become quickly apparent, the documented connections are strong enough to at least justify further discussion and debate. Emphasis is naturally placed on the lengthy careers of Marlene Dietrich and Lotte Lenya, if only because much of cabaret's modern image derives from the work of these two extraordinary performers. The widespread influence of lesser known German artists, however, will be explored as well. Above all, we hope to bridge the artificial barrier that has come to exist between classical and popular music spheres, one which classically-trained composers such as Kurt Weill, Friedrich Hollaender, and Mischa Spoliansky worked tirelessly and tenaciously to break down, with routine tangible results. This gap-bridging quality may in fact represent cabaret's greatest and most durable achievement as a musical and artistic genre.

In previous studies, the author has found himself unwittingly drawn into the timeless debate over the respective importance of the human heart and the human mind in day-to-day affairs of mankind.[24] Ultimately we cannot choose one over the other; both are necessary for a life well lived. If nothing else, it would seem it is better to err, if one must err, in favor of the heart. While cabaret (to its great credit) always resisted any pretense at religious statements, it could never completely escape its spiritual roots in the Expressionist movement of art. No matter how hard it strived to be political or prurient or downright silly, it usually ended up being serious, adult business and, in its own special way, otherworldly. Its best proponents always seemed to be working overtime to strike a kind of perfect, elusive balance between introspective intelligence and mass appeal. One might even say that its two greatest figures — Kurt Weill and Marlene Dietrich — individually symbolized the head and heart, respectively. Weill was as complex a musical mind as the 20th century produced, yet devoted his relatively short life's work to musical theater aimed at as wide an audience as possible. Similarly, during her own time, no performer who walked the stage or stood in front of a camera with sound was more popular on both sides of the Atlantic than Dietrich; nevertheless, even during her most ingloriously compromised moments one could sense an insatiable need to ennoble trite material, to bring to a wide audience something better than passing, ephemeral entertainment. That both Weill and Dietrich always wanted to work together but in the end could not bear each other's foibles might be interpreted almost as a morality tale (see Chapter 11). In its most abstract sense, 20th century cabaret tells the story of how polar opposites usually attract but rarely are able to find common ground, at least for any sustainable length of time.

PART I — BERLIN VIA PARIS

1. *Le Belle Époque* and Überbrettl

"There can be no doubt: the Weimar style was born before the Weimar Republic" — Peter Gay[1]

At the dawn of the 20th century, conventional wisdom held that Germany — not the United States — was the nation-state of the future. Germany at that time had the most powerful military in the world, political allies, trading partners, colonial satellites, a diverse, thriving economy striking an impressive balance between private enterprise and government control, and (above all) a high culture that was beginning to conspicuously surpass its old rival France in this regard. By 1914, this perception was stronger than ever, although fissures were starting to appear in diplomatic relations that had kept Europe in relative peace and prosperity over the previous four decades. Few could have foreseen the multiple disasters that were about envelope the German nation over the next 30 years, and fewer still (if any) anticipated the artistic shock waves from these catastrophes reverberating across the western world. Indeed, the last major disturbance in Europe prior to 1914 (though a mere brush-fire by comparison) had been a quickly fought territorial dispute between Germany and France back in 1870. The fact is noteworthy because, in the respective cases of both France and Germany, musical innovation at home seems to have proceeded in the aftermath of embarrassing military defeat.

For France, the wake-up call came with its thorough drubbing in the Franco-Prussian War of 1870, an unnecessary conflict provoked by Louis Napoleon but whose outcome was dictated by Otto von Bismarck's newly-unified German state, conclusively demonstrating in the process that it should no longer be taken lightly as a world power. The resulting overthrow of Louis Napoleon and foundation of the French Third Republic marked the inauguration of *Le Belle Époque* ("The Beautiful Epoch") in France and throughout the rest of Europe. After an initial period of French political unrest and realignment, things began to happen, especially in the cultural sphere. All of the arts flourished, including music. In 1878, Paris successfully hosted a World's Fair, its first international event since the Franco-Prussian debacle. In 1886, the Statue of Liberty was dedicated in New York City Harbor as a gift of friendship from France to a startled and flattered United States. In 1889, a second *Universelle Exposition* was held in Paris and the Eiffel Tower, the very symbol of Paris, constructed. That same year, to capitalize on this celebration, impresario Joseph Oller launched Le Moulin Rouge ("The Red Mill") in the disreputable Montmartre district of Paris, soon becoming synonymous with modern nightclub entertainment. Here the can-can, originally an obscure courtesan dance, was first widely popularized, then later immortalized on both stage and film. The innovative groundwork paving the way for the Moulin Rouge, however, had appeared in Montmartre several years earlier, at the beginning of the 1880s, when a down-and-out but highly ambitious Parisian entrepreneur realized there was now viable demand for a whole new style of adult musical *divertissement*.

Rodolphe Salis (1851–1897) was the poor son of a French provincial distiller, and following his military discharge after the Franco-Prussian conflict, an aspiring, starving artist. By 1881, however, after realizing that painting would never pay his bills, Salis opened Le Chat Noir ("The Black Cat") in Montmartre, widely considered the first modern commercial artistic cabaret.[2] The basic premise was to let audiences drink during performances, and to charge them for both. Salis' promotional genius immediately manifested itself by forcibly barring at the door anything resembling respectability, while at the same time vaguely promising his patrons only the highest in artistic standards. The venture was a big hit from day one, and soon became a regular gathering spot for the rich and infamous. Thus began cabaret in its preliminary French incarnation, spawning many imitators. Salis himself often acted as emcee or *conférencier* in between acts. Aspiring performers flocked to the cabarets as well, not only to seek paying gigs but also to have their names loudly broadcast to the public, a service which an energetic promoter like Salis excelled at providing.[3] Le Chat Noir would go on to become a venerable brand name for various cabaret venues worldwide, and continues into the present day.

The French connection to cabaret's modern origins would remain important over the next century. Even as *Kabarett* bloomed full flower in Weimar Germany some four decades later, it would continue to pay regular homage to its predecessor's birthplace. It was Marlene Dietrich's trilingual abilities that first impressed Josef von Sternberg when he saw her perform, as she often assumed a French persona both on stage and film, and it was in Paris that she elected to spend the twilight years of her life (see Chapter 5). Kurt Weill wrote French songs for French performers (as well as for Dietrich) during his journey of flight from Germany to America, and viewed French composer Darius Milhaud as both a friend and kindred musical spirit in exile (see Chapter 11). Dietrich and Weill were only the most prominent German-born examples in this regard. Some later, famous *Kabarett* performers such as Margo Lion and Marya Delvard were of French birth and no doubt generated more ticket sales because of it. The Nazis, as one would expect, later came to hate this Francophile aspect of cabaret, as it went completely against their supernationalist agenda, although it would be far more accurate to accuse German *Kabarett* performers of favoring an international or universal outlook, as opposed to being overly biased in favor of France, Germany, or any other particular country. For these brave Weimar performers, any professed admiration for France represented more an overt rejection of fascist nationalism and rampant xenophobia, rather than any denial of love for their own native land. It was also their personal way of simply acknowledging basic truth: the *chanson réaliste* ("realistic song") singing style had in fact originated in Montemarte during the late 1800s.[4]

What grew out of France following defeat in the Franco-Prussian War eventually rebounded on Germany itself, where the sensational new mode of French entertainment did not go unnoticed. By the late 19th century, the philosophical writings of Friedrich Nietzsche (1844–1900) had achieved revered status in the German-speaking world (see Chapter 9). The 1883 publication of Nietzsche's novel *Also Sprach Zarathustra* ("Thus Spake Zarathustra") had introduced the hugely influential and divergently interpreted concept of *Übermensch* ("Superman"). It would be the disciples of Nietzsche who collided with the burgeoning world-wide impact of Parisian cabaret during the 1890s. Foremost among these self-appointed cultural visionaries was the Munich novelist Otto Julius Bierbaum. In 1897, the same year that cabaret pioneer Rodolphe Salis died, Biebaum's novel *Stilpe* presented the story of its namesake narrator advocating an urgent need for (and potential pitfalls of) a distinctive German form of popular entertainment. Bierbaum felt, not too surprisingly in retrospect, that an appropriate Germanic version would be more high-brow and artistically respectable than its French counterpart. Tying this idea into the Nietzschean ideal, Bierbaum wrote (through the voice of his fictional narrator): "We will give birth to the over-man [*den Übermensch*] on the stage boards [*auf dem Brettl*]."[5] Three years later, in 1900, Bierbaum elaborated further on the same idea in his *Deutsche Chansons*. He proposed that German vaudeville or variety show, affectionately known among the masses as *Tingel Tangel*, be used as a starting point to build up something more spiritually elevated and artistically durable.[6] He might as well have been imagining Marlene Dietrich in *The Blue Angel*, some 30 years before that watershed film was premiered (see Chapter 10).[7]

No sooner had Bierbaum gotten specific about what he wanted to see, than it became a reality, or at least seriously attempted to. On January 18, 1901, not long after the death of Nietzsche himself, another admirer of the late philosopher, Ernst von Wolzogen (1855–1934), unveiled in Berlin the *Buntes Theater* ("Colorful Theater" or "Motley Theater"), better known thereafter as Überbrettl ("Superboards" or "Superstage"), a humorous wordplay on Nietzsche's *Übermensch* ("Superman"), possibly stemming from a worshipful Wolzogen having a bust of the recently deceased Nietzsche greeting patrons in his theater lobby.[8] Like Salis, Wolzogen was a frustrated artist, an aspiring poet who would soon write a 1901 libretto for Richard Strauss' forgotten second opera *Feuersnot*, and some of whose poetry, fittingly enough, had been included in Bierbaum's *Deutsche Chansons*.[9] Wolzogen (again, like Salis) discovered an outlet for his energies in popular entertainment; unlike Salis, however, he lacked business acumen, refused to serve his customers alcoholic beverages, and clung to his own creative ambitions.[10] More on the plus side, Wolzogen had a knack for assembling first-rate musical talent, including house composer Oscar Straus, operetta songsmith veteran Victor Hollaender, and a young, then-unknown Arnold Schoenberg on piano.[11] Wolzogen, whose artistic sensibilities were decidedly elitist, had the immediate aim to transform *Tingel Tangel* into a respectable literary vaudeville style, fusing elements of the *Jugendstil* movement and *Kleinkunst* ("Miniature Art") aesthetic, in which the short attention span of general audiences would be accommodated.[12] Wolgozen himself acted as *conférencier*.[13] Nietzsche would be the patron saint of the entire enterprise. The new experiment was destined to be initially successful, but not quite in the manner that Wolzogen had hoped or anticipated.

An enthusiastic house greeted opening night at Überbrettl and the undisputed hit of the evening was *Der lustige Ehemann* ("The Merry Husband"), a skilful, nostalgic musical setting of a Bierbaum text by Oscar Straus.[14] Unfortunately, this initial flush of success seems to have gone to everyone's head, and a series of debilitating disputes broke out between Wolzogen, his investors, and his employees over creative and management differences, culminating in the final closure of Überbrettl only one year later in 1902. Sadly, this setback seems to have brought out a latent anti–Semitic streak in Wolzogen, who in later years insistently wrote that Jews were to blame for the failure of his cabaret. It seems from the very inception of German *Kabarett* that Jews comprised many if not most of its participants, thus making convenient scapegoats. Wolgozen's bitterness and hostility would prove to be a sinister harbinger of the vicious government-sponsored backlash against *Kabarett* performers after 1932.[15]

With respect to the inception of German *Kabarett* at the dawn of the new century, however, the proverbial genie had been let out of the bottle, as a host of Überbrettl imitators soon appeared.[16] Even Otto Julius Bierbaum, the novelist who first publicly pushed for the concept, tried opening his own cabaret in December 1901, but it quickly failed. Then he gave up on the idea and condemned the entire concept, but better promoters than Bierbaum were not so easily discouraged.[17] Wolgozen's catastrophic miscalculation in not serving refreshments was quickly exploited by competitors with the 1901 opening of *Zum hungrigen Pegasus* ("The Hungry Pegasus") by Max Karl Tilke. Tilke, who had been to Paris, shamelessly pitched his enterprise as *Kneipenbrettl* or pub-cabaret.[18] Also in attendance on opening night at Überbrettl had been a 22-year-old Jewish Berliner, Rudolf Nelson, aka Rudolf Lewysohn (1878–1960), a classically trained musician who was both impressed with what he saw on stage and, despite his youth, convinced that he could do the same thing better than Wolzogen. Nelson was especially impressed by the affluence of Wolgozen's well-heeled clientele.[19] After careful planning and preparation, Nelson opened his own club Roland von Berlin in 1904 and then followed it in 1907 with Chat Noir, in homage to the famed original Parisian franchise.[20] Both ventures were successful. Nelson would go on to become a leader in the Berlin cabaret scene over the next half century, somehow barely surviving the Holocaust (see Chapter 6). Similar cabaret theaters soon sprang up in German tourist destinations such as Munich and Vienna, with some making famous names comparable to their Berlin rivals.[21] Both Munich and Vienna produced major cabaret stars, many of whom eventually migrated to the epicenter of the 1920s Berlin scene.

By far and away the most important of the new Berlin clubs appearing in the immediate wake of Überbrettl, however, was co-founded by the soon-to-be world famous Max Reinhardt (1873–1943), a Viennese Jew by birth and established repertory actor in Otto Brahm's prestigious Deutsches Theater.[22] In a simultaneous effort to strike out on his own and break free of all stilted conventions, Reinhardt was instrumental in assembling cast and crew for a new groundbreaking venue, *Schall und Rauch* ("Sound and Smoke"), which opened to the public in January 1901, merely five days after Wolgozen had premiered his Überbrettl.[23] In contrast to Wolgozen's seriousness, Reinhardt's mantra was parody — parody on a level that no one before had imagined, while barely staying within the mandated bounds of Imperial Germany's official censors. Crucially, Sound and Smoke turned a profit and kept turning it.[24] Reinhardt's only other real competitor in this regard was Nelson.[25] By 1903, Reinhardt had opened a second successful Berlin venue, the Kleines Theater.[26] No sacred cow left unprotected by the censors was off limits, and audiences loved it. Even the music of Wagner was hilariously sent up, much to the consternation of apologists for the Master Race everywhere.[27] If Wolgozen loved Nietzsche, adored Nietzsche, hero-worshipped Nietsche, etc., then this only made easier fodder for the likes of Max Reinhardt. As the old adage goes, you have to have real affection for something in order to effectively spoof it, and this was the essence of Reinhardt's irreverent takes on German high *kulture*.

As Peter Jelavich has observed, the Überbrettl fad of 1901–1902 mocked everything and advocated nothing.[28] In this respect, it anticipated the Dada movement of the Great War. It was also taking things to a self-conscious level that Parisian cabaret never dreamed of doing. Some contemporaries viewed it as a clear reaction against the snobbery and elitism of German bourgeois society.[29] By the end of the first decade of the century, serious literary elements had permeated *Kabarett*, which in turn drew satirical ire from outraged Berlin literary critics.[30] In addition to hard feelings caused by cut-throat economic competition, there were retaliatory police crackdowns as early as 1904–1905. Part of the problem was that the new pub-cabarets were using an intellectual façade (not shared by the old *Tingel Tangel*) to circumvent municipal licensing laws, and this violation was often cited as a legitimate excuse to shut them down.[31]

Interestingly enough, the rise of the Überbrettl phenomenon in Germany at the dawn of the 20th century coincided with a conspicuous high-water mark of the German classical music establishment. Not long after many of the new pub-cabarets in Berlin had been suppressed by authorities, Richard Strauss' controversial opera *Salome* premiered at Dresden in January 1906, then five months later moved to Graz, Austria, with a scandalous reputation preceding it. Among those in attendance at that triumphant performance were Strauss, Gustav Mahler. Giacomo Puccini, Alexander von Zemlinsky, Arnold Schoenberg, Alban Berg, the widow of Johann Strauss, Jr., and possibly a 16-year-old Adolf Hitler.[32] As music historian Alex Ross has written, the event "...illuminated a musical world on the verge of traumatic change." To many of his peers, Strauss represented the cutting edge of Wagnerian Romanticism, although to others he was little more than a talented showman and a sell-out.[33] The Jewish Mahler, though himself friendly with Strauss, much more embodied artistic integrity among his students and colleagues. Mahler, primarily a symphonist, also had a low opinion of musical theater, which Strauss had taken pains to make his supreme domain.[34] For a Germany on the brink of World War and catastrophe, the brewing Strauss-Mahler divide in Vienna was a precursor of the insistent fragmentation that would dominate musical tastes for following generations.[35] As Ross summarized the problem, "The split between them [Mahler and Strauss] forecast a larger division in twentieth-century music to come, between modernism and populist conceptions of the composer's role."[36] Apparently unbeknownst to both Mahler and Strauss, Überbrettl was already attempting to fill this breach, and *Kabarett* would more or less accomplish the goal within a few short years. Mahler, however, would not live to see it, dying unexpectedly in 1911.

That the pre-occupied Mahler, who more or less worked himself to death by age 51, seemed unaware of the pre-war origins of German *Kabarett*, should not be too surprising. The case of Strauss, who would live to see the rise, fall and then rebirth of *Kabarett* (see Chapter 8), however, is more troublesome. In addition to being a committed man of the theater, Strauss was, like the founders of Überbrettl, an avid admirer of Nietzsche. For one, he had composed in 1896 his ubiquitous tone poem inspired by Nietzsche's *Also Sprach Zarathustra*. For another, Strauss' inspiration for *Salome*, the work that cemented his reputation and fortune, had been the original 1891 stage version by Oscar Wilde that would go on to inspire Munich-based dramatist Frank Wedekind's *Lulu* plays (1895–1904), in turn becoming touchstones for *Kabarett* during the 1920s and providing a kind of thematic bridge between German Expressionism and cabaret (see Chapter 9). Strauss, however, was also a staunch Wagnerian from adolescence going forward, which tended to make the compressed aesthetic values of *Kleinkunst* rather alien to him, at least in his prime years. As for Nietzsche, it is well documented that his youthful enthusiasm for Wagner later turned into suspicious circumspection as an adult. For opera, Nietzsche later preferred *Carmen* over *Tristan und Isolde*, even though Wagner's operatic dominance clearly prevailed during his lifetime. Alternatively, as summarized by Ross, "Nietzsche declared that music must be liberated from Teutonic heaviness and brought back to popular roots."[37]

Germanic thread-splitting over classical musical theory was, like all of Western civilization, given a jolt of shock therapy by the Great War of 1914–1918.[38] As large swaths of Germany, France, and the Austro-Hungarian Empire became mobilized and devastated war-zones, neutral Switzerland and its largest city Zurich became the temporary capital of satirical-based cabaret. It was here in 1916 that the legendary Cabaret Voltaire opened and, though its existence was brief, acted as an artistic and cultural springboard across Europe both for the duration of the war and long afterwards.[39] Founded by German performance artists Hugo Ball and Emmy Hennings, Café Voltaire was christened in honor of the French Enlightenment philosopher whose very name was equated with freedom of expression. Ball had been an acting colleague of Reinhardt's in Berlin, and after witnessing the horrors of war, relocated to Zurich where he decided to take cabaret satire to the next level of absurdity. The result was the Dada movement, which had its birth at Cabaret Voltaire and went on to influence all popular entertainment into the present day. The basic joke presented by Dada was simple and poignant: mankind was turning itself into machines, and this comedy-tragedy was dramatized nightly on the cabaret stage. Its style was abrasive, calculated to offend, not pander; yet during a time when civilization seemed to be destroying itself, Dada was surprisingly well received. Ball and his Dadaist colleagues in Zurich had direct ties with the German Expressionist movement; it was no wonder then that their influential work acted as a conduit between all public performance art before and after the war.[40]

Almost from the moment that World War I ended, Dada spread to Berlin with a vengeance. Its first and most immediate impact was in the visual arts.[41] In the summer of 1920, much of Berlin considered itself the unfortunate host of the First International Dada Fair, an outrageous proceeding from all accounts, exhibiting work by a nearly who's who of painters going on to make international names for themselves over the next decade — Wassily Kandinsky, George Grosz, Otto Dix, John Heartsfield (aka Helmut Herzfeld), and many others besides.[42] Much of it would later be declared *entartete Kunst* ("Degenerate Art") by the Nazis (see Chapter 8). The Dadaist trend animated and fed directly into the creation of the first Berlin literary cabarets by the early 1920s, many of whose exponents were early hires of the new commercial establishments (see Chapter 2). Thus the progression from Paris to Berlin to Zurich and back to Berlin again had run its course over some four decades. What began as Le Chat Noir in Montmartre had now become something even more revolutionary and defiant.

Often forgotten is that the new post-war political climate in Germany allowed Dada to get away with many of its public antics. With the Kaiser fled into exile, Prussian censorship had finally been lifted, albeit temporarily, and the stage now dramatically set for yet another German renaissance in the arts. This time, however, unlike the pre-war era of Mahler and Strauss, the picture presented by the new generation of artists would not be so pretty. Worse still (and telltale for the future), many Germans would turn away from these innovations in horror and disgust. A defeated, humbled, and previously great nation was not quite ready to take a good hard look at itself in the mirror, especially if the reflection did not conform to the image they had already formed of themselves. Nevertheless, many others were enthralled, and more importantly, willing to pay talented performers able to provide this kind of entertainment. In 1919, Germany suddenly found itself in a position similar to that of France after it had been defeated in Franco-Prussian War nearly half a century earlier. As the first wave of literary *Kabarett* hit Berlin in the wake of the Paris Peace Treaty, word spread that something new was afoot in popular entertainment. The old rowdy *Tingel Tangel* still survived in various shapes and sizes, but now it appeared that some venues were reaching for something classier and, dare it be said, more introspective and spiritual, just as Otto Julius Bierbaum had imagined before the turn of the century. On the other hand, the idealistic Bierbaum could never have predicted what eventually came to pass. The real surprise had come with a shocking new foreign infiltration into the vaunted German music tradition.

2. The Great American Cultural Invasion

"...Germans unquestionably experienced the greatest loss of identity in the years after 1918." — Matthias Eberle[1]

By general agreement the Great War of 1914–1918 was, in the final analysis, brought to a swift, decisive conclusion by the military intervention of the United States in favor of the Allies versus Axis powers. After three initial years of agonizing slaughter and stalemate, the U.S. had been at first stubbornly neutral, then steadily pushed and provoked into active engagement. American troops began to arrive on French soil en masse during the summer of 1918; by the fall of that same year, for all practical purposes, the fight was over. At this precise moment in time, the United States entered history as a dominant world power and has remained one ever since. Nevertheless, the overwhelming force exerted by American military-industrial might achieved far less lasting influence in Europe (particularly in Germany) than did the irresistible weight of American popular culture which flooded into the Old World following the Armistice of 1918 and subsequent Versailles Peace Treaty. When Europe and Germany again exploded into hostilities of unparalleled magnitude some two decades later, by then even the most diabolical of fascist dictators also happened to be a Charlie Chaplin fan.[2] Safe to say, by the end of the 1920s, Weimar Germany, like most of its European neighbors (and whether they liked to admit it or not), had completely fallen under the pervasive spell of American film, music, and dance.

Except for the Dadaist revolution in Switzerland during the war, German cabaret had, not too surprisingly, ground to temporary halt. Then in 1919 it came roaring back with a vengeance. First out of the box (again, not surprisingly) was its most successful pre-war promoter, Max Reinhardt. Reinhardt immediately revived his pre-war Sound and Smoke brand name, opening on December 8, 1919, within the spacious 3,000 square foot basement of the newly-retrofitted Großes Schauspielhaus ("Grand Theater") on the Berlin Friedrichstraße, formerly a horse stable for the old Schuman Circus. Then Reinhardt hired the best creative talent that he could find, including a then-unknown 23-year-old composer, Friedrich Hollaender, along with poets Walter Mehring and Kurt Tucholsky (see Chapter 6), artists George Grosz and John Heartsfield (see Chapter 9), and dancers Valeska Gert and Anita Berber (see Chapter 8), among others.[3] He also brought on board singer-actresses Trude Hesterberg (1892–1967) and Rosa Valetti (1878–1937), both of whom would soon move on to become direct competitors with Reinhardt, despite their perceived female gender handicap.[4] In the unrestrained, newly-liberated atmosphere of the Weimar Republic, such things were possible. With the sudden lifting of all censorship in the aftermath of the war, anything went — and often did.

Postwar opening night at Sound and Smoke was memorable. The reputation of Dada had preceded it as a packed house witnessed the assembled creative team of Mehring, Grosz, and Heartsfield stage a mock puppet show, *Einfach klassisch!* ("Simply Classical!"). The idea was to spoof and deconstruct the alleged and recently-formulated distinctions between "classical" and "modern" art before an amazed or confused nightclub audience.[5] From all accounts, this elaborate headliner was total flop, with the authors themselves, in typical Dadaist fashion, cat-calling their own work and later publishing a formal protest against the inept performance.[6] Had this been the only act on the bill that night, it is possible that Reinhardt's new cabaret venue would have folded more quickly than it had begun. Fortunately for everyone, the young showman had much more up his sleeve to offer, although this involved presenting comparatively young and untested talent to an impatient, inebriated, and potentially hostile Berlin clientele.

Paul Graetz (1890–1937) was born in East Prussia and, along with his compatriot Claire Waldoff (see Chapter 5), destined to represent the embodiment of Berliner combativeness on cabaret stages during the 1920s. Though only 29 years old in 1919, Graetz was a veteran of Reinhardt's Deutsches Theater and knew how to work a crowd. The newly formed, ad hoc songwriting team of Friedrich Hollaender and Kurt Tucholsky had composed for Graetz an extended ditty titled *Der alte Motor* ("The Old Motor") which, without giving too much way, was a parable celebrating human capacity for resilience and adaptability in the face of a hostile, ever-changing world.[7] It was a message that most Berliners certainly needed and many wanted to hear by late 1919. Graetz introduced himself by stumbling through the front door of Sound and Smoke, pretending to be an unkempt, drunken street vendor, then after several loud altercations with various parties, forced his way towards the stage. By the time he made it there and broke into his little inspirational number, the crowd was in on the joke and delighted.[8] Thus *Kabarett*, Weimar Berlin style, was born that night on December 8, 1919, at Max Reinhardt's Sound and Smoke.

There was something poignantly Chaplinesque in this conceit, and it should be recalled that by this time (both during and after the war) Charlie Chaplin's tramp film persona had received international circulation, making him a world-wide celebrity not long before Graetz took Berlin cabaret stages by assault.[9] Because the piece had been written by Hollaender, a classically-trained musician, and Tucholsky, a serious, published poet, the genre was later dubbed "literary cabaret" or *Kabarett* with a "k," as opposed to striptease cabaret with a "c" in the French manner. The Dadaist performance artists, who had ruled supreme in wartime Zurich with their sophisticated, irreverent antics, were suddenly upstaged. The new art form could be sexy, topical, or sentimental, depending on its mood and the mood of its audience. The next three years would see literary cabaret explode across the large urban centers of Germany, but especially in Berlin where, by 1922, no fewer than 38 new venues were documented, many receiving favorable reviews from dumbfounded critics who surprised even themselves at how much they liked the shows.[10] As Weimar historian Peter Gay wrote, Berlin soon became "headquarters for the political cabaret...."[11] In terms of cinematic influence, Chaplin's tramp was not the only purveyor. South America got into the act as well with the Argentine tango, a dance popularized in part by Rudolf Valentino's stunning silent demonstration in *Four Horseman of the Apocalypse* (1921). By the mid–1920s, tango had become part of the standardized arsenal in the Weimar musical scene for both high and low, with some of its best composers offering their own distinctive contributions to the genre.

Not everything, though, was high art. Girlie shows proliferated as well. At their most benign, these were represented by stylized kick lines, ala Moulin Rouge, offered up by widely-applauded acts like the eponymous Tiller Girls. Others were little more than marginal soft pornography disguised as serious dance, the most notorious being the Ballet Celly de Rheidt, whose semi-nude teenage pantomimes included titles along the lines of "Salome" and "Vampyr."[12] So commercially successful were these displays that the infamous troupe was soon dragged into court on obscenity charges and found guilty despite the official Weimar lift on censorship. The judges noted in their decision two key factors justifying the conviction: (1) expert testimony by professional ballerinas to the effect that Celly de Rheidt possessed no artistic merit whatsoever, and (2) the highly intimate, hence provocative, atmosphere of many small cabaret venues in which these dancers often performed, not unlike today's "gentlemen's clubs."[13] As Alan Lareau observed, the cabarets offered patrons both an escape from an unstable economy plus a means of coming to grips with the strange newness of the modern world. The lift on censorship in 1918 was designed to help promote these activities. Lareau then added: "The result, however, was disappointing, for the lifting of restrictions did not bring about a wave of political entertainment, but rather a flood of obscenity and nudity worse than before."[14] Without citing any empirical evidence, it may be added with a fair amount of confidence that this "obscenity and nudity" surely overshadowed the kind of novel serious entertainment being offered by literary cabarets such as Sound and Smoke.

Another singer whose star rose at Sound and Smoke was Gussy Holl (1888–1966), future wife of Emil Jannings, Marlene Dietrich's future co-star in *The Blue Angel*. Holl had already made a name for herself before the war by appearing at Rudolf Nelson's Chat Noir, but after the armistice this gifted performer now found herself being provided first-rate material by Hollaender and Tucholsky.[15] One terrific example of their chemistry together was *Zieh dich aus, Petronella!* ("Take It off, Petronella!"), a nifty burlesque on burlesque designed to poke fun at the trending Berlin permissiveness in nude female exhibitionism. As for Holl's previous mentor Rudolf Nelson, just as before the war, he followed hard and fast in the wake of innovations introduced by his rival, Max Reinhardt. 1920 saw the opening of the no less ambitiously scaled Nelson-Theater on the newly emerging Kurfürstendamm entertainment strip of Berlin, within the same building premises as the fashionable Sans Soucis restaurant. It was Nelson who would later be credited with expanding the role of the *conférencier*, a critical feature of cabaret later immortalized on Broadway and on film (see Chapter 15).[16] Over the ensuing decade, the Nelson-Theater would present to utterly amazed German audiences the latest sensational acts imported directly from *Amerika*.

The first Reinhardt protégé to defect and entrepreneurially strike out on her own was Rosa Valetti (aka Rosa Vallentin), who opened her legendary Café Größenwahn ("Café Megalomania") in late 1920. Valetti, a formidable stage personality in her own right, began by stealing away talent from Reinhardt, including the hit songwriting team of Hollaender and Tucholsky, installing the former as Megalomania's official in-house composer. With Hollaender, as part of the package, came his first wife, the gifted *chanteuse* Blandine Ebinger, aka Blandine Loeser (1899–1993). Almost overnight, Megalomania became unofficial headquarters for prestigious Berlin Expressionist writers while offering an intimate throwback to the Parisian pub-cabarets of the previous century.[17] The dominant original works presented in its programs were brashly pro-working class and unapologetically anti-war in their sympathies; often these were performed by the multi-talented Valetti herself.[18] Within a decade, Valetti would also have the rare distinction of being cast in supporting roles for *The Blue Angel* and the original stage version of *The Threepenny Opera*.[19]

Megalomania drew plenty of attention from audiences and critics alike, but the apotheosis of Berlin literary cabarets came in the fall of 1921 with the opening of the 127-seat Wilde Bühne ("Wild Stage"), situated in the basement of the renowned Theater de Westens, by another Sound and Smoke alumnus, Trude Hesterberg.[20] Hesterberg had been a protégé of both Reinhardt and Nelson, an understudy to operetta star Fritzi Massary, and an alumnus of the Stern Conservatory run by the Hollaender family. While working at Sound and Smoke she was inspired by Valetti and even more inspired when the latter opened her own business.[21] Like Valetti, Hesterberg was a dynamic solo performer, but she also had a sharp eye — perhaps the sharpest of all — for young, up-and-coming talent. She immediately gave employment to the satirist Walter Mehring, despite his being on the verge of leaving Berlin for greener pastures in Paris (as Tucholsky had recently done). Nevertheless, Mehring provided bracing Wild Stage material for a then-unknown singing actor named Kurt Gerron (1897–1944), who would go on to become one Berlin's leading cabaret personalities and later, during World War II, surely its most prominent martyr at the hands of the Nazis (see Chapter 6).[22] It was Hesterberg who hired the envelope-pushing, sexually-indeterminate comedian Wilhelm Bendow, who delighted gay and straight audiences alike with his ridiculous costumes and relentless barrages of double-entendres.[23] It was Hesterberg who first gave a big break to the dashing poet Marcellus Schiffer and his partner-muse, the beautiful singing actress Margo Lion; this odd couple of cabaret would remain at the forefront of the Berlin scene for the next decade. It was Hesterberg who appropriated the brilliant Mischa Spoliansky as Wild Stage in-house composer, after he had first been Hollaender's understudy then successor at Reinhardt's Sound and Smoke. Spoliansky and Schiffer would routinely collaborate for some of the era's best works, including revues that eventually catapulted Marlene Dietrich into superstardom. Hesterberg's biggest discovery, however, may have been a visiting 24-year-old Municher, Bertolt Brecht (1898–1956), several years before Brecht would become a household name on both sides of the Atlantic as controversial poet-playwright and librettist for Kurt Weill (see Chapter 3).[24] With a roster of talent like this, it is not surprising that Wild Stage often lived up to its name and set new standards for unfettered experimentation in Berlin literary cabaret.

Unfortunately for both Wild Stage and Megalomania, their heyday was brief, as was their very existence. Merciless competition and raiding each other's payrolls proved to be the least of their problems. In 1922–1923 came the onslaught of hyperinflation for the German mark, forcing Wild Stage to close and Megalomania to change management, marking the end of politically-oriented literary cabarets in postwar Berlin.[25] Sound and Smoke, along with the Nelson-Theater, managed to hang on, thanks to their willingness in making huge financial and artistic compromises for the sake of maintaining solvency. By 1924, however, conventional wisdom was, not for the first or last time, writing premature obituaries for Weimar *Kabarett*. What critics first failed to take into account was the artists' own steely determination to adapt and survive at all costs, as eloquently expounded in cabaret's maiden tour-de-force credo, *Der alte Motor*. The cultural nay-sayers also seemed oblivious to a new alien phenomenon then being injected into German mainstream society even as they wrote. In addition to vast amounts of American capital flooding Weimar markets to stabilize the economy, American music was now starting to enter the picture as well, just as American cinema had done only a few years previous. The effect would be electrifying everywhere from the lowest beer halls to the most elite conservatories, as musical developments in Germany would quickly bear out. Once again, as it had at the beginning of the century, *Kabarett* would enthusiastically embrace these exotic, foreign influences.

No one knows exactly where German jazz started, but several important things seemed to happen all at once. Peter Jelavich has written, accurately enough, that prior to the Great War, German musicians seemed relatively unaware of American trends; "After the war, however, American music flooded the stages." The technical result was that two-quarter time and syncopation suddenly become dominant.[26] On the other hand, this transformation did not occur immediately. The classic *Kabarett* or couplet songs of the early 1920s (such as *Der alte Motor*), relied on the older, traditional German popular song style, or *Schlager*, as a model.[27] Then American jazz came thundering through Europe and everything changed. One likely impetus for this sudden shift was that the first commercial recordings of Jelly Roll Morton from 1923 to 1924 found wide circulation, around the same period that the German economy was collapsing from hyperinflation.[28] Morton, apart from being a founding father of modern jazz and one of its first prolific recording artists, was (by wide agreement) the first jazz composer-arranger who was musically literate; that is to say, he could write the new style down in notation. This advantage may have weighed heavily in Germany where even the humblest folk musicians tended to be partial for a more written, structured tradition. The other advantage Morton enjoyed was that his music was simply delightful, and people everywhere, regardless of nationality, loved it. Nevertheless, these were only recordings, not live performances. As Alan Lareau rightly observed, "Jazz did not get a true foothold in Germany until after 1924, when American bands began to appear in Berlin."[29]

Berliners got their first documented look at genuine American hot jazz as journeyman bandleader Sam Wooding and his Chocolate Kiddies invaded Hermann Haller's Admiralspalast in May of 1925. Germans had never seen anything like it before. This was true Harlem nightclub entertainment, complete with crack musicians, dancers, costumes, lots of hokum, and at least one Duke Ellington composition on the play list ("Jig Walk").[30] If Berliners were stunned by what they had witnessed with Wooding's barnstorming at the Admiralspalast, however, nothing could have prepared them for the legendary Josephine Baker and La Revue Nègre, direct from Paris, who unveiled their road show at the Nelson-Theater in January of 1926.[31] The light-skinned Baker, rumored to have a German-American father and herself a unique combination of erotic dancer, singer, and musician, would have been quite enough to jar most audiences, but her stage presence was only one facet of the act. In Baker's retinue was another dance phenomenon, Louis Douglas, who shocked and delighted Berliners by mimicking traditional, stilted European choreography in between his own dazzling tap routines.[32] The pit orchestra featured multi-instrumentalist Sidney Bechet of New Orleans, one of early jazz's most nomadic geniuses and acknowledged rival of Louis Armstrong himself. Last came Baker's notorious pet cheetah, sporting a diamond collar, often terrorizing performers and audiences alike. Jelavich discerningly opined that the Weimar "conception of the United States was influenced by what Germans perceived to be black culture, which they considered to be a form of vital 'primitivism' appropriate to modern urban life."[33] In short, jazz had solidly arrived in Germany by early 1926.

Arguably the biggest Berlin musical event of 1926 occurred when the Paul Whiteman Orchestra played Max Reinhardt's Grand Theater — the main theater above the basement cabaret. Whiteman, as his last name advertised, was not African American, but nevertheless a skilled, sympathetic, and tireless promoter of the new music. Included in the program was a performance of George Gershwin's *Rhapsody in Blue*, a work commissioned by Whiteman himself. Among those in the audience listening to Gershwin and Whiteman fuse bordello music with the concert hall was a relatively young and impressionable Kurt Weill, whose advanced compositional style was about to undergo a another dramatic sea-change (see Chapter 3).[34] Music historian Alex Ross has asserted that, among other distinctive qualities, the music of Gershwin and Ellington being heard for the first time by Berliners during this period "had a flair for ambivalence."[35] Ambivalence was what *Kabarett* was all about. German composers of that era were right on the cusp of consciously incorporating into their own popular and serious music diverse innovations that Americans seemed to accomplish effortlessly, instinctively, and without thinking too hard about it — or in the more sophisticated cases of Gershwin and Ellington, at least tried to make it appear that way.

In addition to imported American music, there was imported American technology. Ross succinctly identifies the big three in this regard to be talking motion pictures, electrical recording, and wireless radio.[36] First and foremost, there were the talkies. Gary Marmorstein, in his breezy, witty chronicle *Hollywood Rhapsody*, reminds us that "There is no way to overstate the seismic effect *The Jazz Singer*, quaint as it now seems, had on the movie industry."[37] It also had a seismic effect on the music business. The meteoric stardom of Al Jolson in 1927 had an international impact extending far beyond the U.S. With the introduction of movie soundtracks during the late 1920s, performers and composers alike flocked to this new source of income and potential fame, including those in Germany. Jolson was the rebellious, wayward son of a Jewish cantor who, like many of his contemporaries, fell in love in love with African American music and was talented enough to effectively incorporate it into his repertoire.[38] His overnight smash success made a deep impression on an entire generation and those to follow, including European cabaret performers who had been previously used to eeking out a living in relative obscurity. Now came an entirely new business model in which singers and those providing their material could promote themselves on film and record, and get well paid while doing it, in addition to performing the regular, obligatory live shows. The lesson was not lost on, among many others in Germany, a young, ambitious singer-actress named Marlene Dietrich.

Americanization of *Kabarett* was accelerated during the late 1920s with the arrival of the *Kabarett-Revuen* ("cabaret revue") as the ascendant form of preferred stage show. For Weimar-era Germany, it was the large-scaled, thematically-unified musical revue that epitomized the Roaring Twenties and Jazz Age. Peter Gay labeled this period in Weimar history as "The Golden Twenties."[39] Peter Jelavich was more specific; calling it "the golden age of the Weimar revue" which, he added, "was the most popular form of entertainment in Weimar Berlin."[40] In wake of American jazz's blitzkrieg conquest of Germany in 1926, German audiences now wanted their live acts to be bigger, louder, and sassier, more in the American style, and this is exactly what they got. Pretty girls were essential, and if they could sing, dance, and act anything like Josephine Baker, then better still. This may have been light years away from the comparatively polite and artsy Überbrettl envisioned by Otto Julius Bierbaum and Ernst von Wolzogen before the war, but in truth, it was the logical fulfillment of the Nietzschean "Superstage" dream, adrenalized with an unanticipated dose of African American verve straight from Harlem, Chicago, and New Orleans. Like Wolzogen's pioneering venue, consumption of alcoholic beverages was generally relegated to a separate, serious activity before and after the show; in 1920s Germany there was no Prohibition — such laws were considered insanity by a beer-drinking, central European public. The big revues, however, were more a throwback to the spacious theatrical vaudeville of the previous century, less political and more safe, though still capable of a sharp satirical bite aimed at a wide cross-section of respectable society. The economic formula was simple: bigger productions were capable of producing wider profit margins, especially for those who knew how to give paying audiences what they wanted.

Some of the best creative talent from the earlier, abortive scene of literary *Kabarett* only a few years previous threw itself into the new structural format with gusto. Friedrich Hollaender, Mischa Spoliansky, Marcellus Schiffer, Rudolf Nelson, and others collaborated to produce some of their most durable work over the last five years of the Weimar Republic, even as the national political situation went into a tailspin all around them. Typically at their disposal was the *crème de la crème* of Berlin performing talent, and composer-writers usually took full advantage of it. Above all, there were the songs. Although the atmosphere was no longer intimate, nor the configuration strictly *Kleinkunst*, the spirit of esoteric, miniature art forms lived on in individual numbers often joined together by only the loosest of schematic plots.[41] An brassy duet such as *Wenn die beste Freudin* ("When the Special Girlfriend") from Spoliansky and Schiffer's 1928 hit revue *Es lieg in der Luft* ("It's in the Air") — originally performed and recorded by Marlene Dietrich with Margo Lion — could just as easily fit into a small club as the larger design for which it was originally intended. It also harked back to the early years of the same decade, in which the city Berlin was widely viewed as a unique, licentious hothouse of anything-goes sexuality combined with adventurous artistic creativity.[42]

Concurrent with this explosion in Weimar popular entertainment came revolutions in the sphere of "serious" music. Gershwin toured Europe in 1928 and in the process met, if not influenced, just about every then-major composer, including Igor Stravinsky, Serge Prokofiev, Maurice Ravel, members of the French Les Six, the redoubtable Arnold Schoenberg, Schoenberg's disciple Alban Berg, and, last but not least, Kurt Weill, at that moment himself on the cusp of international fame.[43] The Europeans were particularly impressed with Gershwin's paycheck and ability to find a wide listening public well beyond what they were used to achieving. Ross noted that Gershwin's approach to music was dualistic: "He led at all times a double life ... as highbrow artist and lowbrow entertainer...."[44] He was perfectly capable of playing either Carnegie Hall or the Cotton Club, but as two different, separate artists in one package. Interestingly, Gershwin for his part admired Berg's 1925 avant-garde shock-opera *Wozzeck*, which would later influence the creation of *Porgy and Bess* and, in turn, influence Weill's work for the American stage. As Berg told his American colleague, "Mr. Gershwin, music is music."[45] The problem for Berg was that the majority of elitist audiences who applauded *Wozzeck* at the opera house would not be caught dead listening to *It's in the Air* at the

Theater und Komödie am Kurfürstendamm in Berlin's rough-and-tumble nightclub district. That was still a wide, gaping gap that most "serious" composers were trying in vain to bridge.

There can be no question that 1920s Berlin provided a one-of-a-kind creative environment. The confluence of military defeat, big city atmosphere, lack of censorship or Prohibition, early 20th century technology, and above all, the importation of American music and film, helped to make this time and place in history of special interest to anyone paying attention to the performing arts. Between 1919 and 1927 — eight short years — German cabaret had progressed from the innovative literary *Kabarett* of the early 1920s to the grand extravaganzas of musical revues, a transformation propelled by the rapid success of American popular entertainment throughout Europe. This all seemed worlds away from what progressive classical composers such as Alban Berg were accomplishing with daring works like *Wozzeck*. Nevertheless, around the same time (circa 1927) that *It's in the Air* was shocking and delighting Berlin revue audiences, a 27-year-old, relatively unknown German-Jewish composer, one who had been carefully watching everything from a distance, was about to introduce yet another entirely innovative approach that, for a brief period, seemed to cross the great divide separating musical audiences ever since the Strauss-Mahler rivalry of the pre-war years. The time for building this bridge, he correctly judged, was ripe.

3. Kurt Weill and
Die Dreigroschenoper

"Don't be afraid of banality."— Ferruccio Busoni to Kurt Weill[1]

Not long before Ernst von Wolzogen unveiled his Überbrettl prototype in Berlin, Kurt Julian Weill was born on March 2, 1900, in Dessau, Saxony, today about a 90-minute drive southwest of the German capital. He was the third son of a conservative Jewish cantor, whose family roots in Germany were traceable back to the 14th century. Dessau is also less than an hour's drive north of Leipzig, a city closely associated with the musical legacies of Johann Sebastian Bach (1685–1750), Felix Mendelssohn (1809–1847), and Robert Schumann (1810–1856).[2] In addition, Dessau has long been noted for its rich German-Jewish cultural heritage; for example, as birthplace to the philosopher Moses Mendelssohn, grandfather of Felix. Later in life, after he had become famous in Berlin, Weill responded authoritatively to publishing concerns that his revolutionary style might alienate German provincial audiences. "I know the German provinces. I grew up there...," he wrote, adding that the secret innermost desire of most provincials was to come to Berlin, but in lieu of such travel his distinctively urbane, sophisticated music would provide an outlet for this longing.[3] Indeed, Kurt Weill was that rare kind of artist who seemingly could adapt himself to almost any environment, despite an unassuming appearance and humble background. Such was the man whose songs conquered cosmopolitan Berlin during the late 1920s. As Alex Ross wrote in wonderment, "Kurt Weill's schoolmates probably never imagined him as the cynosure of a decadent city."[4]

Like many of the greatest composers, Weill was a child prodigy. Growing up in a musical household surely helped his development as well.[5] By age 13, he was composing fully-realized, original works. By age 15 (during the war), he was performing public recitals of Liszt and Chopin on piano. He attracted the attention of Dessau's then leading musical personality, conductor Albert

Bing, who took the teenager under his tutelage.[6] By age 17, Weill was playing professionally and giving music lessons to the local nobility. He continued to compose, including settings of poetry by that early prophet of German cabaret, Otto Julius Bierbaum (see Chapter 1).[7] At age 18, Weill was admitted into the prestigious Hochschule für Musik in Berlin, where he studied under Wagnerian disciple Engelbert Humperdinck (1854–1921), composer of the opera *Hänsel and Gretel.*[8] Weill, however, did not fall under the Wagnerian spell, as did so many others of his generation. Instead, he was known to admire the 12-tone experimentation of Jewish-Viennese iconoclast Arnold Schoenberg, as well as the topical modernism of Russian internationalist Igor Stravinsky.[9] At age 19, the serious young student from the provinces fatefully decidedly that musical theater would be his life's work.[10] Weill faithfully adhered to this commitment for the remaining 31 years of his all-too-short life.

Much has been written concerning the vast spectrum of musical influences in Weill's chameleon-like, constantly-evolving style, especially in terms of his contemporary colleagues and the ascendant American jazz idiom of the times. Those need little elaboration within these pages. Brief mention should be made, however, of an old tradition which surely impacted Weill's sensibilities at an early stage and remained with him throughout his nomadic career. This was the inescapable shadow of Bach, whose name had been revered in Saxony since the 1700s, and had been active in Leipzig during his last and greatest period. Bach's music, contrary to a modern, purely instrumental image too often held out, tended to be highly religious, theatrical, and bold, all in one package. It had also been a 20-year-old Felix Mendelssohn, six years before he assumed conductorship of the Leipzig Gewandhause Orchestra, who permanently revived Bach's music drama to-end-all music dramas, the *St. Matthew Passion*, in 1829, roughly a century before Weill would help to rewrite musical history in Berlin. Such regional heritage would have been hard to ignore for any Dessau-born musician of genius. Mendelssohn, a Christianized Jew, was attracted to the insistent universality in Bach's ostensibly Lutheran art, as would have been Weill, raised in an orthodox Jewish household but later as an adult best described as a secular humanist with strong religious instincts. Weill's own compositions, especially from his late Berlin period, have sometimes been aptly described as Neo-Baroque in style, with their arching complexity of structure, rich abundance of detail, and stern, underlying sense of morality. Lastly, he was known to have studied Bach's scores as early as 1917, and Weill's own family moved to Leipzig in 1920, just as he was about to make his own final move to Berlin, where he would be active for the next 12 years.[11]

World War I ended just before the 18-year-old Weill would have likely been drafted. After a brief internship under conductor Hans Knappersbusch followed by an unsatisfying stint as *Kappelmeister* in remote Westphalia, Weill made another remarkable decision: he walked away from a paying job to interview for a Berlin master class in composition presided over by Italian guru Ferruccio Busoni (1866–1924).[12] After the final cut was made, Weill was one of five students accepted. He moved to Berlin in January 1921 and never looked back, supporting himself when necessary by writing music criticism. Weill's biographer Foster Hirsch described Busoni as a "neoclassicist who spurned Wagnerian music drama and the late romantic and expressionist traditions."[13] Alex Ross went further, labeling Busoni "a magnus-like musician who hovered over the early twentieth century like a spider in his web."[14] However one chooses to classify Busoni, one thing is for certain: he made a deep impression on Weill during his final years as a student.[15] It was Busoni who impressed upon Weill that it was no sin for a serious composer to write a hit tune, nor necessarily a sell-out to be financially successful. The composer's job, as Busoni saw it, was to first reach a wide audience and then, if possible, spiritually uplift them in the process. Such an approach was alien to many of Weill's contemporaries, including Schoenberg, who suspiciously viewed mass audiences as blindly enthralled with Wagner or hopelessly obtuse.[16] After Busoni's death in 1924, Weill boldly set out to conquer the highly competitive world of Berlin musical theater, armed with a limitless musical vocabulary and Busoni's catholic philosophy that knew neither theoretical boundaries nor dogmatic constraints.

Between 1924 and 1926, Weill would meet three individuals, all helping to quickly change his life. The first was Georg Kaiser (1878–1945) who, though hardly remembered today, was at that time Germany's leading Expressionist playwright, introduced to Weill through a mutual acquaintance, noted conductor Fritz Busch. Though of different generations and backgrounds, the two hit it off immediately, beginning a fruitful, 10-year creative association, ending only with Weill's forced departure from Germany in 1933.[17] Their first two collaborations were the one-act modernist operas *Der Protagonist* ("The Protagonist") and *Der Zar lässt sich photographieren* ("The Czar Has His Photograph Taken"), the first premiering at Dresden in 1926 (with Busch conducting) and the second at Leipzig in 1927. These works marked Weill's first two noteworthy operatic successes. In between, Kaiser encouraged Weill to work with surrealist poet Iwan Goll for the cantata *Der neue Orpheus* ("The New Orpheus") and another one-act opera, *Royal Palace*, both written in 1925 and hinting at the exciting, uncharted direction in which Weill was about to move as a composer.[18] Around this same time, Weill was heard to express admiration for Mozart's ability to elevate common and banal material to the level of high art, clearly recalling Busoni's earlier advice to him.[19]

It was also through Kaiser and his wife Margarethe that in 1924 Weill met the person proving surely to be the most important figure in his subsequent life and career, aspiring singer-actress Lotte Lenya (1898–1981), then living with the Kaiser family as au pair at their summer home in Grünheide, suburban Berlin. Lenya was not the first woman that Weill had been involved with, nor could the two of them have come from more opposite backgrounds; nevertheless, it was clear from the beginning to all who knew both that they were fellow travelers in life and kindred free spirits.[20] From all appearances, the Kaisers encouraged the romance, allowing the young lovers to live together in the Kaiser's own city apartment for three years. In 1926, the unlikely, star-crossed couple married in Berlin.[21] Weill dedicated the score of *Der Protagonist*, his first mature work, to Lenya.[22] Ross noted that around this same important, transitional period in Weill's artistic development, "His music began to resemble Lenya's voice — that famously unpolished, cutting, wearily expressive instrument. 'She can't read music,' Weill wrote in 1929, 'but when she sings, people listen as if it were Caruso.'"[23] Before meeting Weill, Lenya's talent had been recognized but never fully exploited. She not only served as Weill's inspirational muse over the next three decades, after his death in 1950 became a tireless and uncanny promoter of his legacy for three additional decades during the post–World War II era (see Chapter 4).

The third (and most controversial) artist that helped Weill to fulfill his destiny during the mid–1920s destiny was the irascible poet-playwright from Munich, Bertolt Brecht (1898–1956). Before the two first came face-to-face in early 1927, both had been impressed with each other's work from afar. By the time Weill sought out Brecht as a collaborator for a new commission, he had already praised Brecht's dramas as a critic. Both also admired the plays of Brecht's fellow Municher, Frank Wedekind (1864–1918), whose Expressionist dramas provided inspiration for an entire generation of *Kabarett* artists.[24] Around the time of their meeting, Brecht was in the process of becoming a committed, uncompromising Marxist, a political stance which later made it difficult for Weill to work with him, not only because of ideological differences but also because of Weill's firm belief that music should be far more than mere agitprop or soundtrack for political manifestos. Another problem was that Brecht, from all accounts, was a thoroughly unpleasant individual to socially interact with. These obstacles, however, lay in the future during early 1927 when Weill and Brecht excitedly began work for a scheduled performance at the Baden-Baden Deutsches Kammermusikfest.

Attempts by some scholars to downplay or distance Brecht's connections with *Kabarett* have been overstated. Aside from having performed at Trude Hesterberg's Wild Stage in 1922 (see Chapter 2), Brecht opened his own cabaret in Munich, Die rote Zibebe ("The Red Grape"), where well-known artists such as dancer Valeska Gert and comedian Karl Valentin performed.[25] Cabaret historian Lisa Appignanesi observed that "Brecht really belongs to the satirical New Objectivist [see chapter 9] tradition, a fact that often passes unnoticed."[26] In Munich, according to audiences, Brecht's abrasive delivery as a strolling balladeer was devastatingly effective, sometimes inspiring other writers to fictionally portray Brecht in a this role. Appignanesi noted that "As he [Brecht] claimed, it was to the language of the popular cabaret song that he turned to for a model...," adding:

> The short, sketch-like scenes of the cabaret performance, which were non-consecutive but loosely linked through satirical and political intent, also left their mark on Brecht's work.... Finally, Brecht's use of a narrator who steps out of the fictional dramatic framework to comment on events within the play is reminiscent of the cabaret's voluble conférencier and his running monologue on acts and contemporary events. Many of Brecht's actors, it should be noted, came from the cabaret stage.[27]

By the time Brecht relocated to Berlin during the mid–1920s, the German metropolis had become a Mecca for artists seeking both a broad audience and creative integrity.[28] *Kabarett* attracted some of the best literary talent, especially satirists, and Brecht appears to have been drawn to Weill in turn because the of the latter's known preference for combining serious music with miniature art forms and popular songs.[29]

By 1927, Weill himself was accepted into the ranks of serious composers — figuratively speaking, one of Germany's "great white hopes" against the recent incursion of American jazz; nonetheless, he was ready to try something completely different.[30] In 1926, he heard Paul Whiteman's Orchestra perform George Gershwin's *Rhapsody in Blue*, became intrigued with jazz, and wrote about it favorably in his published criticism. His 1925 opera *Royal Palace* had shown hints of jazz, and then in 1927 Weill's Berlin colleague Ernst Krenek enjoyed notable success (and publicity) with his so-called jazz opera *Jonny spielt auf* ("Johnny Strike Up"), essentially by tacking on a rousing Dixieland combo at the conclusion of the piece.[31] As Ross correctly judged, however, "...Krenek's engagement with African American music went about as deep as the blackface painted on the singer Jonny."[32] No doubt, Weill thought he could do much better, at least in terms of integrating jazz instrumentation into the European tradition. As far as that older tradition went, Weill considered Alban Berg's *Wozzeck* (1925) the culmination of an era, in his review of the work calling it "a masterpiece of tremendous power" and "the grandiose conclusion" to "the Wagnerian tradition."[33] Berg, for his part, was the only member of progressive Second Viennese School who did not disparage Weill's music; Berg also happened to be on friendly terms with the commercially successful Gershwin.[34] By the time that Weill contacted Brecht to express interest in working together, Weill had been widely accepted into the smart ranks of young and upcoming German composers including the likes of Krenek, Paul Hindemith, Hanns Eisler, and Stephan Wolpe.[35]

Earlier in 1927, Brecht had published five *Mahagonny Songs* as part of his
Die Hauspostille collection, two of which were English language parodies
(including the famous "Alabama-Song"), both probably written by Brecht's
Girl Friday, Elisabeth Hauptman.[36] The basic premise was a mythical sin-
city in the American West to which almost everyone is attracted but where
no one lives happily ever after.[37] Ross described *Mahagonny* as "...Brecht's
uncanny prophecy of Las Vegas" written decades before modern Las Vegas
actually appeared on the map.[38] As critic Christopher Hailey observed, "Weill's
last-minute decision to write the *Mahagonny Songspiel* for the Baden-Baden
Music Festival of 1927 was the turning point of his career."[39] Lotte Lenya, by
then Mrs. Kurt Weill, was immediately recognized by Brecht — always possessing a good eye and ear for new talent — as a crucial stage asset, happily
casting her to sing in the lead role of Jenny. The July performance in Baden-
Baden, one of several notable premieres that festival year, was a resounding
hit with audiences and critics alike, turning Lenya into an overnight star.[40]
Weill's musical contribution was nothing short of brilliant. Replacing the traditional operatic aria with the German popular *Schlager*, Weill chose to link
his name with contemporary Berlin cabaret songsmiths rather than "serious"
German composers of the era.[41] The "Alabama-Song" has itself been aptly
described as an "electrifying synthesis" (Foster Hirsch) and continues to be
re-interpreted by artists into the present day (see Chapter 19).[42] After Baden-
Baden, as bar-crowds enthusiastically sang their songs, Brecht and Weill, contrary to their high-brow credentials (in the words of critic John Fuegi), were
"in considerable danger of becoming a popular success."[43]

The buzz generated by *Mahagonny Songspiele* immediately created a
steady stream of small commissions for Weill. The biggest of all came the following year in 1928, but almost did not happen but for a strange confluence
of circumstances. Brecht had been hired to produce a new Berlin musical for
the out-of-the-way, comparatively small Theater am Schiffbauerdamm by its
new owners, Ernst Josef and Margot Aufricht.[44] First, Aufricht rejected
Brecht's own idea for a production; then English-speaking Elisabeth Hauptmann again came to the rescue by suggesting a semi-updated German version
of John Gay's 1728 play, *The Beggar's Opera*.[45] Aufricht liked the idea, and
Brecht naturally wanted to bring Weill on board for the music but Aufricht
resisted because of Weill's conservative, traditionalist reputation. Aufricht
wanted excitement, not tradition. Accordingly, Kurt Weill, recent toast of the
Baden-Baden festival, was forced to audition on piano for the job. Being
notoriously soft-spoken and reticent, Weill was on the verge of failing this
test when Lenya, with her newly acquired celebrity, assured Aufricht she
would sing in the production.[46] It was therefore reluctantly decided that Weill
would be given a chance. Deutsches Theater alumnus Erich Engel was brought

on as director. Designer Casper Neher, who had worked on *Mahagonny Song-spiele*, along with conductor Theo Mackeben and his jazzy, scrappy, seven-piece, multi-instrumentalist, pseudo-American "Ruth Lewis Band" were all retained as well. Finally, the risky decision was made to hire an entire cast of singing actors like Lenya rather than more expensive opera stars, thus the door thus opened for some of the best cabaret talent such as Rosa Valetti, Ernst Busch, and Kate Kühl to secure key supporting roles.[47] At the time, no one involved had any idea what *Die Dreigroschenoper* ("The Threepenny Opera") would later become, although Weill believed it had possibilities.[48]

Opening night for Weill and Brecht's *The Threepenny Opera* took place on August 31, 1928. Very few at the time expected it to succeed and some thought it would not open at all. Before the curtain went up, everything seemed to be falling apart. Leading man Harald Paulsen threatened to quit if his character did not receive a special introduction, so on very short notice Weill wrote "Die Moritat von Mackie Messer" ("The Ballad of Mack the Knife"), then Kurt Gerron (in the role of Tiger Brown), perhaps Berlin cabaret's most versatile talent, stepped up to the plate and delivered a world premier of the song by which Weill is now best remembered.[49] Carola Neher (no relation to Casper) was scheduled to sing "Seeräuberjenny" ("Pirate Jenny") in her role as Polly Peacham but had to be replaced by an understudy due the sudden death of her husband. The song was instead given to Lenya's character (again named Jenny) and has been associated with her ever since. The printed program, however, by accident omitted Lenya's name, and more confusion was created. In short, everything seemed poised that evening for Weill and Brecht to be victims of a sophomore slump, but the show somehow went on. The result was a sensation — the biggest hit anyone had ever seen, eventually becoming what Foster Hirsch described as "a symbol of Weimar Berlin."[50] In the audience that night was a young American, the future celebrity agent Robert Lantz, dragged to the show against his will by an older relative. Many years later Lantz reminisced that "Lenya ... was interesting beyond belief. *Nobody* else had her particular quality and sound ... the entire production was strictly first-class; major avant-garde theatre. The impact cannot be over-stated."[51] The cumulative impact of *Mahagonny Songspiele* and *The Threepenny Opera* in Germany and beyond, was to thrust their creative team, especially Weill and Lenya, to the very top of their respective professions.

Weill's mature style was light years ahead of its time in terms of variety, complexity and attitude, yet still managed against all odds to find a mass audience. Comparing this watershed work to Kern and Hammerstein's *Show Boat* (1927), Alex Ross noted that "...*Threepenny* sits on the border between classical and popular genres, combining 'hit' numbers with modernistic textures and socially critical themes."[52] The music was neither jazz nor classical nor cabaret, but seemingly incorporated bits and pieces of everything into a seamless, integrated whole, and then, for good measure, presented it as musical theater. Underpinning everything (in an unlikely manner) was a tremendous seriousness of purpose, no doubt aided by Brecht's unsentimental text. The "Neo-Baroque" descriptor later adopted by some critics well applied to these solemn, thoughtful, yet exuberantly catchy stage tunes which Weill later happily authorized into breezy dance arrangements. In one sense, *Mahagonny* and *Threepenny* represented an unprecedented injection of "high-brow" influence into "low-brow" entertainment. As a result, today it is still not unusual to find classical or operatic stars collaborating with pop and teen idols in the re-interpretation of Weill's songs (see Chapter 19). These two works also seemed to represent the aesthetic triumph of German *Kabarett*, American jazz, and anti–Wagnerian modernism — in short, everything in progressive music that the Nazis later came to hate so vehemently.

The sad thing in retrospect is that, in wake of *Threepenny*'s blockbuster triumph, many of Weill's progressive music colleagues, some livid with jealousy, attacked him as well. Foremost among these was Arnold Schoenberg, who had formerly approved of Weill's compositions before 1927. To the iconoclastic Schoenberg of the late 1920s, all popular music was, by definition, a commercial sell-out. As for Weill, who admired Schoenberg during his student days, the old accusation of his late mentor Busoni, that Schoenberg had thrown out the baby with bathwater, began to manifest itself. The falling out started with Weill, who had already decided that the Second Viennese School was beyond the capabilities of most listeners, making vague references in print to elitist composers who disdained the public; Schoenberg took it personally and the two were soon exchanging public barbs, though both would be kicked out of Germany by the Nazis in less than four years.[53] Even after Weill and Schoenberg arrived in the United States, Weill was still taking pains to distance himself from Schoenberg's style. Schoenberg, to his great credit, was a big enough man to later admit error in his critical judgment, possibly recalling that once upon a time, before the war, he had been a cabaret pianist-bandleader and composer of cabaret-style songs.[54] Shortly after the Schoenberg feud erupted, Brecht then turned on Weill with his formidable powers of insult, confrontation, and tantrum-throwing, taking full compositional credit for many of their hit songs (including "Mack the Knife"), publicly calling Weill a "phony Richard Strauss" and refusing to be photographed with him.[55] As for poor Richard Strauss, whose operas had ruled supreme in Germany only two decades previous, by the 1920s his ambitious stage works were receiving mixed reviews and struggling to find commercial audiences while *The Threepenny Opera* played to full houses night after night.[56]

Despite Brecht's sudden antagonism towards Weill (along with instigating litigation over film rights to *The Threepenny Opera*), he still saw fit to continue collaborating with Weill for a stunning series of stage works over the next four years. The biggest of these follow-ups was a full-blown operatic version of *Mahagonny*. Max Reinhardt was rumored as producer and Marlene Dietrich to star, but neither came to pass.[57] Instead, *Aufstif und Fall der Stadt Mahagonny* ("The Rise and Fall of the City of Mahagonny") premiered early 1930 in Leipzig, again with Lenya starring.[58] It was both applauded and controversial, with the Nazis Party attempting to disrupt performances via demonstrations and protests. More Weill and Brecht miniature masterpieces came in short order: *Das Berliner Requiem* ("The Berlin Requiem") in 1929; *Der Lindberghflug* ("The Lindberg Flight") in 1929; *Happy End* in 1929; *Der Jasager* ("The Yes-Sayer") in 1930; and *Die sieben Todsünden* ("The Seven Deadly Sins") in 1933, the last a visionary Parisian singing-ballet featuring legendary lead performances by Lenya and Tilly Losch. In 1931, the celebrated film version of *The Threepenny Opera* was released, directed by G.W. Pabst (see Chapter 10). As Weimar Germany went into its death throes in 1932–1933, Weill somehow still found time to create additional large-scaled works with other librettists besides Brecht. These included *Die Bürgschaft* ("The Pledge") in 1932 with Casper Neher, and *Die Silbersee* ("The Silver Lake") in 1933 with Weill's first and perhaps favorite Berlin collaborator, Georg Kaiser. The Leipzig premiere of *Die Silbersee* was well received, despite Nazi protests, but 10 days later the Reichstag burned down under suspicious circumstances. Then, with Chancellor Hitler's endorsement, all civil liberties were suspended. Shortly thereafter, all of Weill and Kaiser's works were officially and summarily banned.[59] On March 21, 1933, Kurt Weill fled Germany for Paris, never to return again, even after the dust had settled from World War II.

Weill's two-year sojourn in Paris and London during 1933–1935 demands far more space than is within the scope of this study; nonetheless, several items deserve passing mention. First and foremost is that Weill and Lenya long before this exodus were living apart and in 1933 agreed to divorce.[60] Their separation, however, proved temporary and remained amicable, with Lenya still performing Weill's works when not otherwise tending to his financial matters in Germany as best she could. Meanwhile, in Paris, there was no time for self-pity: Weill wrote some of his most memorable pieces while biding time in the City of Light. Even before moving there, he had become very popular in Paris, where his music was admired by the likes of Stravinsky, Cocteau, and Picasso.[61] New commissions came immediately. For French chanteuse Lys Gauty (who had already recorded a French-language "Chant de Barbara" from *The Threepenny Opera*) he composed several works, including the timeless *Je ne t'aime pas* ("I Don't Love You") with lyricist Maurice Magre.[62] Upon request, he wrote songs for Marlene Dietrich which, unfortunately, were never recorded. For the French music-hall, he composed *Marie Galante* (1934) with lyricist Jacques Deval, including a song later turned into an anthem for the wartime *Resistance, J'attends un navire* ("I'm Waiting for My Ship").[63] Weill's biggest, yet most elusive, project during this period, however, was *Der Kuh-handel* ("Shady Dealings"), a German-language music drama, modeled on Parisian light operetta, but eventually premiered at London's Savoy Theatre in a revised, English-language version (with a Shakespearean flourish) titled *A Kingdom for a Cow* (1935).[64] It succeeded in retaining the political conscious-ness of German *Kabarett* while moving in a new stylistic direction.[65] The cha-otic production was not a success but, as many critics have noted, this opera, like all of Weill's Parisian work, helped to artistically pave the way for his later triumphs on Broadway.[66] *Kingdom* yet again demonstrated his baroque-like facility for rapidly delivering commissions by any means necessary, plundering and rearranging his own past work with almost Handelian ruthlessness.[67]

At the time of *The Threepenny Opera*'s commercial breakthrough (1928), Weill had only had 22 years left to live, but his worldwide influence during that short remaining period would be extraordinary. The diverse, inclusive style of his music — one of cabaret's hallmarks — came at a point in history when many fascist regimes were attempting to aggressively exclude all per-ceived undesirable elements from privileged society. By the time Weill fled Germany in 1933, then Europe in 1935, he had accomplished what probably no one else could have, incorporating cabaret into the "classical" repertoire while simultaneously bringing it to mass audiences worldwide. Obviously, he had considerable help from others along the way in this regard. His early asso-ciations with Albert Bing, Ferruccio Busoni, Fritz Busch, Georg Kaiser, and Bertolt Brecht were all indispensable. Among all of Weill's helpers, however, the most important was clearly Lotte Lenya. Though they were no longer officially man and wife by the time Weill made his passage to the United States, their lives and careers were once again about to intersect in epic fashion. For that matter, in retrospect, Weill's Berlin and Paris periods, great as these were, represented merely the first of at least three different phases in the spec-tacular advancement of his musical legacy. The remarkable individual who served as a crucial catalyst for all three of these career phases, which total combined spanned over half a century, merits separate, detailed treatment within these pages.

4. Lotte Lenya, Future Tony Award Winner

"And I believe I'll find my life's work in making this music known ... so that he [Kurt Weill] won't be forgotten too quickly in a time which has no time to remember what happened yesterday." — Lotte Lenya[1]

Lotte Lenya, future Tony Award winner, was born Karoline Wilhelmine Charlotte Blaumauer, on October 18, 1898, in a lower class neighborhood of Imperial Vienna, then capital of the fading Austro-Hungarian Empire. Hers was an impoverished, dysfunctional family with an alcoholic, abusive father and submissive, long-suffering mother doing the best she could to protect her children from the countless horrors and pitfalls of a sordid, dangerous environment, both in and out of the house. If this dealt hand in life were not bad enough, Karoline's namesake was an older sister, formerly her father's favorite child but tragically dying in infancy. There is every indication that the younger daughter could never live up to the diseased, grief-stricken father's expectations, and therefore spent the rest of her life trying to overcome an unconscious, unjustified sense of guilt because of this perceived failure.[2] No one at the time would have dared predict that 28 years after her birth, young Karoline was destined to become Mrs. Kurt Weill, let alone an international star in her own right. Nevertheless, this was the same woman who would serve as goodwill ambassador to the world for the high-brow, sophisticated, and artsy version of cabaret music during latter half of the 20th century.

In the years leading up to the Great War, according to her own frank, undisputed revelations from an unpublished memoir, Lenya by age 13 was doing what many unfortunate girls in her time and place often did, namely, dropping out of school and turning to street prostitution for subsistence.[3] Like Louis Armstrong in New Orleans around this same period but on another continent, young Karoline had essentially become a street waif by the time she was a teenager. At this point in her life, there was no reason to believe that she was destined to live anything other than a brief, tragic, and completely obscure life. Although showing an aptitude for singing, dancing, and acting from a tender age, these qualities did not guarantee her escape from the Viennese ghetto; in fact, far more often than not, they did not provide a ticket out of poverty even for the fortunate few who possessed them. Then at age 14, a *deus ex machine* arrived at the disintegrating Blaumauer household in the form of a childless maternal Aunt Sophie from Zurich. In what can only be described as a service to humanity, the aunt took a shine to niece Karoline and brought the girl back to Switzerland, placing her in the middle class home of some elderly friends, the Ehrenzweigs, If all this were not enough, the thrilled, enthusiastic teenager was then enrolled in ballet school.[4]

For Lenya, like so many young artists of her generation, neutral Switzerland proved to be a perfect safe haven during the Great War. While there is no firm evidence that Lenya ever visited the legendary Cabaret Voltaire in Zurich or any of its spin-offs (see Chapter 1), she was known to consort with plenty of other people who did. In all likelihood, she was exposed to the early Dada movement, then all the rage in Zurich.[5] In Zurich she is known to have met Ferruccio Busoni, soon-to-be musical mentor of her future husband (see Chapter 3). Ballet quickly segued into acting and singing, her two biggest talents. She also had lovers, but was very choosey and discriminating, only taking up with men who would willingly help her career. She then landed in repertory acting at the prestigious Schauspielhaus, performing Shakespeare, Sophocles, Shaw, Wedekind, Kaiser, and even a non-singing role in Strauss' opera *Der Rosenkavalier*. Noted producer Richard Révy, a personal friend of Georg Kaiser — another mentor-to-be of her future husband — was impressed by Lenya's acting talent and encouraged her to read the classics. One friend later recalled that Lenya by then already had a wild reputation, but was very popular and an excellent performer besides.[6] After the war, as word spread that Berlin was becoming the Brave New World of modern performing arts, Lenya and a girlfriend made the decision in 1921 to board a train from Zurich to the German capital. There were no firm prospects, only dreams. By this time, she was 23 years old and calling herself Lotte Blaumauer, "Lotte" being short for her middle name Charlotte, obviously representing an effort to distance herself from an unhappy first name never wanted nor asked for.[7]

In Berlin, the first thing she did was to look up Révy, who gave her whatever work he could.[8] Under Révy's direction, one of the first things she did was to drop her last name in favor of "Lenja" (later becoming Americanized with "Lenya"). Lenja was a Russian bowdlerization of her Viennese nickname, Linnerl, reflecting leftist political sympathies that she would adhere to for the rest of her life, as well as yet another distancing from the memory of an unloved biological father.[9] Additional work in Berlin, however, proved scarce. When not working, Lenya recalled getting an eye-full of modern, uncensored street life in Berlin, including S&M prostitutes publicly advertising themselves with whips and high shiny boots along the Tauentzienstrasse near the city's largest department store, the Kaufhaus des Westens. As a lifelong fan of mass entertainment, she frequented Berlin's most popular variety theater, La Scala, and attended light operetta extravaganzas.[10] In 1922, she unsuccessfully auditioned for a role in the musical pantomime *Zaubernacht* ("Magic Night") by a then-unknown composer, Kurt Weill. The two never made visual contact, only by voice, she being on stage and he in the orchestra pit; for the audition she betrayed her Viennese roots by requesting Weill play on piano the *Blue Danube Waltz*, with which he bemusedly complied.[11] Lenya later managed to land a role as Maria in Shakespeare's *Twelfth Night* in 1923, and through Révy, made re-acquaintance with playwright Georg Kaiser, in whose works she had performed in Zurich. Kaiser, again intrigued by the 25-year-old singing actress, did want to discuss his own plays; instead, he pretended to be ignorant about Shakespeare and began quizzing Lenya regarding her then-current role. According to her own recollection, she blithely talked her head off at length, much to the amusement of both Kaiser and Révy.[12] It would prove to be one of the more important conversations in the history of 20th century theater.

By 1924, in wake of Germany's economic collapse from hyperinflation, Lenya's Berlin acting career had stalled as well. At this point, she could have easily packed her bags but instead, rather miraculously, received an offer from Kaiser and his wife Margarethe to be a live-in family au pair for their children at suburban Grünheide, outside of the city.[13] The Kaisers may have had a premonition that Lenya was a woman of destiny; instead of objecting to an attractive young actress in the house with a husband known to be occasionally unfaithful, Margarethe Kaiser struck up a life-long friendship with Lenya. That same summer, Weill arrived at Grünheide by invitation to work with Kaiser on their opera *Der Protagonist.*[14] Lenya met Weill at the train station and together they rowed out to the Kaiser family's lake house.[15] It appears to have been mutual attraction at first sight, even though they had seemingly little in common besides musical theater. By 1925 they were living together in the Kaiser's Berlin apartment flat, and Weill dedicated the finished score of *Der Protagonist* to her. If the Kaisers encouraged the romance, however, Weill's conservative parents strongly disapproved. In the understated words of biographer Donald Spoto, "...Kurt's parents were not members of the cabaret crowd...."[16] In their critical eyes, Lenya was Viennese, Catholic, poor, older, uneducated, and of dubious reputation. In spite of all these objections, Weill and Lenya were married in a Berlin civil ceremony on January 28, 1926.[17] It was an open marriage almost from the beginning, with Weill telling Lenya frankly that his music came first, and she second.[18] If one must keep score,

Lenya was probably unfaithful first, perhaps in part provoked by Weill's inattention.[19] By 1927, they had decided not to have children, although whether Lenya was capable of having any has remained an open question.[20] As time would prove, however, this was no ordinary couple.

The next two years, 1927–1928, launched both husband and wife into the stratospheres of world celebrity and notoriety. In 1927 they teamed up for the first time with Bertolt Brecht to produce their smash sensation, *Mahagonny Songspiele*, for the prestigious Baden-Baden festival. Lenya, for whom Weill had written the lead singing role, received her proper due for putting the whole thing across. Although she was musically illiterate and willing to learn, Weill told her to stay the way she was, perceiving it as an advantage in reaching broad audiences. It was Lenya who first sang the "Alabama-Song" and in the process winning life-long artistic approval from Brecht, a rare distinction to be sure.[21] Spoto notes perceptively that "Her lack of pretense, her apparent vulnerability as well as her nervousness — she fought stage fright all during her life — were a refreshing contrast to a great deal in the tradition of florid and elaborate 'stage presence.'"[22] These qualities set Lenya apart from other singers in Berlin such as Marlene Dietrich, herself then in the process of becoming famous.

Work on a full-scale opera by the same creative team as a follow-up to the success of *Mahagonny* was interrupted by a new commission to produce yet another opera for the recently reopened Theater am Schiffbauerdamm in Berlin. On incredibly short time frame, *The Threepenny Opera* was written and orchestrated during a chaotic summer holiday on the French Riviera and premiered to the world in August 1928, the 200th anniversary of the English play on which it was based, *The Beggar's Opera* by John Gay.[23] According to all accounts, everyone involved had deep reservations on whether the curtain should go up on opening night, but Lenya, once again singing lead with a part written specifically for her (plus being rewritten right up until the 11th hour) led the charge of cast and crew onto the Überbrettl of the intimate Schiffbauerdamm. Audiences and critics were astounded and delighted; within a few months, almost everyone involved with the production was financially secure and being asked to do more work. More importantly, music history was made that evening, with German *Kabarett*, in its multiple guises and incarnations, beginning to take international center stage.

For the next five years, Lenya the singer-actress was in constant demand both as a performer and recording artist. Foremost among her notable starring roles was in the operatic version of *The Rise and Fall of the City of Mahagonny* in 1930, often performed in the face of open Nazi Party hostility.[24] These protests made such an impression on her that she forever after associated the work with Nazi ascendancy in Germany during that period.[25] In 1931 came the classic G.W. Pabst movie version of *The Threepenny Opera* in which Lenya was immortalized on film singing "Pirate Jenny" (see Chapter 10). Around this same time, Weill began to have a prolonged affair with Erika Neher, wife of Caspar Neher, the gay set designer for many of Weill and Brecht's most famous and successful works.[26] By 1932, Weill and Lenya were living separate lives, Lenya openly carrying on her first prolonged extra-marital affair with the Italian tenor Otto von Pasetti, her co-star in the Vienna production of *Mahagonny*.[27] During her Vienna homecoming, admiring critics noted how she was able to marvelously humanize the character of Jenny, world-weary prostitute and fair-weathered friend.[28] Whether these critics were aware of Lenya's personal past on the streets of Vienna only two decades prior is unknown; there can be no doubt that personal experience informed Lenya's tragic and realistic "Jenny" stage persona — one used to such tremendous effect in both *Mahagonny* and *Threepenny*—which very few actors were able to duplicate in such convincing manner.

In 1933 Weill, both as a Jew and leading cultural symbol of everything loathed by the new-ruling Nazi regime, was forced to flee Germany for Paris. Lenya, still on friendly terms with Weill, stayed behind, helped to look after his financial affairs, and tried to keep a low profile in Vienna. The two were quickly united in Paris later that year for Lenya's performance in Weill and Brecht's *The Seven Deadly Sins*, a singing-ballet directed by a young up-and-coming choreographer, George Balanchine.[29] Lenya's co-star, stage alter ego, and off-stage lover in this memorable production was the beautiful Austrian dancer and actress, Tilly Losch. Lenya had been introduced to Parisian gay social circles by admiring film director Jean Cocteau, although coming from Weimar Berlin, alternative lifestyles in the performing arts would have certainly been nothing new to her.[30] Earlier in 1932, Lenya filed for divorce, and in 1933 the settlement was finalized. It was a move that she would regret for the rest of her life, although at the time there appears to have been an element of political necessity.[31] In order to be an effective friend to Weill in German business matters, she also had to make an appearance of distancing herself from him.[32] Such were the terrible times in which they lived.

Weill, after leaving Germany for Paris, though busy and earning a living, had lost most of his material possessions, as well as his country of birth, and was bitter about it, to say the least.[33] By 1934, Lenya was a star celebrity but adrift, no longer Mrs. Kurt Weill. Despondent that their world had crumbled, she reportedly attempted suicide while in Zurich. Then friends intervened. Correspondence, which had never ceased being cordial, grew warmer and more frequent. By 1935, they were reconciled and reunited in France. Weill invited Lenya to join him on a trip to America to participate in the projected opening of his new work, *The Eternal Road*, a topical, elaborate, musical allegory-extravaganza on the Jewish diaspora then unfolding across the world stage. The huge production had been mostly organized by Weill's fellow-in-exile and cabaret pioneer, Max Reinhardt. *The Eternal Road* would eventually prove to be an expensive commercial flop for its investors, but succeeded in getting Weill and Lenya (among others) out of Europe and into the States just before the political situation in the Old World grew much, much worse. On September 4, 1935, the excited couple sailed from Cherbourg to New York City, arriving on September 9th.[34] It marked the beginning of an extraordinary second phase in the development of Weill's artistic legacy, one in which Lenya, yet again, would be right by his side.

Weill's American career would thrive over the next 15 years, but Lenya's did not, or at least did not seem to at the time. Whereas Weill adapted to Broadway with startling alacrity (see Chapter 11), Lenya seemed out of her element. She was slower to learn English, and publicity attempts to glam her up Hollywood-style only came across as awkward and ill-conceived. Her persona of Jenny the Prostitute which had conquered European stages was incomprehensible or offensive to most American audiences. Weill later tried writing an American vehicle specifically for her, *The Firebrand of Florence* (1945), but, much to his chagrin, it bombed badly — his only American failure after landing on U.S. soil. In a final act of pathetic resignation, Lenya resolved to retire from the stage and focus on being a good house wife. Despite these disappointments, however, there were bright spots. Lenya and Weill officially remarried on January 19, 1937, and this time stayed married. After Weill's massive 1941 commercial success with *Lady in the Dark*, they bought a delightful old residence (Brook House) in suburban New York. Although the marriage arrangement itself remained open by mutual consent, there was never again any question as to personal or professional loyalties. In public life, they were strictly a couple, and both seemed to like it that way.

There were also musical consolations. From the moment they set foot in America, both were often treated like artistic royalty. No sooner had they arrived in 1935 than both were invited by George Gershwin to witness dress rehearsals for the historic premiere of *Porgy and Bess*, with Lenya sitting next to Gershwin himself in the audience.[35] In 1937, Lenya performed in the radio opera *I've Got the Tune* by Marc Blitzstein (1905–1964), a young American composer who later, during the 1950s, would play a central role in reacquainting the public with Weill's works.[36] In 1938, Lenya took a modest cabaret gig at New York City's Le Ruban Bleu and, star-struck, discovered the likes of Marlene Dietrich and Cole Porter sitting in the audience admiring her performance.[37] Later she admitted that "I never sang in cabarets.... I was approached many times ... but I never could."[38] In 1941, American playwright Maxwell Anderson — next door neighbor and friend, wrote a part for Lenya in a touring production of his drama *Candle in the Wind*. It was during this tour, according to Lenya, that she first saw the American heartland, giving her valuable insight into Midwestern audiences that many star performers even nowadays seem to lack.[39] After U.S. entry into World War II, she appeared in 1943, with Weill providing piano accompaniment, at a wartime fundraiser ("We Fight Back") hosted by Hunter College in Manhattan (see Chapter 12). The program featured old and new songs, including the topical Weill and Brecht meditation on their former homeland, *Und was bekam des Soldaten Weib?* ("Ballad of the Soldier's Wife"), plus *Lost in the Stars*, a full six years before the same-titled Weill and Anderson musical opened on Broadway. Six songs from this recital became Lenya's debut U.S. recording soon afterwards.[40] In 1944, she became a U.S. citizen. In 1945, however, came *Firebrand* and she was savaged by critics. Utterly convinced that she had become an artistic liability for Weill, Lenya decided to give up her singing career.

In the aftermath of the war, Lenya seemed permanently settled into a quiet life outside of the public eye when in 1950, after a brief illness, Weill died of heart failure. His will left absolutely everything to her.[41] All friends from that time agree that Lenya was inconsolable with grief and guilt, fearing for her life as well since she neither showed nor expressed much interest in living.[42] Lenya recalled, "After Kurt died, I really sank to the bottom of the ocean." At this critical juncture, in May 1950, an old friendship was renewed with writer-editor George Davis, who had first met Lenya during a photo shoot for *Harper's Bazaar* in 1936.[43] Though openly gay, Davis was destined to become, in the words of mutual friend Milton Caniff, "the architect of the entire Lenya enterprise in the 1950s."[44] The two soon became constant companions and in 1951 entered into a marriage of warm friendship and business convenience. The third phase in the promotion of Kurt Weill's musical legacy was about to commence. In 1950, Lenya had resolved to dedicate her remaining career to the preservation and promotion of Weill's artistic legacy.[45] High-profile gigs followed in short order. In 1951, old friends organized a "Kurt Weill Concert" at New York City's Town Hall in which she performed.[46] Later that same year, Anderson wrote another dramatic part for Lenya as the wife of Socrates (*Barefoot in Athens*).[47] In 1952, she was invited to sing the role of Jenny in concert, this time in a brand-new English translation of *The Threepenny Opera* by Marc Blitzstein at Brandeis University, with Leonard Bernstein conducting.[48]

Encouraged by a favorable reception, Lenya agreed in 1953 to reprise her *Threepenny* role, this time in a full-blown musical stage version of the Blitzstein translation at the recently-converted, 299-seat, off–Broadway, Theatre de Lys in Greenwich Village.[49] Amazingly, Blitzstein had persuaded his fellow Marxist Bertolt Brecht to grant permission for mounting of the new production.[50]

The show opened on March 10, 1954.[51] By this time Lenya was 55 years old and her voice was a shadow of its former self. She went through with the premier only to honor the Weill's memory, and because Davis and Blitzstein had insistently badgered her into it. An earlier (1933), inferior English-language version of *Threepenny* on Broadway had failed miserably. Despite exceptions like the 1948 success of Tennessee Williams' *Summer and Smoke*, all off–Broadway shows at that time were considered risky financial affairs.[52] The political reign of terror in the U.S. imposed by McCarthyism on anything remotely associated with leftist politics had only recently begun to abate.[53] There was no reason to hope for anything better than a modest, small-margin profit. Nevertheless, an energized Lenya, with her graying hair dyed Technicolor red, hit the American Überbrettl that evening one more time as *Threepenny* Jenny, a role she had originated 26 years earlier in Weimar Berlin.[54] From day one, the production was a massive sell-out, overwhelming everyone involved with cascading audience demand. *The Threepenny Opera* went on to log in 2,611 shows over the course of seven years, the first real blockbuster off the main strip, and up until that time the longest continually running musical in history.[55] Then, on March 1, 1956, a more-than-deserving Lotte Lenya, former Viennese street waif known as Karoline Blaumauer, was presented a Tony Award by grateful peers for her near single-handed creation of the off–Broadway music industry, still flourishing to this day.[56]

In retrospect it is striking how none of these events appeared inevitable, and may well have never occurred but for the individual, heroic efforts of Lenya, Blitzstein, and Davis. As a young composer touring Europe in the 1920s, Blitzstein, like many of his elders, was hostile and disparaging towards Weill's populist approach to music. He managed, however, to catch *The Three-penny Opera* in its premier run, and by the 1930s had changed his mind completely.[57] Shortly after Weill and Lenya arrived in America, an admiring Blitzstein attended their Group Theater workshop in which *Threepenny* music was played.[58] In 1937, the same year he invited Lenya to perform in his radio opera, Blitzstein achieved everlasting fame with his pro–Labor, Orson Welles collaboration, *The Cradle Will Rock*. By the 1950s, however, leftist politics had gone out of fashion and Weill's music, despite being successful during his lifetime, was now being ignored on both sides of the Atlantic.[59] Add to these, the ascendancy of television. What Weill would have thought of the new medium is difficult to say; mostly likely, he would have adapted to it just as he had successfully adapted to everything else in his life. The American revival of *Threepenny*, however, seems only to have happened because of dogged persistence from a very small group of artists led by Lenya, not in search of fast profits but rather out of sheer conviction and belief in the work itself.

Following the American *Threepenny's* unlikely triumph in 1954, Lenya was lured back to the recording studio. First came an original cast LP. "Nobody thought it would work," she later recalled.[60] Instead, like the musical, it was a massive hit, going on to influence an entire generation of American songwriters (see Chapter 18). Then in 1955 came her first return to Germany since 1935. Lenya resisted the trip, according to a friend, because she still hated most Germans after her exile. Meeting Brecht in Berlin, she made him weep with her singing, then it was on to Hamburg for recording sessions featuring songs from *Threepenny* and other Weill and Brecht classics.[61] After returning to the U.S., she joined Louis Armstrong for his breakthrough "Mack the Knife" sessions (see Chapter 14). While Lenya's extensive post-war recording legacy is often criticized due to her voice no longer being beautiful in the conventional sense, the fact is that doing what she did took tremendous courage and dedication; moreover, it was accomplished long before preserving Weill's musical heritage became a fashionable thing to do. Marlene Dietrich she was not; whereas Dietrich was, by the mid–1950s, the leading diva of Las Vegas, receiving material from some of the best songwriting talent of the day (see Chapter 13), Lenya was past her prime, both in looks and voice, attempting a comeback (after a long hiatus) by performing works of a dead composer recently on the verge of being forgotten. That Lenya, hailing from the humblest circumstances in Vienna, succeeded in becoming world ambassador of concert-hall cabaret, while Dietrich, the daughter of middle-class Prussian respectability, became the cinematic queen of *Tingel Tangel* low-brow entertainment, makes a noteworthy contrast. Add to this that Lenya, with Weill's insistence, remained musically illiterate and did everything mostly by rote, one must surely have a better appreciation for her overall achievement. On one hand, Billie Holiday was her favorite singer; on another, Benjamin Britten her favorite modern composer.[62] Unusual dichotomies such as these underscore Lenya's uniqueness as an artist, both on record and in her own day as a performer.

Lenya's extraordinary post-war comeback temporarily paused in 1957 with the death of her second husband and business benefactor, George Davis, from a sudden heart attack, the same malaise that killed Weill (at nearly the same young age) seven years earlier. Though shocked and staggered, Lenya forged ahead with her rejuvenated career, and within a short time was back in the limelight. On November 14, 1961, back at the Theater de Lys, she headlined the premier of *Brecht on Brecht*, a revue including both songs and dramatic readings.[63] Lenya, the actress who had caught the eyes of both Georg Kaiser and Richard Révy some four decades earlier, began to reassert herself on the theatrical stage. Soon, she was landing major film roles, the most famous proving to be her sinister portrayal of James Bond-nemesis, Rosa Klebb, in *From Russia with Love* (1963), a part in which she, at age 64, did her own on-screen hand-to-hand stunts with Sean Connery.[64] Then in 1966, producer Hal Prince offered her the role of Fräuline Schneider in *Cabaret*, the new pioneering Broadway musical by John Kander and Fred Ebb (see Chapter 15). She accepted instantly, and the rest is history. Lenya had long been a fan of Christopher Isherwood (see Chapter 7) and later flatly stated that "I loved doing every minute of *Cabaret*."[65] Composer John Kander recalled with amazement that Lenya, as elder stateswoman of that production, when not on stage, seemed intimately acquainted with all of the dives and marginal performers in New York City.[66] By the time *Cabaret* became an Oscar-honored movie in 1972, she was 74 years old and only performing sporadically. She still found time, however, to promote the opening of *Berlin to Broadway with Kurt Weill*, once again at the Theater de Lys, site of her many past triumphs.[67] Two more husbands (both gay) and lovers of both sexes came and went.[68] In 1978, at age 80, she made her last public appearance singing songs from *Cabaret* in a celebrity-packed Kander and Ebb concert at Avery Fisher Hall. Curiously, late in life, Lenya, by then the living embodiment of alternative lifestyle, showed little interest in 1960s and 1970s counterculture. "Women's liberation bores me to death.... I was born free and remain that way," was about all that she had to say on the subject.[69]

The elderly Lenya was fond of quoting an old Viennese proverb: "In Berlin the situation is serious but not hopeless. In Vienna the situation is hopeless but not serious."[70] Whether this favorite quip reflected the gloomy mood of many Americans during the late-Jimmy Carter administration, or a premonition of her own impending demise, we are not prepared to say. All that is documented for certain is that on November 27, 1981, after a long fight with multiple illnesses, the self-created woman known to world as Lotte Lenya passed away, according to witnesses, whispering the names of many loved ones known throughout her lengthy sojourn in life.[71] She was buried next to Kurt Weill in upstate New York. Did Weill's long, close relationship with Lenya, a true daughter of the proletariat, steer him more towards entertainment for the masses? This seems more than likely. Weill otherwise may well have ended up just another mostly-forgotten, modernist composer from the early 20th century, despite his brilliant, versatile talent. As for Lenya, her surprising disdain for women's liberation calls to mind another ex-patriot German cabaret diva, a near contemporary, and in many ways, artistic foil, despite both women having professed mutual admiration for each other's extraordinary theatrical and musical abilities.

5. The Long, Strange Journey of Marlene Dietrich

"Nevermind those old German songs—we are in America now and Broadway is tougher than the Kurfürstendamm."*—*Kurt Weill to Marlene Dietrich[1]

In early 1930, around the same time that Lotte Lenya was recording the "Alabama-Song" from Weill and Brecht's *The Rise and Fall of the City of Mahagonny*, a work whose Leipzig premier was disrupted by Nazi demonstrators, a brand new movie was being released across Germany and the U.S. This film, *Der Blaue Engel* ("The Blue Angel") would prove to be the breakthrough for another young German singing actress destined to become the very symbol of her time and place in history. If Lotte Lenya later became (rather improbably) cabaret's good-will ambassador to the world, then it might well be said that Marlene Dietrich embodied, to most international audiences, cabaret itself in all of its glory and infamy. Good will had nothing to do with it; Dietrich was there for all to see and hear whether we liked it or not — and most of us still like it quite a bit. Explaining to the uninitiated how exactly such a phenomenon came to into being is no easy task. The best that we can hope to accomplish in this limited space is to reiterate a few generally agreed-upon facts, interject commentary at regular intervals, and then allow patient readers to judge for themselves as to the precise cause-and-effect relationships that drive such seemingly irresistible forces of nature.

Maria Magdalene Dietrich was born in the fabled Schöneberg district of Berlin on December 27, 1901, the same year that saw Berlin's first explosive wave of cabaret arrive on the scene (see Chapter 1). Her father, Louis Erich Otto Dietrich, was a decorated veteran of the Franco-Prussian War, a respectable career police lieutenant, and upright member of the Berlin middle class. Her mother, Wilhelmina Elisabeth Josephine Felsing, came from a cultured, well-to-do family of Prussian artisans. There was also an older sister, Elisabeth, born one year before. The mother had wanted a son when the second daughter arrived, and reportedly treated Maria Magdalene somewhat like a boy, nick-naming her "Paul" and teaching the girl resourceful self-reliance in all things. Older sister Elisabeth liked dolls and games. Maria Magdalene liked music, drama and poetry.[2] From an early age, the younger daughter was taught to play violin, and demonstrated considerable aptitude.[3] Despite having the same biological parents and upbringing, and despite being only a single year apart in age, by adolescence it was becoming increasingly difficult to view the Diet-rich sisters as having much in common besides a gene pool. Even their hand-writing was opposite. Elisabeth favored the formal, old-fashioned style while Maria Magdalene opted for a more modern flourish, a type of script that the Nazis would later in fact take trouble to officially ban.[4]

When Maria Magdalene was six years old, her father fell unexpectedly ill and died relatively young.[5] Briefly, during World War I, the mother remar-ried another German officer, but by 1918 had been made into a widow again.[6] Like the mother, teenage daughter Elisabeth married into the German military, and this husband survived the war. Meanwhile, younger daughter Maria Mag-dalene stayed unattached, attended music school and then, sometime during her late teens (no one agrees exactly when), combined her two first names into "Marlene"—at the time a relatively novel conceit. Rather than worship male movie stars, she idolized German actress Henny Porten, whose uncon-ventional, do-it-yourself screen persona popularly reflected the necessities of independent German womanhood during wartime.[7] By 1916, Marlene's family relocated to provincial Dessau, also then-home to future composer Kurt Weill's family (see Chapter 3). Though belonging to opposite social worlds in Dessau, it is quite possible that the young Kurt Weill and the young Marlene Dietrich knowingly or unknowingly crossed each other's path. One thing is for certain: before the war ended and before she came of age, and despite her unassailable "Germanic" credentials (including physical appearance), the 17-year-old Mar-lene Dietrich had become the proverbial black sheep of her family. She was a good example of what Weimar historian Peter Gay termed "insider-outsider" rebellion to the respectable Prussian society in which her mother and older sister seemed to move so naturally.

Little is known of Dietrich's activities during the turbulent post-war years in Germany of 1919–1920, but by 1921 she was back home in Berlin, on her own, and taking on any work she could find in the burgeoning entertain-ment industry. As the Greek historian Plutarch once wrote with respect to Julius Caesar, steady, irresistible progress began with the most meager of beginnings, and the same observation applies to Dietrich. First came a job as violinist in a *Kabarett* pit orchestra, then more tellingly, as a chorus line show girl in Guido Thielscher's *Girl-Kabarett* revue.[8] In 1922, like a guided missile, she zeroed in on Max Reinhardt's famed acting studio, but failed her first audition, much to Reinhardt's later embarrassment.[9] This setback, however, proved temporary. Dietrich frequented Rosa Valetti's Café Meglomania (see Chapter 2) where she got to know both Valetti and her house composer, Friedrich Hollaender. Hollaender's uncle Victor worked for Reinhardt, and through this connection was finally accepted into acting school, this time with private acting lessons thrown into the bargain.[10] Partly out of gratitude and partly out of respect for his talent, Dietrich later made the younger Hollaender her personal songwriter of choice over the next half century. As biographer Donald Spoto wrote, "Holla[e]nder's tunes became identified with Dietrich's voice and presence, and composers for her other films invariably turned to those recordings for inspiration."[11] Valetti, already by then a seasoned professional stage veteran, was used to seeing good-looking, aspiring female performers come and go, and was at first, like so many others, unimpressed with the young Dietrich. Then Valetti heard her sing, and, as millions of others would later react, marveled at Dietrich's voice.[12] Bear in mind what Valetti heard in those early days was not the powerhouse delivery of Enrico Caruso or Fritzi Massary, but rather a simple, direct instrument both distinctive and confident well beyond its 22 years.

Dietrich was of course not the only young, attractive, talented performer in Berlin at that time; many others, like her, were triple threats (that is, singer, dancer, actor). Lenya, for instance, had similar credentials, yet her career had nearly derailed by 1924. In Dietrich's case there seems to have been some intangible factor at work as well. Whether it was her relentless drive, boundless energy, street smarts, plain luck, or all of the above—whatever it was, not only did she seem to always find work, she took on as much work as she could get away with at any given moment. As early as 1922, Dietrich was landing bit parts in silent films, then in 1923, a larger role in *Tragödie der Liebe* ("Tragedy of Love"), shortly after which she married the associate producer, Rudolf Sieber (1897–1976) who had helped her land this part.[13] A daughter was born shortly afterwards in 1924, but the new mother's work schedule did not decrease; rather, it seemed to accelerate. Her first important stage role, albeit a small one under Reinhardt's banner, came in 1922–1923 with Frank Wedekind's *Die Büchse der Pandora* ("Pandora's Box"), directed by her future film songwriter, Friedrich Hollaender.[14] By the mid–1920s, she had added Shakespeare and Shaw to her résumé, even as she continued to appear on screen in no fewer than 10 minor movie roles between 1924 and 1927.[15]

In spite of all this, however, and as Spoto has observed (accurately enough): "there was nothing particularly polished or impressive about Dietrich in the early 1920s, and she was not singled out for special attention onstage or in cabaret."[16] Her first real critical recognition did not come until 1927 for a small role in *Die Schule von Uznach* ("The School of Uznach") by Carl

Sternheim, then Germany's leading comic playwright. That same year she was made a cast member for the European premier (in Vienna) of *Broadway*, the new hit American play by George Abbott and Philip Dunning.[17] When not performing on stage or film, Dietrich established a highly visible, see-and-be-seen presence in some of Berlin's most fashionable (and notorious) cabarets.[18] As Dietrich gradually gained notoriety and became a fixture within Berlin's controversial *Girl-Kulture* of 1920s, her bohemian lifestyle also lost the approval of her conservative mother, who favored more the conventional norms of provincial marriage and parenthood adopted by eldest daughter Elisabeth.[19]

During this formative period, Dietrich came into close contact with one of Weimar Berlin's most dynamic performers, the inimitable Claire Waldoff, aka Clara Wortmann (1884–1957).[20] In appearance, Waldoff could not have been more different than Dietrich the cabaret show-girl—short and plump with frizzy red hair and working class demeanor. Waldoff was also openly gay and, according to some, one the very first female performers in Germany to regularly dress like a man.[21] Above all, she had a powerhouse vocal delivery that could flatten even the most indifferent audiences at long-distance ranges. Extant recordings support her legend. Amazed critics at the time tried in vain to analyze Waldoff's technique as she stood still as a statue except for her eyes which constantly rolled and darted across the room while singing the most bawdy or politically incorrect songs imaginable, all at piercing decibel levels. The people loved it. Dietrich struck up an unlikely friendship and learned a lot fast: a female singer did not necessarily need a wide vocal capacity or even a feminine look to mesmerize an audience. According to cabaret star Curt Bois, it was Waldoff who also taught Dietrich the all-important "backstage" arts of appearance and image.[22] It was also around this same time that Dietrich purportedly began to experiment with alternative, bisexual lifestyles in which she would continue to indulge for the rest of her long career. Austrian starlet Tilly Losch, rumored to be among Dietrich's lovers (and soon to become one of Lenya's as well), later recalled that Dietrich adopted a "glamorous" masculine look early on, and that she cultivated a reputation for outrageousness both on and off stage. Even before she became famous, everyone agreed that Dietrich stood out in a crowd. Losch also noted, however (almost incredulously), that Dietrich did not do drugs and was a light drinker—in her Berlin days at least—quite contrary to the zeitgeist of that particular time and place (see Chapter 8).[23] Whatever she later may have become, Dietrich the aspiring star (and, lest we forget, married mother) appeared uniquely capable of harnessing her instilled Prussian discipline and self-control whenever it came to career advancement.

With the late 1920s came Dietrich's final, astounding vault into the stratosphere of superstardom. After Al Jolson's game-changing performance in *The Jazz Singer* (1927), along with the overnight ascendance of talking motion pictures, the market value of talented singing actresses suddenly shot up. Concurrent with this trend was the triumphant infiltration of American jazz into European musical entertainment, especially in Germany where the intimate literary cabarets of the early 1920s were quickly replaced by large-scaled, thematically-related extravaganza stage revues. The very same performers who in 1923 were lucky to be singing in front of 100 people were now facing much larger audiences, and good ones (of which there were many) adapted very well to increased exposure. Dietrich, by 1928, had become a charter member of this elite group. To her great fortune, or thanks to her savvy, or both combined, she successfully auditioned for a musical revue by the crack songwriting team of Mischa Spoliansky and Marcellus Schiffer (see Chapter 6). With Spoliansky himself at the piano, Dietrich initially had trouble navigating the composer's ambitious key ranges and was on the verge of being dismissed by the director when, on the spot, Spoliansky took trouble to improvise a lower octave more friendly to Dietrich's distinctively deep voice. She promptly nailed the tune (to her own astonishment) and was accordingly grateful to Spoliansky for the rest of her life.[24] *Es Liegt in der Luft* ("It's in the Air") opened at the Komödie Theater in 1928, Dietrich co-starring with Schiffer's wife Margo Lion, and German film-stage veteran Hubert von Meyerninck. The show was a resounding and scandalous success, the best-known number being a duet of thinly-disguised homosexual love between the lead female characters played by Dietrich and Lion, *Wenn die beste Freudin* ("When the Special Girlfriend").[25] Lion — the tall, skinny, glamorous, and sometimes campy parodist, appears to have been another major influence on Dietrich during this crucial phase of her early career. Along with Claire Waldoff, it was Margo Lion who helped to shape Dietrich into the risqué, outrageous performer of world celebrity that she was then on the cusp of becoming.

Another Spoliansky-composed revue followed in 1929 to capitalize on the rousing success of *It's in the Air*. Now Spoliansky collaborated with Georg Kaiser, recent Berlin mentor for both Kurt Weill and Lotte Lenya. The result was *Zwei Krawatten* ("Two Bow Ties"), another vehicle featuring Dietrich, this time co-starring with cabaret-film stars Rosa Valetti and Hans Albers.[26] As fate would have it, both Valetti and Albers had been recently cast by the Austrian-American director Josef von Sternberg to appear in his rapidly approaching Berlin film shoot of *The Blue Angel*, and Sternberg made it his business to attend their current stage show. At this late date, a choice had still not been made for the lead role of Lola Lola, although every high-profile starlet in Germany was publicly rumored to be interested.[27] Dietrich was a proverbial dark horse, but as soon as Sternberg saw her on stage, he was floored by her beauty, intelligence, talent, and toughness. The decision was immediately made to cast Dietrich in the lead, and Sternberg insistently stuck with his handpicked star in the face of persistent, doubting associates. *The Blue Angel* was filmed in late 1929 and released to international acclaim in early 1930. The rest, as they say, is history (see Chapter 10).

No sooner had the preview party for *The Blue Angel* been thrown in Berlin than Dietrich sailed for America and Hollywood to continue her partnership with Sternberg for six more films over the next five years. Not only had she instantly become Germany's biggest movie star, Dietrich now challenged the biggest American stars in terms of pure celebrity, including Greta Garbo (1905–1990), who before that moment had reigned supreme as Hollywood's undisputed number one European import. Plus Dietrich was a devastatingly effective singer and now began to regularly prove it in the recording studio. American audiences received an eyeful and earful of things never before experienced, such as Dietrich in *Morocco* (1930), including a scene in which her French cabaret persona dons top hat and tails, delivers a *chanson réaliste*, kisses a gorgeous female patron on the lips, then affectionately tosses a carnation at Gary Cooper while inciting the indignation of his startled girlfriend. In *Blonde Venus* (1932), Dietrich enters a New York speakeasy wearing a gorilla costume, accompanied by half-naked savages and jungle music, before stripping down to show-girl bare essentials, sporting a blond wig (though she is already a blonde), and singing, Josephine Baker–style, "Hot Voodoo" to a smitten gangster played by Cary Grant in his breakthrough role. These are representative samplers of early Dietrich film numbers. In Berlin such things were commonplace, but for the American heartland, it came as a shock. Dietrich's movie antics, often orchestrated and encouraged by Sternberg, have been postulated as an indirect cause of the Hollywood censorship code then coming into existence, and this writer sees no reason to dispute that opinion. For certain is the fact that by 1930 Dietrich, almost single-handedly, had bravely imported the wildness and freedom of German *Kabarett* onto the Hollywood big screen, and, for better or worse, there would be no going back after that, either for audiences or other performers.

Meanwhile, back in Germany, the political situation was beginning to rapidly deteriorate. By the time that Dietrich filmed *The Song of Songs* in 1933, Hitler and the Nazis had completely taken over the reigns of German government. Anyone previously affiliated with cabaret now had three unsavory choices: flee, join the bad guys, or die. For Jews, who comprised the majority, there only two choices. Dietrich was not Jewish, but her hatred for the Nazis was early, pronounced, and consistent. When she came to Hollywood in 1930, husband and daughter joined her. Mother, sister, and other relatives, however, stayed behind. She briefly returned to Berlin in 1934, had a bizarre meeting with Joseph Goebbels (whom she openly loathed), and then avoided Germany for the next decade. There were rumors that Goebbels had forced the interview by making veiled threats against her relatives.[28] The Nazis simultaneously panned Dietrich's film work in public while trying to lure her back home for conversion into a Third Reich media symbol. In 1937, she applied for U.S. citizenship, which was granted two years later. In 1938, she traveled to Switzerland to meet with her mother and sister's family in one last attempt to get them out of Germany.[29] They elected to remain. Back in the States, Dietrich, written off by some industry experts because her box office had begun to flag, came charging back in 1939 with *Destry Rides Again*, co-starring James Stewart. Featuring music and words by fellow German émigré Friedrich Hollaender and German-American Broadway stalwart Frank Loesser, Dietrich proudly reassumed her shady French cabaret persona (via New Orleans), now transplanted to the confines of a western frontier saloon, as she sang "See What the Boys in the Backroom Will Have."

Dietrich's laudable, combat-zone activities during World War II are best treated elsewhere in this study (see Chapter 12), but the coda for this heroic period in her career brought personal disappointment and tragedy. Even after ceasefire, for her the war was not quite yet over. With German surrender in 1945 came first a short-lived reunion in France with her favorite pre-war lover, French matinee idol and Resistance-hero Jean Gabin (1904–1976), who announced to Dietrich that he wanted to discontinue their relationship in favor of conventional marriage and family, preferably with a younger woman. This public humiliation, possibly the first and greatest romantic rejection that she ever experienced, was only the beginning of her sorrows. Thanks to U.S. Army connections, she was able to track down her mother and sister's family, both of whom were still alive. Throughout the war Dietrich had harbored a fantasy in which she would triumphantly return to Germany, rescue her relatives from the evils of fascism, and everything would go back to the way it was during the 1920s. Instead, she discovered that her relatives did not want to be rescued. The mother was living in bombed-out, occupied Berlin, and after an emotional reunion, informed her world-famous daughter that Germany was her home, and always would be. Then came the real shock. Sister Elisabeth and her husband were stationed at Bergen-Belsen, not as inmates in the concentration camp, but rather as part of the civilian support apparatus for the *Shutzstaffel* ("SS"). They may have not been pulling the triggers, but they were certainly catering to war criminals who did. Not long after Dietrich returned to the U.S. that same year, she was denying the very existence of her sister, and Elisabeth followed suit by doing the same in kind.[30] Only six months after Dietrich left Germany, her mother died, still proudly bearing the surname of von Losch (rather than Dietrich), the name of her second husband (for two years) during the first World War.[31] For the great prodigal daughter Marlene, then 44 years old, the whole family saga had to have come as a profound shock that changed her for the rest of a long remaining life.[32]

Dietrich returned to Hollywood and went back to work. In 1948 she reunited with Hollaender and fellow German ex-patriot, director Billy Wilder, to film *Foreign Affair*, a classy production set in post-war Berlin, yielding no fewer than three classic Dietrich standards — "Ruins of Berlin," "Illusions," and "Black Market." Otherwise, her late 1940s career seemed lackluster. She studiously avoided Broadway, whose critics had recently savaged Lotte Lenya (see Chapter 4), perhaps recalling Kurt Weill's stern warning to her a few years previous. Then in 1950 she teamed up with Alfred Hitchcock to give a creepy, unforgettable performance as the villainess in *Stage Fright*. When not playing the public persona of Marlene Dietrich for Hitchcock, she delivered an over-the-top, burlesque rendition of Cole Porter's "The Laziest Gal in Town" — a song written especially for Dietrich that would remain on her standard play list. The opposite truth of course was that Dietrich was well-known among industry insiders as the hardest working woman in show business. In 1950, for her distinguished war-time activities she was awarded the French Legion of Honor — the most rarely bestowed medal among western countries.[33] Then the template she successfully experimented with in *Stage Fright* was built upon further to reinvent a whole new image, one that would proceed to dominate the international post-war entertainment world. After recording a series of duets with a young and yet-to-be-famous Rosemary Clooney in 1952, Dietrich accepted an enormous offer to do a three-week engagement in Las Vegas, then still a relatively undeveloped backwater not known for presenting quality acts. Going against the advice of her colleagues, she opened at the Sahara Hotel in 1953 and was a smash sensation, in the process initiating the true transformation of that city into its modern version (see Chapter 13). This American triumph in turn provided her with a springboard for a touring cabaret show that conquered most of Europe during the 1950s.[34]

As the 1950s wound down, Dietrich, ever on the lookout for new talent, took a young, unknown, Jewish-American composer-arranger named Burt Bacharach under her wing. Bacharach assisted in raising her already peerless stage show to even new and greater levels of sophistication). Finally in 1960, she decided that the time was ripe to return to Berlin and tour Germany. Biographer Steven Bach summarized the logic of the decision: "She was German, the most famous German woman of the century, their one true world star, a culture symbol whether she wanted to be or not. She was an emblem of the Weimar Republic and embodied ideals of duty and discipline bred in the bone of the empire."[35]

The decision proved to be one of her rare professional miscalculations.

Although the German government publicly and officially fawned over her, the German *Volk* did not. While some fans cheered enthusiastically, many others greeted her with "Marlene Go Home" signs or simply boycotted the concert halls. The low point came in Düsseldorf, site of the Nazis' "Degenerate Music" exhibition 23 years earlier (see Chapter 8), when an 18-year-old girl approached Dietrich outside of the theater, shouted "Traitor!" and spit in her face.[36] Had Dietrich been Jewish she might have been "forgiven" by the German people for giving comfort to the enemy during the war; as it was, her pure Prussian heritage and upbringing helped to condemn her. The same good-girl-gone-bad image so fascinating to Berlin audiences during the 1920s, now continued to be a liability for her in Germany a full 15 years after the war had ended. Although Dietrich would continue to appear before non–German audiences for almost two more decades, her performing days in Germany were over. Not until her own wartime generation of Germans began to die out, did she begin to regain massive popularity on native soil.[37]

After 1975, Dietrich's redoubtable career as a live performer finally came to a halt with failing health and cumulative, nagging injuries.[38] In 1976, somewhat to the surprise of friends, she was totally grief-stricken by the deaths of former lover Jean Gabin and then her husband of 53 years, Rudolf Sieber, for whom she always had nothing but good things to say. Despite a freewheeling lifestyle and reputation, Dietrich had married only once and chose to stay married. Financially, she supported her daughter, her husband, and her husband's mistress. Then, just when everyone thought she was finished, Dietrich rallied to make a riveting, brief appearance in the 1979 film *Just a Gigolo*, starring David Bowie. She was paid $250,000 for three days of work in early 1978 to portray the fictional Baroness von Semering, Madame of a post–World War I Berlin ring of male prostitutes, and to sing one chorus of the film title song. When she arrived on the set looking aged and feeble beyond her 77 years, no one recognized the famed star and thought another huge mistake had been made. The old pro, however, knew exactly what she was doing. Disappearing into a dressing room, Dietrich had in tow celebrity make-up artist Anthony Clavet, who had previously impressed her with his uncanny ability to create Marlene Dietrich look-alikes for *Vogue Paris*. She emerged as an older version of Marlene Dietrich, announcing with Prussian imperiousness to everyone present, including director David Hemmings, that she would now sing "that horrible old German song."[39] The cameras rolled. For a few moments, 1920s Weimar Berlin cabaret came breathing back to life in all of its profound sadness and desperation. The tango-like "Schöner Gigolo, armer gigolo"— politely translated for American audiences as "Just a Gigolo" by Irving Caesar in 1929 — was originally written in 1928 by Austrian songwriters Leonello Casucci and Julius Brammer. It was a massive hit on both sides of the Atlantic. Some of the more famous German versions circa 1929 were by the Dajos Béla (aka Leon Golzmann) Tanz-Orchester, the Paul Godwin Tanz-Orchester, and one of Dietrich's old personal friends, opera star Richard Tauber. All were forced out of Germany during the early 1930s. Wherever the inspiration came for this last effort, the candle of her genius burned brightly one final time for all to see, adding a fleeting moment of poignancy to an otherwise forgettable film.

After this appearance, Dietrich retreated to her Paris apartment, where she lived secluded the last 14 years of her life, excepting an occasional interview, celebrity phone call, or trip to the doctor.[40] She wanted the world to remember her as she was, citing her work with Sternberg on *The Devil Is a Woman* (1935) as her favorite movie role, since (as she put it) that film made her appear the most beautiful. In 1990, she publicly expressed happiness at the reunification of Germany.[41] She died on May 6, 1992, was given a public funeral in Paris with an American flag-draped coffin, and was buried, fittingly enough, near her birthplace in the Schöneberg district of Berlin next to the grave of a mother from whom she never seems to have won full approval. Dietrich out-lived her great Hollywood rival and fellow recluse, Greta Garbo, by about two years. Their lives make an interesting contrast. Though the Swedish-born Garbo was younger than Dietrich, she made it to Hollywood five years earlier, and was not particularly musical. She retired in 1941, age 36, at the height of her celebrity, and spent the rest of her life in New York City, where her wid-owed mother immigrated to join her. She was not publicly political, before, during, or after the war. Like Dietrich, she was bisexual, but never married and had no children. Dietrich, on the other hand, continued to make films and records right through the 1970s, influencing everyone in sight and earshot while doing so. She was an early, vocal opponent of fascism, and continually put herself at risk during the war by performing on the front lines. Though a naturalized U.S. citizen, she preferred to live in Paris.

In the final analysis, the mysterious, turbulent journey of Marlene Diet-rich through life defies rational explanation. By the time she made her perma-nent mark on western culture, Dietrich had somehow become, simultaneously, both a displaced, nomadic exile and prominent citizen of the world. Perhaps a bit of truth can be found in one of her movies. During the final frames of *Stage Fright*, after having been exposed and caught in a mousetrap-like plot sequence, Dietrich's evil character delivers a chilling monologue reflecting on her life and behavior. Bitterly recalling once owning a dog that repaid kindness with a bite, she coldly remarked that the animal consequently had to be put down, adding that the whole experience was like being slapped in the face by one's own mother. Did art mirror real life in this case? One cannot help but wonder; moreover, Hitchcock had to be aware of this connection. In any event, we will never know for certain. It can be safely said, however, that Dietrich was not alone among her generation in these wrenching personal experiences. For one, the man who wrote many songs forever associated with Dietrich had his own long, strange journey through the 20th century, though one far less high-profile in the public eye.

6. Hollaender, Spoliansky and Their Doomed Associates

"In many respects, Jewish political songs created on the eve of the Holocaust have become songs of the twentieth century."— Philip V. Bohlman[1]

As music historian Alex Ross once observed, "The Holocaust accomplished the murder not only of millions of individuals but entire schools of [musical] composition."[2] Fortunately for civilization, cabaret was not among those compositional schools completely wiped out, but it did have to take a big hit, thanks in large part to the majority of its best creative artists being Jewish. In addition to ethic and religious persecution within the Third Reich, anyone who dared to associate with Jews either personally or professionally often suffered a similar condemnation. For example, two of cabaret's biggest stars, Marlene Dietrich and Lotte Lenya, had to flee Germany during the mid–1930s on pain of death, despite both being as purely "Aryan" in birth and upbringing as any Nazi could possibly demand. Nevertheless, Lenya was married to a prominent Jewish composer, Kurt Weill, in addition to being a leading proponent of "degenerate music" (see Chapter 8). As for Dietrich, by 1930 arguably the biggest German celebrity in the entertainment world, there were no Jewish familial connections; however, her alleged crime in the eyes of the Nazis was similar — she willingly, happily consorted with Jewish composers, musicians, and actors, and worst of all, made absolutely no apologies for it. Rather, she seemed proud of it.

Not counting Dietrich's post-war American partnership with Burt Bacharach, the most famous and productive of her German-Jewish musical collaborations was with Friedrich Hollaender (1896–1976), an association lasting from their first meeting at Berlin's Café Megalomania in the early 1920s right up to Dietrich's retirement from the stage in the mid–1970s, shortly before Hollaender's death in 1976. Born into an established Berlin musical family, Hollaender was trained at the prestigious Stern Conservatory operated by his uncle Gustav, and where, like Kurt Weill after him, he counted Engelbert Humperdinck among his teachers.[3] His father Victor was an accomplished operetta composer and one of the first German professional cabaret songwriters at the dawn of the Überbrettl era (see Chapter 1). Being old enough to serve in the German army during World War I, Hollaender found himself assigned to duty as a bandleader for troop entertainment on the western front. Surviving the conflict, he landed at Max Reinhardt's path-breaking Sound and Smoke cabaret in Berlin, then in 1920 was hired away as house composer by Rosa Valetti for her new venture at Café Megalomania and later freelanced for Trude Hesterberg's Wild Stage as well.[4] By 1922, Hollaender had rubbed shoulders with the finest talent then blooming in the first wave of Berlin's literary *Kabarett* explosion, including his first wife and muse, *chanteuse* Blandine Ebinger, specializing in her populist "poor little street girl" persona.[5] His biggest new acquaintance from this period, however, would prove to be the young Dietrich, freshly arrived in Berlin to seek fame and fortune. Through Hollaender's family connections, Dietrich was able to get her foot into the door of Reinhardt's acting studio, her first major step towards achieving world celebrity (see Chapter 5).

From the very beginning of the Weimar era, Hollaender was a prolific composer of cabaret classics. Peter Jelavich, citing Hollaender himself, analyzed his work with the observation that "Hollaender's formula — the serious aspirations of elite 'theater,' the framework of the 'variety show,' and the 'political tribunal' of local antiauthoritarian sarcasm — was the recipe for Berlin cabaret."[6] Philip Bohlman rightfully asserted that "At the beginning of the twenty-first century, Holländer's songs are central to a canon for the revival of German-language cabaret and film music," judging him as "One of the most celebrated composers of the first generation of film music."[7] Hollaender's most famous film music was written for Dietrich's 1930 breakthrough film *The Blue Angel*, and included Dietrich's signature song, "Ich bin von Kopf bis Fuß auf Liebe eingestellt," better known in the loose English translation by Sammy Lerner, "Falling in Love Again." Hollaender's prime songwriting, however, began much earlier during the early 1920s as he churned out one masterpiece after another for the literary cabarets. In particular, Alan Lareau has written that "Hollaender's magnificent music for the Wilde Bühne ["Wild Stage"] has dramatic quality and sophistication that surpass any of the work that he did before or after this period."[8] By the late 1920s, Hollaender was also fronting Weintraub's Syncopators, one of Germany's leading jazz ensembles and selected by film director Josef von Sternberg to be the on-screen pit orchestra in *The Blue Angel*.[9]

In addition to his essential film work, Hollaender's career as a Berlin stage musician ended with a flurry of activity during the late 1920s and the early 1930s. A series of stunning *Kabarett-Revuen* began in the mid–1920s and culminated in 1931 with *Spuk in der Villa Stern* ("Ghosts in the Villa Stern").[10] This last piece dared to mock Adolf Hitler and all anti–Semites, including the poignant "Münchhausen"—a song which nonetheless suggested that the only real option for anti-fascist political sentiments in Germany was escape into fantasy and illusion.[11] If this were not defiance enough, Hollaender opened his own Berlin cabaret venture in 1931 within the old space formerly occupied by Trude Hesterberg's Wild Stage, dubbing it "Tingel-Tangel" in homage to the German vaudeville tradition that he himself had done so much to immortalize in *The Blue Angel*. He then used this high-profile location as a personal bully pulpit to lampoon the Nazis.[12] When the National Socialists finally took over Germany in 1933, Hollaender wisely fled to Hollywood, where his German film scoring credentials enabled him to earn a living.[13] Although his long, productive career still had over four more decades to run, by the time he left Germany, he had already created an enormous, diverse body of work absolutely central to the legacy of Weimar cabaret and film music.

Not too far behind Hollaender in importance as a Weimar-era cabaret composer was Mischa Spoliansky (1898–1985), born in Bialystok (then part of Russia, later Poland). By age 14, Spoliansky settled in Berlin as his Jewish relatives, like so many others, fled Eastern Europe to avoid persecution and war. Though only a teenager, he found work as a musician in the wartime cafes and cinemas of Berlin before being noticed by Hollaender's father Victor, who enabled the talented young refugee to enroll in the family-run Stern Conservatory.[14] After the war, Spoliansky was recruited by son Friedrich Hollaender to work in Reinhardt's Sound and Smoke, once again proving itself to be a magnet for top cabaret talent later dominating the Berlin scene during the Roaring Twenties. Once again following Hollaender's energetic example, Spoliansky first succeeded him as house composer for Sound and Smoke, then was quickly lured away to become house composer for the Wild Stage. Here he encountered an all-star lineup of Weimar talent, especially the poet-lyricist Marcellus Schiffer and his comic-chanteuse partner, Margo Lion. In 1922, after the trio persuaded impresario Hesterberg that Lion should perform a Spoliansky-Schiffer test pilot composition, the act drew raves and this important creative team was off to races for the next decade.[15] Even before Spoliansky met Schiffer, however, he was composing songs with controversial subject matter. The earliest of these included what is generally regarded as the first open celebration of same-sexuality, *Das Lila Lied* ("The Lavender Song"), written in 1920 under the pseudonym "Arno Billing" and dedicated to Magnus Hirschfeld, the pioneering sexologist whose work was destined to attract a young Christopher Isherwood to Berlin some 10 years later (see Chapter 7).[16] Another was the haunting instrumental *Morphium* ("Morphine"), written for

Anita Berber, the tragic, provocateur dance sensation of Weimar Germany, (see Chapter 8). Spoliansky himself married the dancer Elspeth Reinwald in 1922, and this marriage lasted over six decades until their respective deaths in 1980s.[17] Counted among his fans was Kurt Weill, himself then in the process of finding a wide audience.[18]

Spoliansky's golden Berlin period arrived during the late 1920s with a group of masterful cabaret revues which, in short order, first helped to make an international star out of Marlene Dietrich, then placed Spoliansky near the top of the Nazis' most-hated list, not only because of he was a Jew, but also because of occasional satires aimed at them by lyrics set to his music. After the rousing success of *It's in the Air* in 1928 and *Two Bow Ties* in 1929, Spoliansky's partnership with Schiffer reached its zenith with several more thematically-unified revues, including a 1932 work in touted as *Kabarettoper* ("cabaret opera"), remote ancestor to the popular "rock operas" garnering widespread media attention some four decades later (see Chapter 17). *Rufen Sie Herrn Plim!* ("Call Mr. Plim!") perhaps represented the ultimate satire on affluent consumerism in Weimar Germany, and its topicality remains sadly relevant in today's world.[19] Concurrent with these large-scaled revue productions, which numbered no fewer than four in three years (1931–1933), Spoliansky began regularly scoring and writing songs for German-language films, with his hit tunes being recorded by the likes of Dietrich and Margo Lion. In spite of these accomplishments, however, Spoliansky, like Hollaender and countless others, was forced flee Germany in 1933 upon Hitler's ascent to power.

Both Hollaender and Spoliansky, upon their exodus from Germany, were able to find employment in the American and British film industries, respectively, because of their adaptable talents and track records. Both were fortunate in this regard because leaving continental Europe early on probably saved their lives. Many of those who stayed in Germany or opted for France, Holland, or Eastern Europe, were not so lucky. As Europe geared up for world war during the 1930s, however, the two leading composers of *Kabarett* music began to make new names for themselves among foreigners who had never heard of German cabaret, let alone places like Sound and Smoke, Megalomania, or the Wild Stage. Around the same time that Kurt Weill reestablished his career as a composer of Broadway musicals (see Chapter 11), Hollaender reunited with Dietrich to write several Hollywood soundtracks, including *Desire* (1936), *Angel* (1937), *Destry Rides Again* (1937), and *Seven Sinners* (1940).[20] As early as 1932, however, American Jewish film composers such as Leo Robin and Ralph Rainger (aka Ralph Reichenstahl)—a successful team admired by Hollaender—were tipping their hats to the Weimar style by providing Dietrich with cabaret-like songs in *Blonde Venus*.[21] Meanwhile in London, Spoliansky quickly obtained British citizenship because of his musical celebrity, then proceeded to become a fixture on the British film soundtrack scene. His international breakthrough came in 1932 with *Das Lied einer Nacht* ("Song of the Night"), also released in French as *La chanson d'une nuit* and, more importantly, in English as *Tell Me Tonight.* The title song, another collaboration with Schiffer, helped to bring Spoliansky international recognition just in time to escape Germany. More notable film songs were later written by Spoliansky for English movie appearances by African American singers Elizabeth Welch in 1939 (*Over the Moon*) and Paul Robeson in 1935–1937 (*Sanders of the River* and *King Solomon's Mines*).[22]

The first important cabaret casualty of that troubled era was the multi-talented Marcellus Schiffer (1892–1932). Schiffer was the most brilliant, prolific, and, ultimately, unstable of all the Weimar song lyricists. After being discovered by Hesterberg in 1922 and becoming house writer for the Wild Stage, Schiffer went on to produce texts for Spoliansky, Hollaender, Rudolf Nelson, and Werner Richard Heymann (among others), as well as for more serious composers such as Paul Hindemith.[23] It was his bold work with Spoliansky for the revue *It's in the Air* that first brought Dietrich widespread attention, and it was his successful text for *Song of the Night* (better known as *Tonight or Never*) that probably helped to save Spoliansky's life by helping to get the latter welcomed into England by 1933. Nevertheless, Schiffer was, among all of his artistic colleagues, the least well situated to survive the impending rise of Nazism. He was a cabaret satirical writer, gay, and Jewish — three big strikes against him even before adding to these handicaps his known struggles with depression and substance abuse. His marriage to Margo Lion was mainly one of personal friendship and professional convenience; they both worked well together with most of the prominent composers from the period, including Hollaender.[24] Schiffer was a visionary who could see everything clearly except himself. By 1932, he no doubt foresaw what was about to engulf Germany. Unwilling or unable to flee, combined with despondence, terror, and loneliness (according to his relatives), he overdosed on sleeping pills. He was 40 years old. Berlin papers gave him a sympathetic, respectful obituary, then he was forgotten until over half a century later when renewed academic and artistic interest in Weimar *Kabarett* rediscovered his genius.[25] As sad and tragic as Schiffer's end was, it was certainly more humane than anything the Nazis would have later had in store for him. With his death, Schiffer's widow (and stage advocate) Margo Lion departed to Paris where she lived out the rest of her long life.

Unlike Schiffer, Hollaender's former colleague Kurt Tucholsky (1890–1935) wrote openly and energetically about German politics from Paris, where he had lived since 1924.[26] Having personally witnessed the horrors of World

War I as a young man, Tucholsky was outspoken in his pacifist views and unwavering opposition to the Nazis. In 1930, he moved to Sweden, home of the Nobel Peace Prize, partly lured there by a fleeting romance, and hoping to stay out of harm's way while helping like-minded friends back in Germany. By 1933, he had been officially condemned by the Nazis (along with others) as having exposed Germany's secret rearmament, and his books were publicly burned. Tormented by poor health, an unhappy personal life, and guilt over having failed to help his activist friends as the fascist cloud spread across Europe, Tucholsky, like Schiffer three years earlier, ended his life with sleeping pills in late 1935. A little over a year later, in early 1937, cabaret star singer Paul Graetz, having fled to America and Hollywood in 1933, died from a heart attack at age 46, soon after having landed his first high-profile role in a Greta Garbo film.[27] Thus by the mid–1930s, the two artists — Tucholsky and Graetz — who had collaborated with Hollaender to produce the first big hit song of the Weimar *Kabarett* era (see Chapter 2), were no more.[28]

The combative Claire Waldoff, unquestionably Berlin cabaret's biggest singing star during the 1920s, survived fascism and the war but otherwise fared little better. Unlike Trude Hesterberg (see Chapter 12), she made no overtures to the Nazis or apologies for her alternative lifestyle, despite having solid "Aryan" credentials. After 1933, her glory days as a performer were finished. When war came, she and her life-long partner moved to the Bavarian provinces and kept a low profile except when called upon to entertain German troops, which she still could do with aplomb. Nevertheless, she was destined to die after the war in relative obscurity, impoverished and forgotten. Even more melancholy was the case of Rosa Valetti, founder of Megalomania, co-film star of Dietrich, stage colleague of Lenya, and early patron of Hollaender. Being Jewish, she fled to Vienna in 1933 where she died in 1937, age 59, after returning from a sojourn to Palestine. In this, as in many other things, Valetti was a pioneer, anticipating the great Jewish post–Holocaust migration to the Middle East. Mercifully, she did not live to see the 1938 *Anschluss* and Nazi takeover of Austria, though she most likely saw it coming. Her Viennese gravesite, like that of Mozart, has since disappeared.

Valetti's former employer Max Reinhardt, though of Viennese birth, fled directly to America in 1933, where he tried to break into Hollywood. Excepting a notable film version of Shakespeare's *A Midsummer Night's Dream* (1935), Reinhardt could not replicate his German success in America, partly because he was too much a man of stage.[29] He became a U.S. citizen in 1940, but died in 1943 at age 70, possibly comforted by the fact that the Nazis by then had suffered crushing defeat on the Eastern front. Nevertheless, the founder of Sound and Smoke, artist and impresario at the forefront of the German cabaret scene since 1901, the one who gave Hollaender his first big chance, did not live to see Hitler's final demise. Somewhat more fortunate was Reinhardt's long-time competitor Rudolf Nelson (1878–1960). The ultimate survivor in both business and life, Nelson left Berlin in 1933 and by 1934 had arrived circuitously in Holland, which had a thriving, original cabaret scene of its own. In Amsterdam, Nelson shrewdly depoliticized his show and, more importantly, knew how to be very popular with the general public. By the time the German army arrived in 1940, Nelson was among a small group of Jewish-Dutch entertainers allowed to continue performing for segregated audiences. When the "Final Solution" came in 1942, however, he accomplished what millions of others had attempted and failed, namely, survival. Nelson's documented whereabouts in 1942–1945 are murky, but one possible scenario is that he first went underground into hiding, then at some point became an inmate at Westerbork, which tended to be an intermediary stop before final transit to the eastern death camps. Westerbork was also known to be more preferential and indulgent towards cabaret stars because of its theater-loving commandant. In any event, by the time Westerbork was liberated by Allied troops in early 1945, Nelson was still alive.[30] Through unbelievable luck and savvy, the showman who had introduced the Josephine Baker to Germany and worked with almost every major figure in Weimar *Kabarett* (including Hollaender), somehow managed to outlast his persecutors.[31]

If Rudolf Nelson was cabaret's most prominent Holocaust survivor, then surely its most famous victim was Kurt Gerron (1897–1944). Unlike Nelson, Gerron ran only with reluctance and then refused to hide, perhaps in the mistaken belief that his status as a decorated German war veteran and international film celebrity would cause the Nazis to overlook the fact that he was Jewish. This was the man who premiered Weill and Brecht's "Mack the Knife" to world in the original 1928 production of *The Threepenny Opera*. Two years later he starred along side of Dietrich in *The Blue Angel* as Hollaender's music filled cinemas on both sides of the Atlantic.[32] After being practically shoved out of Germany in 1933 by the Nazis, Gerron reluctantly settled in Holland where he joined the burgeoning, relocated community of Jewish entertainers. In 1940 came German invasion and in 1942, the beginning of deportations. Both Dietrich and Sternberg, among others, tried to get Gerron out of Europe and into the U.S., but he repeatedly declined their offers. In 1943, he was detained and sent to the Westerbork camp, again joining many of his performing colleagues. In early 1944, he was transferred to the infamous Theresienstadt concentration camp in Czechoslovakia, and later that same year, along with thousands of others, transported to Aushwitz in Poland where he perished in the gas chambers.[33] He was 47 years old.

Before Gerron departed for Auschwitz, however, he had one last command performance to give, and it was a memorable one though not in a good way. Theresienstadt's infamy partly rests on its dubious distinction of hosting the Nazi propaganda film, *Der Führer schenkt den Juden eine Stadt* ("The Führer Presents a City to the Jews"), part of a concerted, highly-coordinated effort to dupe the wartime Red Cross and German populace into believing that no Holocaust was taking place.[34] A key component of this sinister plan involved recruiting Gerron as film director and cabaret entertainer. Obviously believing that some lives, including his own, might be spared as a result of this project, he cooperated. The ethical propriety of this agonizing decision has been widely debated ever since, and we will not insult the memory of the dead by attempting to address it within a limited space such as this. The documentary record, however, is there for all to see, and was recently re-summarized in the 2003 Canadian PBS documentary *Prisoner of Paradise*. For his coerced camp audience, Gerron created a cabaret motif titled *Karussell* ("Carousel"), using his multiple talents to direct cameras and crowds while singing "Mack the Knife" and other *Threepenny* hits. Additional songs performed touched upon, fittingly enough, the favorite *Kabarett* themes of illusion and escape.[35] Some of Gerron's "Carousel" song texts were written by Leo Strauss, son the same operetta composer who wrote the very first Berlin cabaret hit in 1901 for Wolzogen's Überbrettl (see Chapter 1).[36] In a final symbolic tragedy for German cabaret art, Strauss was included among those transported with Gerron from Therensienstadt to Auschwitz, where he too was murdered.[37]

There is no real happy ending to this saga; only perhaps that after the war, some artists were still left alive to tell their stories. In America, Hollaender earned a living but his career never found the same traction enjoyed during the Weimar era. His only musical fault was that, like most other notable German composers of his generation, he was not Kurt Weill. In 1947, Hollaender's fellow German émigré Billy Wilder paid him a visit at his failing nightclub on Sunset Strip, still named "Tingel-Tangel" as it had been before the war in Berlin.[38] Wilder recruited Hollaender to write songs and play piano for Marlene Dietrich's 1948 film noir *Foreign Affair*, which included three Dietrich classics — "Black Market," "The Ruins of Berlin," and "(Want to Buy Some) Illusions." Then he went back to churning out competent soundtracks for mostly forgettable films, with a few exceptions like *The 5,000 Fingers of Dr. T* (1953) and *Sabrina* (1954). In 1956, he made a bold and unusual move for a German-Jewish ex-patriot by returning to Germany, settling in Munich (of all places), which during the 1920s had been Hitler's first great bastion of power. For the last two decades of his life he enjoyed being a native cultural institution, and wrote books, including his yet-to-be-translated autobiography, *Von Kopf bis Fuß: mein Leben mit Text und Music*, in 1965.[39] By that time his melody which first made Dietrich famous had been recorded by countless artists, including the Beatles while performing live in Hamburg (see Chapter 17). Somewhat fittingly, by the time that Hollaender passed away in 1976, age 79, Dietrich's active performing career had more or less ceased.

Most of Hollaender's surviving cabaret associates had one surprising thing in common: they stayed in Europe after the war and spent a lot of time in Germany. Spoliansky was invited to write a song for Dietrich in *Stage Fright* (1950) and obliged with "Whisper Sweet Little Nothing to Me." He divided time between his London home where he continued to write movie soundtracks, and West Germany where he helped to mount stage works. His final film score before retirement, appropriately enough, was for *Hitler: The Last Ten Days* (1973), starring Alec Guinness as the scourge of humanity who destroyed the world of Spoliansky's youth. After the world had been rid of Hitler, the irrepressible Rudolf Nelson, despite being advanced in years and nearly exterminated by his countrymen, went right back to mounting lavish revues in Berlin, even though this type of show was then in the process of being retrofitted for American mass consumption (see Chapter 13). Later, Nelson was awarded the Ordre national du Mérite, the second highest level of recognition in France after the Legion of Honor, the latter distinction having been previously given to Dietrich. Claire Waldoff, a non–Jew, chose to live out her remaining days in the southern provinces and became, like many other elderly Germans of the postwar period, destitute. In 1953, her fanciful, yet-to-be-translated memoir, *Weeste noch...! Aus meinen Erinnerungen*, was published. Upon her 70th birthday (in 1954) she was awarded a small government pension, but died three years later in 1957, seemingly forgotten as the dynamic performer who had made such a big impression on the young Dietrich while belting out women's liberation anthems like Hollaender's "Raus mit den Männern!" to delighted Weimar audiences.

Peter Jelavich reminds us that "The National Socialist takeover in the spring of 1933 nearly destroyed the cabaret movement, for most of the entertainers had been liberal, leftist, or Jewish."[40] Indeed, the better-known examples recited in this chapter only represent the tip of the iceberg. Many other outstanding cabaret artists were killed or had their careers prematurely ended. In a few isolated, unusual cases, they successfully adapted their art to the New World or stubbornly, against all odds, kept performing, writing, and organizing shows. Above all, the collective memory of their talent and achievements managed not only to survive, but prosper and grow during the second half of the century, despite ferocious persecution during the 12-year terror of the Third Reich. Perhaps the singular aspect of this catastrophe most often forgotten is that Jews, Communists, and Liberals were not the only ones persecuted. Alternative sexual lifestyles, one of the sociological hallmarks of Weimar art, tended to be proscribed as well. Often overlooked is how this short-lived era of sexual freedom in Weimar Germany led a young, aspiring English writer to the heart of Berlin itself, and whose later literary work would in turn help to immortalize the image and myth of German cabaret for the English-speaking world and far beyond.

7. Christopher Isherwood, Reporting from Berlin

"The sun shines, and Hitler is master of this city."— Christopher Isherwood[1]

While most movie and music lovers are familiar with the melody of Friedrich Hollaender's *Falling in Love Again*, far fewer know of the composer who wrote it, and fewer still are aware of the historical context in which the song was written. Much more prominent in the popular contemporary imagination are sights and sounds of this era drawn from a semi-fictional work of literature not published until several years after most cabaret artists had been driven out of their homeland. Around the same time that Josef von Sternberg and Marlene Dietrich were filming *The Blue Angel*, a young, wayward Englishman arrived in Berlin, attracted by the famed licentious freedom and decadence of the city, combined with a need to gather material in furtherance of his own writing ambitions. When most of the free world was willfully ignoring ominous events in late Weimar Germany, this slumming English adventurer decided to see things for himself and then reported back with striking accuracy and objectivity. His achievement was not unlike that of Alexis de Tocqueville, whose *Democracy in America* (1835) was published exactly one century before the first installment of an extraordinary travel journal, thinly-disguised as fiction, in which the universe of Weimar cabaret would be coolly replicated and analyzed by a talented and sympathetic foreign observer. To repeat, this is how most of us eventually came to visualize the cabaret world of Weimar Berlin.

Christopher William Bradshaw Isherwood (1904–1986) was the son of a provincial British army officer killed during the Great War, and the young Isherwood's pacifism, deep mistrust of official authority, and hatred for all warfare remained with him for the rest of his life. He was also openly bisexual, and coming from a comfortable middle class background, found "respectable" civilian life in England during the 1920s and 1930s to be awkward, if not intolerable. Everyone early on could see that Isherwood had exceptional abilities, but conventional paths to achievement seemed unsuitable for him. First, he was accepted into Cambridge University, but dropped out; next followed a brief stint at King's College before he dropped out again. He wrote poetry and came to the attention of the W.H. Auden, who became Isherwood's enthusiastic literary champion and occasional partner in vice. In 1928, an unexceptional first novel was published. Then in 1929, Auden excitedly insisted that Isherwood join him in Weimar Berlin, where they could freely partake in the many forbidden pleasures offered by that cauldron of a metropolis. On a slightly more intellectual plane, both Isherwood and Auden, as age 20-somethings experimenting in alternative lifestyles, were keenly interested in the pioneering work of Berlin sexologist and gay-rights activist Magnus Hirschfeld (1868–1935), whose Institut für Sexualwissenschaft ("Sexual Research Institute") had become a huge repository for books, studies, data, educational services, and medical references nearly impossible to find elsewhere.

Isherwood arrived in Berlin during the Spring of 1929, initially taking up residence in the apartments of Hirschfeld's Institute. The following year, in 1930, he moved into the boarding house of Fräuline Meta Thurau at Nollendorstraße 17 in the Schöneberg district of Berlin, the same neighborhood in which Marlene Dietrich had been born 29 years previous before achieving world celebrity in 1930, just as Isherwood was about to begin achieving his own.[2] In almost no time he became romantically involved with a working-class German youth. Isherwood later faithfully recounted his personal experiences in Germany and beyond over the next decade with the 1976 publication of his second memoir, *Christopher and His Kind*, some four years after the 1972 movie version of *Cabaret* had taken his literary fame to even greater heights (see Chapter 15).[3] As he wrote in the preface to a later edition of his collected Weimar fiction, "From 1929 to 1933, I lived almost continuously in Berlin...."[4] Originally, Isherwood planned another novel, this one with a working title, *The Lost*, an appropriate choice given the desperate character of humanity that the gentile young Englishman was about to intermingle with. The projected novel soon transformed into a group of literary vignettes, not unlike the miniature art forms playing such a central role in the aesthetic development of German cabaret music. Among the misfits that Isherwood encountered in Berlin was the aspiring British singer Jean Ross, eventually becoming the model for his boldly delineated, semi-fictional Sally Bowles. The name Bowles was itself based on the soon-to-be American ex-patriot author, scholar and composer, Paul Bowles (1910–1999), who during the early 1930s counted among Isherwood's distinguished visitors in Berlin.[5] There he also encountered the effete British critic, writer, and world traveler, Gerald

Hamilton, upon whom was based the mysteriously eccentric, hopelessly inept, and quintessentially English "fictional" character of Arthur Norris. Isherwood's landlady Fräuline Thurau also proved to be quite a personality (and ultimate survivor); her unforgettable portrayal as Frau Schröeder in many ways represents the main plot trajectory and connecting thread within the author's series of short stories.

To fully appreciate Isherwood's later achievement, it is perhaps useful to pause and consider his methods, as well as the milieu in which he moved. Although Berlin at this moment in history was one of the great artistic capitals of western civilization, Isherwood was not willing or able to interact with celebrities. He did not meet, insofar as we know, Marlene Dietrich, Lotte Lenya, Kurt Weill, Friedrich Hollaender, Mischa Spoliansky, or any of the other outstanding artists who later came to represent German cabaret in the popular field. Instead, he opted to consort with the margins of society (normally typical cabaret audiences), would-be stars and intellectuals at best, or at worst, urban low-life and the dispossessed — the same unhappy individuals who often captured the attention of talented German painters from that era (see Chapter 9). Another unique aspect of his work — one surely not planned by Isherwood but unique nonetheless — is that he gives us a snapshot of barely civilized society on the verge of political collapse and irretrievable descent into evil. Typically, works about this historical period deal with the years immediately leading up to World War II, specifically, the late 1930s. A good example of this genre is Erik Larson's recent non-fiction *In the Garden of Beasts: Love, Terror, and an American Family in Hitler's Germany* (2011), a fine book by a fine writer. Nevertheless, Larson addresses the gradual American realization of Nazi intentions during the late 1930s, which was indeed very late in coming, and continues to be a favorite topic among historians.[6] The events leading up to the Nazi takeover of 1933, however, including how and why it occurred, tend to be far less scrutinized by English-language readers, and this is precisely where Isherwood excels and becomes invaluable as a perceptive eye-witness. Upon Hitler's ascent to power in 1933, Isherwood, like his fictional narrator, sensibly left Berlin.[7] Later that same year, Hirschfeld's library was sacked and his books burned by the Nazis. In 1935, on his 67th birthday, Hirschfeld died of a heart attack while in French exile.

After returning to England, Isherwood's short stories were published in two installments: *Mr. Norris Changes Trains* in 1935 (dedicated to Auden), and *Goodbye to Berlin* in 1939, the latter work opening with Isherwood's famous line "I am a camera..." — alluding to his famously detached point of view.[8] These works still make a gripping read over eight decades after the fact. For newcomers expecting something akin to "Cabaret, the Book" or perhaps a sentimental journey into the nostalgic past, be forewarned. Whereas Bob

Fosse's 1972 movie version of *Cabaret* strove to make the film more faithful to the literary original, the original story in its unvarnished, un-expunged form could probably be presented only as an R-rated feature to a strictly adult audience difficult to shock or offend. Isherwood's large, unforgettable cast of degenerate misfits is enthusiastic for any and every type of vice catalogued, and those who are not (or at least not openly) tend to be anti–Semites and Nazi-sympathizers. The only characters who seem to have a clue about anything are Jews, and these figures are often presented by the novelist as tragic, passive victims of escalating persecution. As Isherwood's autobiographical narrator tours the cabarets and seedy haunts of early–1930s Berlin, readers are given an unpleasant but edifying glimpse of a crumbling society on the brink of implosion. There is no question as to who the bad guys are, or where events are heading — only how ordinary human beings can behave or misbehave under stressful, deteriorating economic and political conditions.

In the opening pages of *Mr. Norris Changes Trains* readers are introduced to the first-person narrator, William Bradshaw (Isherwood's two middle names), as well as his fussy landlady, Frau Schröeder, and their mutual English acquaintance, Mr. Arthur Norris. Norris constantly has irons in the fire, but we are never quite sure on any specifics, while his vague, elaborate schemes always seem to miscarry. In contrast to Bradshaw's precise, unemotional penchant for objectivity, Norris has trouble getting a fix on reality. He becomes emblematic of everyone in the free world whom either underestimated or misunderstood the imminent Nazi threat. Norris' persistent vanity and overly fastidious appearance calls to mind the cabaret song lampoon "L'heure bleue" ("The Blue Hour"), written by Spoliansky-Schiffer around the same time that Isherwood was arriving in Berlin.[9] In the story, both Bradshaw and Norris feel superior enough to poke fun at Frau Schröeder's unaffected manners and dress, recalling another satirical Spoliansky-Schiffer composition, "Song of the Trendy Set."[10] The overbearing sense of elitism and entitlement that infects many of Isherwood's middle class characters sometimes includes the novelist himself. The same applies to any of their German counterparts who are not working class. Thus from the very beginning of the narrative, there is a distinct correlation between Isherwood's descriptive powers and favorite cabaret songwriting themes from the period.

Isherwood's characters frequent the Berlin cabarets throughout the stories. All of these venues, like the characters themselves, are given fictional names. The first of these presented is the Troika, named after a Russian word meaning "threesome" and having intentional, multiple connotations.[11] Many of the early Berlin cabarets did in fact have Russian affectations and, in some cases, mostly Russian ex-patriot clientele, which proved to be a draw for talented Russian-born Weimar artists such as Spoliansky (see Chapter 6). The novelist's photographic descriptive powers for these locales provide readers with a documentary (and often less than pleasant) glimpse into the atmosphere of 1920s Weimar nightlife. At the Troika Bradshaw meets playboy and man-about-town, Fritz Wendel, who figures prominently throughout the tale, and later the stage and movie versions of *Cabaret* as well.[12] It is also at the Troika where Bradshaw is introduced (through Norris) to the shady, secretive Kuno (aka Baron von Pregnitz). Against this backdrop of international espionage and political intrigue, Isherwood gives us a flash portrait of Troika's claustrophobic, conspiratorial environment overlaid with a veneer of nightclub entertainment: "The dancers, locked frigidly together, swayed in partial-paralytic rhythms under a huge sunshade suspended from the ceiling and oscillating gently through cigarette smoke and hot rising air."[13] This scene strongly calls to mind the well-know Max Beckmann painting *Dance in Baden-Baden*, circa 1923 (see Chapter 9), although it is unlikely that the novelist was familiar with this earlier work at the time of writing. The important thing is that Isherwood, like Beckmann, was an eyewitness to these scenes and presents readers an image consistent with those produced by other artists active around the same time and place.

The most memorable character creation from *The Berlin Stories*, however, is the novelist's astringent portrayal of the free-spirited, uninhibited, and completely unpredictable Sally Bowles. By the time Isherwood's second-half narrator ("Chris") is introduced to Sally through Fritz, some readers may mistakenly believe that they have already been shown the most unusual oddities that Weimar Berlin had to offer, but this proves not be the case.[14] Sally is an English cabaret performer trying to make a go of it in Berlin, and despite her limited musical talent has a definite knack for gaining the spotlight. Lovers come and go. An abortion procedure is sought out with devastating matter-of-factness. Some 50 pages (and three years) later, around the time of the Nazi takeover in 1933, Sally exits the narrative as abruptly as she first entered it, leaving for Paris and Rome after becoming involved with a teenage Polish-American con artist. Isherwood's narrator, writing approximately six years after the fact (circa 1939) notes that he never saw her again but fondly sends out his felicitations should she ever read the book — an unlikely occurrence, it is rather strongly implied.[15]

In between her comings and goings, Sally sings (badly, we are told) at the fictional Lady Windermere cabaret, for which Isherwood provides a vivid, lengthy description. The Lady Windermere — a moniker with disreputable Oscar Wilde-associations — as the narrator informs us,

> ... (which now, I hear, no longer exists) was an arty "informal" bar, just off the Tauentzienstrasse, which the proprietor had evidently tried to make look as much as possible like Montparnasse. The walls were covered with sketches on menu-

cards, caricatures and signed theatrical photographs — ("To the only and only Lady Windermere." "To Johnny, with all my heart.") The Fan itself, four times life size, was displayed above the bar. There was a big piano on a platform in the middle of the room.[16]

Isherwood's Lady Windemere club appears to be an amalgamation of several well-known Berlin cabarets from the period, and is located at the intersection and epicenter of the Kurfürstendamm entertainment-vice district that so disgusted a malcontented Joseph Goebbels in his 1928 journal.[17] This is the same locus on the Berlin city map where Sally Bowles is most in her element. The novelist catalogues other fictional Berlin cabarets as well, each usually introduced to the astonished narrator through Fritz: the Alexander Casino (a tacky pick-up bar), the Salomé (another "dives" gay bar), and an unidentified "communist dive" which Chris and Fritz enjoy frequenting despite their decidedly apathetic, non–Marxist political beliefs.[18]

Overt sadomasochism appears throughout *The Berlin Stories* at regular intervals. Norris keeps an extensive library of S&M literature, and likes to engage in unspoken recreational antics with his German friends Anni and Olga.[19] Later, Norris and British correspondent Helen Pratt refer to the S&M prostitutes prominently hanging around the Kaufhaus de Westens department store on the Tauentzienstraße, which seems to have become a tourist attraction of sorts in 1920s Berlin.[20] At this point, it is worth pausing to recall that, according to some sociologists, this form of sexual deviancy first found full public expression during the late 1800s and early 1900s in Germany. Its original literary apologist and namesake, at least in the popular imagination, was the Austrian journalist and novelist Leopold von Sacher-Masoch (1836–1895), a contemporary of Nietzsche, whose *Venus in Furs* (1869) would go on to inspire (if that is the right word) future generations of musicians and writers interested in the extreme margins of society (see Chapter 19).[21] From the first-hand accounts left by Isherwood, Lenya, and others, it is clear that Weimar Berlin by the late 1920s had found a secure niche for this sort of thing as part of its torn social fabric. Weimar painters and photographers were apparently intrigued as well (see Chapter 9).

On a far more sinister level, *The Berlin Stories* pointedly and repeatedly captures the festering anti–Semitism of the Weimar period. Frau Schröeder's friend Fräuline Mayer is blatantly and unapologetically anti–Semitic, while their acquaintance Frau Nowak shares this attitude but tries to softens it with a fantasy belief that Hitler would not actually kill any Jews.[22] The wealthy, cultivated, young, beautiful (and Jewish) Natalie Landauer is sympathetically portrayed despite her disapproval of the narrator's lifestyle, and her first social meeting with Sally, as one would expect, proves to be an ungraceful disaster.[23] Nevertheless, these minor altercations are implicitly portrayed as nothing compared to what the Landauer family will most certainly suffer over the next decade at the hands of the German nation. It is noteworthy that Isherwood's formidable powers of observation recorded these sentiments and attitudes during a period (the 1930s) in which an industrial-scaled Holocaust still lay in the future and most of the world would not even become aware of the situation until after the war. He thus shares good artistic company with the likes of Friedrich Hollaender and Mischa Spoliansky, both of whom had recently incorporated social commentary on racism and xenophobia into their musical cabaret songs and stage revues before they too were forced to leave the country.

Perhaps the most distinctive feature of the late Weimar Republic captured by Isherwood is the covert political espionage that seems to permeate every level of daily life, even in the cabarets. At one disorienting point in the tale, almost everybody seems to be a secret agent for someone else.[24] Norris' own secretary, the grim and humorless Schmidt, is obviously a Nazi spy; moreover, as the narrator puts it, "He was quite prepared to say anything to anybody."[25] Schmidt personifies the moral bankruptcy of Weimar Germany. The narrator's Marxist friends, all arch-enemies to the fascists, are nonetheless pathetically inept and painfully out of touch with reality, much like Norris himself. They do not even seem to realize they are about to be crushed. After the Reichstag burns, Frau Schröeder easily buys into the Nazi version of events (i.e. the fire being caused by the Communists) and speaks reverently of "Der Führer."[26] Soon afterwards, Chris overhears a drunken Nazi exclaim to his girlfriend, "Blood must flow!" The girlfriend, instead of trying to calm things down, reassures him that blood will indeed flow, as confrontations between Nazis sympathizers and Marxists escalate all along the Tauentzienstraße.[27] One of the last images that readers encounter (remember, this is a 1939 book based on things witnessed in 1933) are Nazis chanting in fervent mockery pacifist slogans as they raid bookstores and confiscate perceived subversive material, later to be burned.[28] After hurriedly departing for Mexico City, Norris laments in a letter that "It is indeed tragic to see how, even in these days, a *clever* and *unscrupulous liar* can deceive millions."[29]

The late–1930s publication of Isherwood's Berlin journalism barely camouflaged as fiction was immediately successful, although most people outside of Germany did not fully acknowledge the threat of all-out war until the cumulative events of 1939–1941 laid military aggression and devastation right on their doorsteps.[30] Long before these occurrences, accurately anticipating that war was about to once again engulf England, Isherwood traveled to America in 1939 and opted to stay there. Despite his openly pacifist stance, he managed to become a U.S. citizen in 1946, having settled in Santa Monica, California, while dividing his time between producing serious literature and earning his living through Hollywood. In 1951, his *Berlin Stories* were adapted into a very subdued but popular stage play by John Van Druten, *I Am a Camera*, earning a young Julie Harris (as Sally Bowles) the first in her long string of Tony Awards. Later, in 1955, Harris also starred in a rather tepid and tame movie version of the same stage drama, this time receiving mixed reviews. Before that, however, during the early 1950s (in wake of the play's success), Isherwood returned to post-war Berlin, where he encountered old acquaintances, some of whom greeted him jovially as if nothing had happened. No mention was made that only a few years previous in Germany, Isherwood, as an un-closeted homosexual, would have been carted off to the death camps. Reflecting in a hotel bar along the Kurfürstendamm, Isherwood tactfully recalled that he found himself "surrounded by thick-necked cigar-smoking businessmen who might have stepped right out of the cartoons of Georg Grosz. It was I, not these people, who had changed...."[31] Fräuline Thurau, still identified as the "fictional" Frau Schröeder and hailing him with "Herr Issyvoo" as merrily as ever, was slightly upset with the novelist, not because he had recorded her pro–Nazi sentiments, but for describing her in print as being a bit overweight. She had since slimmed down, he was careful to note.[32]

Isherwood later went to achieve even greater literary triumphs, including his novel *A Single Man* (1964), considered by many to be his masterpiece and made into a stylish feature film in 2009. Even as he was writing his post-war Berlin impressions circa 1954, the off–Broadway revival of Weill and Brecht's *The Threepenny Opera* (see Chapter 4) was beginning its phenomenal surge to the forefront of commercial pop culture, thereby laying the groundwork for the later success of *Cabaret* as both musical (1966) and movie (1972). Consequently, by the mid–1970s, Isherwood found himself, probably much to his own surprise, routinely included in the upper echelons of living English-language writers. Seemingly lost in the shuffle, however, was his uncanny, prophetic accomplishment with the Berlin short stories which first brought to him worldwide celebrity. Regardless of all his touted objectivity and distance, Isherwood had succeeded in doing best what countless other writers later tried to do in a much more heavy-handed manner — he eloquently exposed the growing spiritual void in pre-war Germany. Despite obvious affection for many of the characters — some innocent victims and some passive collaborators — the novelist mainly recorded minute facts and observations, dispassionately allowing readers to draw their own conclusions, which tend to be the type most strongly retained. Their verdict was (and remains) firm: Weimar Germany was a society in which everyone's moral compass had gone badly awry.

8. Total Collapse of the Moral Universe

"Two thousand years ago, the catacombs provided a place of refuge for the first Christians; today it is a place of refuge for the last."— Werner Finck[1]

Not often remarked upon is the documented fact that the German Weimar Republic (1919–1933), despite its chaotic, precarious history, lasted some 14 years, two years longer than the Third Reich (1933–1945). Which period produced greater artistic and cultural achievements with a more widespread, lasting influence across western civilization is never debated. While World War II hobbyists and secretive, neo-fascist admirers of Adolf Hitler may spend considerable time obsessing over Nazi-era symbols and slogans, the aesthetic remnants of Weimar Germany continue to be before our very eyes and ears in everyday life, omnipresent and inescapable. Nonetheless, many Germans at the time considered Weimar Berlin to be "a modern Babylon" and refused to live there, in part because of the city's large Jewish population and partly because of its ingrained reputation for unrestrained vice, an established and continuing reputation stretching long before and after the existence of the Republic itself.[2] Others, particularly visiting foreigners such as Christopher Isherwood (see Chapter 7), were drawn to Berlin precisely because of this same shady, corrupted and corruptible image. It would therefore seem, at least at first glance, that creativity and vice might go hand in hand in this case. Whether this disturbing combination, however, should be regarded as a necessary axiom remains an open question for many of us.

By the time Isherwood landed in America and Hollywood during the late 1930s and early 1940s, the American film industry had elected to impose upon itself a new censorship code, designed to promote generally-accepted notions of decency and discourage all forms of copycat immorality. The Motion Picture Production Code (MPPC), better known as the Hay's Code, named after its Hoosier-born sponsor, Will H. Hays, was first enacted in 1930 as an attempt to reign in the cinematic licentiousness of the Roaring Twenties and mollify a growing chorus of stateside critics, particularly in the wake of movie soundtrack innovations after 1927.[3] During the first four years of its existence (1930–1934), the Hay's Code was essentially un-enforced, but its architects nevertheless took themselves very seriously as self-appointed guardians of family values. In 1930, the very first film selected for official scrutiny was none other than *The Blue Angel* (see Chapter 5). After having been heavily censored upon its American premier in Pasadena, California, the final verdict in the first test case for the Hay's Code was an enthusiastic thumbs up for the unedited version of Marlene Dietrich's sexually-charged on-screen performance.[4] Whether this was due to director Josef von Sternberg's considerable skill at navigating the Hollywood system, or the new censors' desire to appear not too harsh, or the growing realization that to censor a film was only to increase its market demand, or all of the above, we are not prepared to say.[5] Certainly Dietrich and Sternberg were not the only suspected offenders in this regard; and yet this very same period (the early 1930s) in which the Hay's Code was being initially tested, also witnessed the collaboration between Dietrich and Sternberg grow increasingly daring (see Chapter 10). By 1935, full and strict enforcement of the Hay's Code had arrived, although by that time, the cat had been let out of the bag, so to speak.

Meanwhile in Nazi Germany, 1935 saw the forced closing of perhaps the most famous and legendary Berlin cabaret of them all, *Die Katacombe* ("The Catacombs"), although its great contemporary, the *Kabarett der Komiker* ("Cabaret of Comedians") or "Kadeko" for short, had preceded it and would continue to operate for another decade.[6] Co-founded in 1924 by the impresarios Kurt Robitschek, Max Hansen, and Paul Morgan (aka Georg Paul Morgenstern) the Kadeko had appeared almost immediately after the demise of Berlin's famed literary *Kabarett* scene during the early 1920s (see Chapter 2). From almost day one, its entertainment featured political themes with former Megalomania proprietor Rosa Valetti delivering parodies aimed at Hitler and the Nazis, at that early stage still widely viewed as a group of marginal fanatics.[7] Other musical members of Valetti's troupe soon became Kadeko regulars, including *Threepenny Opera* veteran Kate Kühl (see Chapter 3) and Marxist agitprop specialist Ernst Busch. Innovative dancers were brought in as well, among them the cutting-edge pantomime stylist Valeska Gert, and composer Friedrich Hollaender's second wife, Heidi Schoop.[8] After some moving around, the Kadeko settled into permanent, custom-designed digs on the Kurfürstendamm in October 1929, just as the American stock market was crashing (see Chapter 9).[9] Despite the immediate onslaught of a world-wide Great Depression, the new venue survived and at times even thrived, being initially hailed by critics as representing the true rebirth of cabaret.[10]

Edgy stand-up comedy had always been an integral part of the German cabaret scene from the moment Max Reinhardt first discovered that paying customers would flock to laugh at send-ups of artistic pretension. As Peter Jelavich observed, "Joking was one of cabaret's major attributes." Moreover, Berlin had long tradition of rough, subversive wit going all the way back to Thirty Years War of 17th century.[11] After Rudolf Nelson helped transform the MC role of *conférencier* into one of cabaret's most distinctive features, this raucous style of "Jewish" humor would go on to heavily influence professional comedians into the present day.[12] As one would expect, sometimes such an approach would step well beyond the boundaries of good taste, but that did not necessarily make it any less popular. For example, following hard upon the Kadeko's initial success came the *Kabarett der Namenlosen* ("Cabaret of the Nameless"), founded by Erwin Lowinsky (stage name "Elow") in 1926.[13] Here, members of the general public were invited to try their hand at performing before sadistic Berlin audiences who, far more often than not, hooted, humiliated, and sent packing unfortunate aspirants whose delusions of grandeur were cruelly and publicly crushed. This Weimar precursor of *American Idol* and *The Gong Show* disgusted all connoisseurs of good taste, but was a big commercial hit nonetheless. At more high-minded venues such as the Kadeko, however, clever and biting socio-political humor (interspersed between musical acts) helped to diversify popular nightclub entertainment into a far more sophisticated form of miniature art, seemingly outpacing even the impressive achievements of literary *Kabarett* from a few years earlier.

Opinions vary on when exactly the Kadeko began to decline in artistic quality but most agree that its heyday was brilliant and brief, before eroded by Nazi political ascendancy. Just as the Kadeko's impertinent brand of humor was considered undesirable by the National Socialists, so were the stylistic roots of that humor, both Jewish and non–Jewish, as catalogued by Weimar historian Peter Gay:

> The unrestrained political satire that entertained and frightened visitors to the Kabarett der Komiker ... traced back its manner and matter to Heinrich Mann's *Der Untertan*, to Walter Mehring's early political chansons, to Frank Wedekind's eccentric dramas ... and to Carl Steinheim's clipped, mannered dissections....[14]

All of these pioneering German Expressionist writers were early role models for cabaret performers, and all who those lived to see the Third Reich did not fare well under it. In 1931, Kadeko co-founder Robitschek wrote an article attributing a recent downturn in business to superior theatrical skills on the part of the Nazis, maintaining his sense of profound, caustic humor even though (as a Jewish entrepreneur) he had been financially hurt by the sudden shift in public opinion.[15] After 1933, though Cabaret of the Comedians remained a viable brand name with the general public, the club's acts downshifted into a more middle-of-the-road and less politicized mode, which helped it continue doing business. Robitschek had long since departed for the U.S., while Max Hansen successfully posed as an Aryan and survived the war. Paul Morgan was not so fortunate. After unwisely choosing to return to Europe from a Hollywood trip in 1930, Morgan tried settling back in his native Austria, only to be caught up in the German *Anschluss* of 1938. As a Jewish anti–Nazi entertainer he was promptly arrested and transported first to Dachau, then Buchenwald, when he died before the end of the year at age 52, making him one of the earliest high-profile cabaret victims of the Holocaust. It is said that he continued performing almost until the very end.[16] Morgan thus also became one of the first (and many) Jewish performers who irrepressibly took cabaret with them all the way to the death camps.

If Kurt Robitschek could be viewed as the godfather of the Kadeko, then German comedian Werner Finck (1902–1978) might well be considered the symbolic patron saint of Weimar comedy. Finck was perhaps the bravest performer of them all, yet somehow managed to survive the Third Reich with a unique combination of pure "Aryan" credentials, luck, guile, a veneer of harmlessness, and (crucially) unabated popularity with the German general public. As founder and guiding spirit behind the Catacombs of 1929, Finck's true calling in life was to see if the Nazis were capable of laughing at themselves, which they were not.[17] After gradually working his way up through the cabaret ranks of 1920s Berlin, Finck woke up one day to find himself in demand as the most controversial jokester of Weimar Germany. His sketches and skits were so bold that foreigners had to see and hear to believe them, such as an outrageous, prurient parody of the Hitler Youth movement, or a known penchant for offering to slow down his motor-mouth delivery for the alleged benefit of Gestapo agents in the audience frantically trying to take notes. After Hitler assumed power in 1933, and unlike the Kadeko, the Catacombs maintained its more militant, anti-fascist stance, and its final 1935 program openly mocked the Nazis, after which it was permanently shut down.[18] Finck's archnemesis, Nazi Propaganda Minster Joseph Goebbels, who fully recognized the subversive comedian's threat to lockstep socialist order, personally ordered the closing of the Catacombs in 1935 and had Finck imprisoned. While incarcerated, however, Finck first succeeded in winning over his jailors with in-house command performances, then after learning that *Luftwaffe* chief Hermann Göring counted among his fan base, played upon this connection (and Göring's well-known animosity towards Goebbels) to secure his early release. After a brief period of keeping a low profile, Finck was right back in the public sphere selling jokes at the expense of the German government. Finally, by 1939, Goebbels had enough and publicly denounced Finck, who responded to an alleged want of patriotism by enlisting in the *Wehrmacht*, where he also happened to have a huge following. Like Claire Waldoff (see Chapter 6) he survived the war as a front-line entertainer for the Germany armed forces.[19] By the time Finck died in 1978, still performing and making irreverent jokes, a new entertainment franchise in America evolving into *Saturday Night Live* began to hit its stride.[20] Whether Finck was ever aware of *SNL*, or the creators of *SNL* conscious of a huge artistic debt owed to its Weimar prototype in Finck's Catacombs, is uncertain.

Having less to do with comedy and more with music, despite their moniker, were the Comedian Harmonists, by far and away Weimar Germany's most beloved singing group. A sextet consisting of three "Aryans" and three Jews, their amazing story was retold in the excellent 1997 German film *The Harmonists* (English language title). Originally inspired by the Revelers, an American jazz vocal quintet, the Comedian Harmonists were given their first big break in 1928 by Berlin celebrity director Erik Charell (see Chapter 12), then quickly established themselves as European superstars by the end of the decade. Before being forcibly disbanded by the Nazis in 1934, the Harmonists left an extensive, compelling recorded legacy. In addition to their dazzling musicianship, the lyrical content of their arrangements often disguised frank sexuality with sugarcoated, sly respectability, much to the delight of German and non–German audiences alike. It was perhaps for this reason that strict moralists among the Nazis turned against them, even more so than for their mixed-race membership, as well as a likely reason why many Nazis were originally fans to begin with.[21] Had they been an all-Jewish group appealing only to non-fascist audiences, their success would have probably been less offensive in the eyes of the Third Reich.

In contrast to a superb film achievement like *The Harmonists*, with its realistic, contradictory nuances and irreconcilable complexities, *Swing Kids* (1993) presents 1930s German popular music in a more simplified, palatable version for typical modern American viewers. This over-earnest and heavy-handed tale (with an underlying factual basis) is set in Hamburg during the late 1930s — a historical period much easier for today's audiences to grasp — but thematically having much more to do with the Lindy Hop revival of the late 20th century than actual events leading up to World War II. The *Swing jugend* ("Swing Youth") counterculture had risen in opposition to the *Hitlerjugend* ("Hitler Youth") during the final years of peacetime before finally being suppressed by the Nazis in late 1941 as world war enveloped Germany. As an interesting side note, however, the inland port city of Hamburg would, less than two decades later, become fertile development ground for a young Liverpool group befriended by local students who closely identified themselves with pre-war Existentialist values cultivated by German free-thinkers of a previous generation (see Chapter 17).

Before leaving the subject of Weimar counterculture and its frequently contentious expression in cabaret entertainment, it would be remiss not to mention the short, tragic life and career of Expressionist dancer Anita Berber (1899–1928), who in many ways embodied everything both widely feared and admired in Weimar culture. Before her premature death from alcoholism and substance abuse at age 29, this fiercely talented performer had turned herself into a kind of demonic poster girl for the decadent lifestyle associated with her epoch. Lotte Lenya, no slouch herself in this department, many decades later recalled in awe Berber's brilliance and beauty with "So, if you think we are far ahead now with the nudity, no, we had it all in Berlin forty years ago."[22] With the art of Anita Berber (a regular performer on the Berlin cabaret scene), suffice it to say that no boundary went un-pushed, no taboo unexploited. She was a classically-trained dancer of unlimited abilities and unlimited capacity for self-destruction. The proverbial "rock and roll lifestyle" began, not in America during the 1950s, but rather in Weimar Berlin during the 1920s, an era in which unfettered performance artists did things never before witnessed by audiences, both pleasant and unpleasant. Berber's premature illness and death, occurring on the eve of international success by near-exact contemporaries such as Lenya and Marlene Dietrich, calls to mind the punitive cost often attached to celebrity and notoriety. She was, in many respects, the Jimi Hendrix of her own generation. In addition to the unforgettable portrait of her painted by Otto Dix (see Chapter 9), a good place to begin exploring this once nearly-forgotten personality is the intriguing 2006 biography by Mel Gordon, *The Seven Addictions and Five Professions of Anita Berber: Weimar Berlin's Priestess of Debauchery*.

None of this, of course, went unnoticed by the rising Nazi tide.[23] After the new regime assumed power in 1933, it systematically went to work silencing and discrediting anything that Goebbels or his censors believed a threat to public morality and conformable behavior. After many "undesirables" had been compelled to leave Germany during the first three years of the Reich, 1937–1938 saw a pronounced effort to step up persecutions against those who remained behind, especially Jews and Marxists. Regarding the visual arts, the year 1937 saw the unveiling in Munich of the notorious touring exhibition Entartete Kunst ("Degenerate Art"), representing a virtual who's who of Weimar post–Expressionist painting, including over 500 condemned works by Max Beckmann, a non–Jewish, non–Marxist, heterosexual German World War I veteran, and arguably the greatest German artist of the period.[24] The following year (1938) came Entartete Musik ("Degenerate Music") in Düsseldorf, which singled out mostly Jewish composers for censor. In addition to condemning some of the greatest names in early 20th century music (Schoenberg, Mahler, and Weill), cabaret was considered Exhibit A in this category as well. The official poster advertising the exhibition featured a caricature of a semi-human black musician wearing the Star of David around his neck and playing saxophone, an instrument of French origin, much like cabaret itself.[25] Some accounts, however, have these displays raising more hackles among famous German artists than creating new Nazi converts. Perhaps the best-known example of this reaction was the 73-year-old Richard Strauss, who dutifully attended the Degenerate Music spectacle, but was not impressed. As he gazed around, Strauss realized with irritation that to be considered degenerate in the eyes of the Nazis was also to be viewed as cool and cache by many others, especially younger audiences. On the spot, Strauss asked the curator why his own compositions were not considered "degenerate" or subversive (as they had been many years before), and was matter-of-factly informed that it was because the Führer liked his music.[26] Struggling to regain popularity ever since the Great War had broken out (see Chapter 1), Strauss returned to writing his final opera *Capriccio*, subtitled "A Conversation Piece for Music"—a rarified chamber work premiering to a small audience in late 1942 just as multiple catastrophes began to envelope Hitler's Germany and the industrial scale of the Holocaust reached stupefying proportions.[27]

One odd thing about this infamous government attempt to act as arbiter of musical taste was that behind the scenes it never missed an opportunity to appropriate the popularity of cabaret music for its own purposes. Moreover, non-sanctioned composers often found themselves influenced by proscribed styles in spite of themselves. Perhaps the best examples of this contradiction were the late Berlin-period operas of Kurt Weill and Bertolt Brecht. Both Weill and Brecht had to make a very quick exodus from Germany by 1933, the former because he was a Jew and the latter because he was a Marxist, and yet even by that time several of their works had been praised by reactionary political elements within Weimar. The first of these misinterpreted Weill and Brecht operas was the 1929 radio cantata *Der Lindberghflug* ("The Lindbergh Flight"), celebrating Charles Lindbergh's historic, 1927 trans–Atlantic sojourn. Lindbergh, himself a future Nazi apologist, was held up by many in Germany as an exemplary "Aryan" *Übermensch* ("Superman") and role model for the young. When an exasperated Brecht later learned how the work was being used politically, he changed the title to *Ozeanflug* ("Ocean Flight"). One year later, in 1930, a similar thing happened. Weill and Brecht's children's opera *Der Jasager* ("The Yes-Sayer") was originally conceived as a complex meditation on the debatable merit of individual sacrifice for the good of society, but ended up being touted as a straightforward argument in favor of individual sacrifice.[28] Given distortions such as these, it is no wonder that Weill's operatic themes became more radical and uncompromising even as the Nazis continued to gain power. After the fall of the republic in 1933, and after leaving for

France and parting ways with Brecht (see Chapter 3), Weill was still drawn to projects with unambiguously anti-fascist themes such as *Die Silbersee* ("The Silver Lake") and *Der Kuhhandel* ("Shady Dealings").[29]

The other odd aspect of this strange episode in history is that the very same censors who condemned the moral foibles of Weimar artists were themselves then preparing to commit some of the greatest crimes in the history of humanity. In retrospect, the tragedy of, say, Anita Berber destroying her own talent while corrupting a handful of imitators (most of whom were more than willingly corrupted) seems far less egregious than the premeditated slaughterhouses of Auschwitz and Stalingrad. The purpose here is not to preach but rather to note a possible connection between censorship of perceived immorality and actual immorality of the censors — these pages hardly representing the first place where such a connection has been made. If the moral universe of German society seemed to be in a state of total collapse during the Weimar era, then the Third Reich certainly represented a preview of Doomsday for civilization itself. Stranger still is that such a bleak milieu was so vividly captured in the music from that troubled period. Voices were certainly raised in protest, but attentive audiences proved scarce until it was too late. Then, just as mysteriously, after the storm had passed, many wanted to pretend that prior warning signals had not been obvious or, worse still, downplay the importance of those voices that had been raised. This seems hardly any different or better than the travesty of visionary artists during their own lifetimes being condemned as degenerate, irreligious or unpatriotic.

9. A Field Day for
the *Neue Sachlichkeit*

"The best art of the 1920s, so full of rage and passion, was denounced as 'degenerate' because it showed the dark side of human life, its impurities, its ugliness."— Ian Buruma[1]

The Great War has been called "the quintessential twentieth-century catastrophe" and in retrospect this view is difficult to argue with. Not including the Bolshevik Revolution in Russia, it was defeated Germany which bore the greatest brunt of suffering: five million dead, one million invalids, two million orphans, and one million widows, not counting a wrecked, crippled economy, plus the unquenched animosity and vindictiveness of its neighboring former enemies.[2] Somehow, out of this national misery emerged one of the greatest and most influential aesthetic movements of the century, if not *the* greatest. The Weimar Republic was, in the words of Sabine Rewald, "a time of creative ferment that saw innovative accomplishments in literature, film, theater, design, architecture, and other visual arts unparalleled elsewhere in Europe. It was perhaps the most creative period in the history of twentieth-century Europe."[3] To this long list one could easily add music (the focus of this particular study), although music naturally tended to overlap with accomplishments in these other fields — hence, the slight detour of this chapter into the fine arts of the period. Why exactly this phenomenon occurred is well beyond the scope of this investigation, but many historians agree that national suffering somehow also produced intellectual liberty, which in turn fostered widespread vice, originality, or in some cases, both simultaneously. As Ian Buruma summarized, "The collapse of moral strictures gave people freedom. Depravity was one consequence, an extraordinary flowering of art and sciences was another."[4]

The term *neue Sachlichkeit*, often translated as "New Objectivity" or "New Matter-of-Factness," was the coinage used most frequently to label the aesthetic innovations of the Weimar period. It was first adopted in 1925 by

Gustav Hartbaub, director of the Kunsthalle Mannheim, to advertise a new traveling exhibition at his museum featuring many of the most soon-to-be-famous painters of the era.[5] Among experts, however, precise terminology can be controversial. At the risk of over-simplification and annoyance to some of these professional critics, we offer the following modest descriptors. *Neue Sachlichkeit* rose in the 1920s as a reaction against the more extravagant artifices of German Expressionism from the late 19th and early 20th centuries, which, as most will probably agree, was usually very personal and subjective in its artistic impetus, at least in comparison to that which came before.[6] For those who had survived the horrors of the Great War (at least from the defeated German point of view), as indeed most of these artists had, harsh objective reality had to be re-explored or, at minimum, distinguished from self-imposed personal illusions. Thus the greatest art of 1920s Germany tended to embrace realism in all of its repulsive ugliness or, alternatively, unapologetically escape into the world of abstraction. In any event, there would be less opportunity for confusing the two. Nevertheless, so closely was the New Objectivity associated with the Expressionist movement against which it originally rebelled, that to this day it is not unusual to hear these very same artists referred to as Expressionists, so much so that some occasionally attempt to classify the former as a subset of the latter. Further muddying the waters is that New Objectivity proponents would often borrow elements from other contemporary trends such as Surrealism, Cubism, Dadaism, and all of the other "isms" which happened to serve their larger purpose. Some, including perhaps the greatest of them all, Max Beckmann, rejected all attempts to pigeon-hole himself into the category of *neue Sachlichkeit*.

Strictly speaking, painted representations of cabaret (like cabaret itself) began during the late 19th century in France with the fabulous works of Henri de Toulouse-Lautrec and other French Impressionists. True groundwork for the breakaway innovations of Weimar era, however, came before the war as German Expressionist painters established their own original styles. The most prominent of these groups were Die Brücke ("The Bridge") and Der Blaue Reiter ("The Blue Rider"), the latter including a young Russian émigré, Wassily Kandinsky (1866–1944), from whose eponymous 1903 painting the group took its name. Tragically, two of the most talented members of the Blue Rider, Franz Marc and August Macke, were killed in battle during the Great War.[7] After the armistice, Kandinsky and fellow Russian import Alexej von Jawlensky, along with two Germans, Paul Klee and Lyonel Feininger, reformed a loose association under the umbrella of Die Blaue Vier ("The Blue Four"), retaining their favorite color blue as a symbol because, as Kandinsky once explained, he considered it the color best representing spirituality. Kandinsky, however, elected to pursue abstraction and did so spectacularly, before fleeing, like so many others, to Paris in 1933 after the Nazi takeover. Interestingly, Kandinsky had known Arnold Schoenberg in Berlin before World War I (see Chapter 1), reputedly shared some artistic aims, and painted a few his early abstract masterpieces inspired by Schoenberg's musical pioneering.[8] Neither of these great artists, though, would opt to confront head-on the ugly, repulsive realities of 1920s Germany in their later creations.

The artistic innovations of the pre–1914 period were later put to brutal or sublime effect by Weimar painters during the 1920s and 1930s. Memorable works tended to be either a direct, unpleasant confrontation of reality or a beautiful, psychological escape from reality into the realm of abstraction. Prominent representatives of the New Objectivity generally belonged to the former group. Whereas French Impressionists of the previous generation had portrayed Montmartre cabaret as a dreamlike wonderland, Weimar post–Expressionists often presented an unflattering, nightmare vision of Berlin *Kabarett*, tending to throw a harsh light on both audiences and performers. George Grosz, aka Georg Groß (1893–1959), an alumnus of the Dada movement and perhaps the most politically-driven of the New Objectivists, judged Weimar Berlin to be "a completely negative world" that in reality was a sinister and superficial tourist trap.[9] In this respect, he was in surprising agreement with his Nazi persecutor Joseph Goebbels. Unlike Goebbels, however, and in common with many other painters of the era, Grosz believed that this "negative world" needed to be portrayed and preserved on canvass in all of its crassness and venality. Buruma correctly noted that "This underlying seam of loathing is one of the distinctions of Weimar Period art, what makes it different from Parisian depictions of sexual objects." This distinctive element in German art had roots going back for centuries, but was also "…a sign of the artists' humanity. Injecting their bile into their paintings was a way of coming back from the dead."[10] Indeed, contemporary artists from France (who had not lost the war) did not follow suit in this regard.[11] Another distinctively German factor in this process was a long tradition of Berliner sardonic wit (see Chapter 8), with which these painters were right in tune.[12] The unforgettable images they created may appear like caricatures to us today, but were not considered such at the time.[13] Above all, Weimar post–Expressionist painters strove to resist modern mechanization while debunking perceived roles and stereotypes in society, often including those of the artists themselves.[14]

This is obviously a subject that deserves its own separate treatment, but the relationship to cabaret music of the period is tangible and worth brief commentary. A good overview can be provided by surveying the 2006 exhibition (and accompanying book) sponsored by the New York Metropolitan Museum of Art titled "Glitter and Doom: German Portraits from the 1920s," including works from the biggest names of the period, beginning with perhaps the most intimidating figure of them all, Max Beckmann (1884–1950). Having already made a name for himself as a painter before he was 20 years old, Beckmann marched off to war in 1914 only to return from service after suffering a nervous breakdown while working as a front line medical attendant. Through painting, he slowly brought himself back to sanity, and by the 1920s was again a leading figure on the German scene, interspersing his trademark, cool emotional tone at regular intervals with devastatingly subjective self-portraits.[15] Having been influenced in his youth by the "Superman" ideal of Nietzsche, Beckmann later turned to older German masters for quasi-religious inspiration, announcing that he wanted to help build a kind of "new church" through his art.[16] Although Beckmann never set out to chronicle the visual atmosphere of the cabarets, two of his early post-war works give intriguing glimpses into this world. The first of these, his haunting *Self-Portrait with a Champagne Glass* (1919), shows the shell-shocked, tipsy artist drinking alone at a table in a claustrophobic, indoor environment, surrounded by the subtlest hints of human misbehavior and misdeeds in every corner.[17] For *Dance in Baden-Baden* (1923), Beckmann captures the same locale that would later bring initial fame to Kurt Weill (see Chapter 3), with various well-to-do, tango-dancing couples portrayed in the most unsympathetic, unromantic light imaginable.[18] When the art of Beckmann — lionized by the German government only a few years before — was declared "Degenerate" by the Nazis in 1937, he and his wife left first for Amsterdam, then later, America.

Rivaling Beckmann in "pure" Germanic credentials, if not raw talent, was Otto Dix (1891–1969), a hardened and decorated four-year combat veteran of the Great War who sketched macabre scenes at the front when not manning a machine gun post from the trenches. Focusing on portraiture during the 1920s, Dix's paintings were compared by one critic (not inappropriately) to warrants issued by the artist for his subjects' arrest.[19] Like Beckmann, he had been heavily influenced by Nietzsche and the old German masters, but with a different focus. Dix was more interested in capturing the status quo, no matter how squalid and undesirable, rather than any idealized notions about mankind.[20] His shocking portrayal of Anita Berber (see Chapter 8) from 1925, looking twice her actual age due to hard living and substance abuse, but still a professional dancer to the very core, has become one of the most famous artistic images from the Weimar period.[21] His unsettling portrait of journalist Sylvia Harden (1926) has become iconic as well, and was later used as a kind of stylistic inspiration for the film version of *Cabaret*.[22] In addition to these, Dix, himself a cabaret dance enthusiast, gives us two scenic depictions, both often held up as representative of their time and place. *To Beauty* (1922) is a not-too-flattering self-portrait of the artist as cabaret entrepreneur and hustler, flanked by his employees, including a waiter, dancers for hire, a prostitute, and African American musician (with a Native-America drum logo), all over-shadowed by his personal favorite, a female mannequin.[23] Still more grandiose (and outrageous) is *Metropolis (Triptych)* from 1928, with a central panel of riotous cabaret dance revelry, flanked by street scenes of unspeakable squalor, including a legless, disfigured war-veteran beggar giving the military salute to aloof, indifferent prostitutes parading by.[24] Otto Dix was able to survive multiple tours of combat duty in the Great War, but his art was unable to survive more than a few days under the Nazis after 1933. After hundreds of his works had been confiscated, Dix retreated to the countryside and painted innocuous landscapes until the Second World War had subsided.[25]

Last but not least among the major Weimar figures was George Grosz. Partly because of his questionable, non-combatant war record, and partly because of a short flirtation with the Communist Party, but probably more due to the explosive political content in many of his canvases, Grosz was an early target of the Nazis, and, like Dix and Beckmann, had hundreds of his works seized before immigrating to the U.S. in 1933.[26] His stunning large-scale allegories such as *Eclipse of the Sun* (1926) give a pretty good sense of the toxic political environment in which Weimar cabaret had to function. Grosz also painted two portraits (1925/1927) of his friend and cabaret drinking companion, the poet and literary critic Max Herrmann-Neiße, a deformed hunchback whose blameless integrity nonetheless is fully captured in these sympathetic treatments.[27] *Inside and Outside* (1926) is very similar in theme to Dix's *Triptych* (which came two years later), but finds little or nothing attractive in a single brick wall dividing a dissolute cabaret lifestyle from the casualties of war subsequently abandoned by society to the city streets. The grotesque and frightening *Lovesick Man* (1916), strictly speaking, predates the *Kabarett* era but nonetheless anticipates it with a brutal (self?) depiction of male narcissism, lust, and violence in a cabaret setting. These are but a sampling.

Though not quite in the same league as paintings by other giant figures of Weimar art, one other large-scale canvass deserves special mention because of its subject matter. *Death of the Poet Walter Rheiner* (1925) by Conrad Felixmüller, currently displayed at the Art Institute of Chicago, offers a symbolic depiction of Rheiner's then-recent suicide in Berlin at age 30. Rheiner was a minor Expressionist writer who, despite the interesting quality of his surviving works, suffered from acute poverty, depression, and substance abuse. Like Anita Berber, he is sometimes viewed as one of the earliest artistic casualties of the Weimar era. Felixmüller's painting depicts Rheiner leaping from a window into the urban night lights of Berlin. The scene would be merely considered sadly eccentric were it not for the grim fact that several of German cabaret's most talented lyricists also chose to end their lives over the next decade, including Marcellus Schiffer and Kurt Tucholsky (see Chapter 6). To stand before this canvas as a viewer is to naturally ask the question whether to be a gifted German artist during this period necessitated a constant struggle against self-implosion, with or without drug use. Obviously (it would seem), many of these far-sighted individuals foresaw what was about to engulf Germany (as well as themselves), and consciously chose another mode of escape besides immigration, rather than risk the foreseen horrors of the future.

While it may be arguable whether some of these artists self-destructed out of perceived desperation for the future or simply overindulged themselves in an age of excess, there can be no question that by the mid–1920s, past and futuristic film images of horror were being projected on big theater screens in Germany for everyone to see. Just as painting was beginning to depart from the fantastical reveries of Expressionism, movies were enthusiastically adopting them. For one, it was in early 1920s Germany that the modern horror movie was more or less invented. Prominent examples of this new genre included F.W. Murnau's *Nosferatu: A Symphony of Horror* (1922), Robert Weine's *The Cabinet of Dr. Caligari* (1920), and Paul Wegener's *The Golem: How He Came into the World* (1920).[28] All of these influenced the later classic horror films of Hollywood, as well as the German cabaret scene, and still present jaw-dropping visual experiences nearly a century after the fact.[29] Another visionary German director touched by Expressionism and the New Objectivity was Fritz Lang, whose silent masterpiece *Metropolis* (1927) takes the urban jungle of Weimar Berlin to its logical, frightening conclusion. After the arrival of sound, Lang probed the diseased psyche of a serial child killer in *M* (1931), and the perceived overlaps between criminal behavior, insanity, and supernaturalism in *The Testament of Dr. Mabuse* (1933).[30]

In retrospect, perhaps the most striking aspect of Weimar film Expressionism is that it seemed to influence both directors later driven from Germany (such as Lang), and those who stayed behind, collaborating (to varying degrees) with the new Nazi regime. G.W. Pabst, in addition to helping immortalize film images of cabaret stars in *The Threepenny Opera* of 1931 (see Chapter 10), was an early auteur in melding together New Objectivity with topical social themes. *The Joyless Street* (1925), while helping to launch the international career of Greta Garbo, also allowed Pabst as director to explore difficult contemporary questions regarding economic hyperinflation, forced prostitution, and hoarding of wealth. On a more extreme level, Leni Riefenstahl, destined to become Hitler's favorite filmmaker, first came to directing prominence in 1932 with *The Blue Light*, freeing drawing upon Expressionism's favorite symbolic color for its title, as well as for some of its more fanciful and whimsical artifices. Thus many Weimar artists who later embraced or tried to reconcile with Nazism could often still not help but be profoundly influenced by the new aesthetic, even as their leaders routinely condemned it. As a skeptical Richard Strauss was bluntly informed in 1938 (See Chapter 8), so long as the Führer liked your work, you were golden.

Another conspicuous victim of German National Socialism was the Staatliches Bauhaus ("School of Building"), founded by Walter Gropius in 1919 as a cooperative business, and later put out of business by the Nazis in 1933. During its brief lifespan (roughly coinciding with the existence of the Weimar Republic), Bauhaus would succeed in establishing its permanent, world-wide legacy in the field of international architecture and design. As Weimar historian Peter Gay wrote, "Just as the Weimar style was older than the Weimar Republic, so was it larger than Germany."[31] No artistic establishment illustrated this point better. Relocating progressively from Weimar (1919–1925) to Dessau (1925–1932) and finally to Berlin (1932–1933), Bauhaus attracted some of the best talent in Germany, eventually becoming the alma mater of such distinguished names as Ludwig Mies van der Rohe, Josef Albers, and László Moholy-Nagy.[32] Painters were on staff as well, including Kandinsky, Klee, and Feininger (three members of Die Blaue Vier group).[33] In relation to the cabaret scene, the international aesthetic was employed with stunning, spectacular effect in Bauhaus alumnus Erich Mendelssohn's 1929 modernist design for the permanent 950-seat Berlin Kadeko (see Chapter 8), a venue unfortunately leveled by Allied bombing near the tail end of World War II.[34] The Jewish Mendelssohn, along with his non–Jewish mentor Gropius and just about every other important Bauhaus figure of the era, were all forced to leave Germany during the early 1930s. The one offense they shared in common with each other (and with the cabaret community) was bold, unfettered artistic freedom and innovation.

Not surprisingly, vestiges of Expressionism and New Objectivity are found throughout the canon of Weimar *Kabarett*, opera and musical revue. The song lyrics of Marcellus Schiffer, strongly reinforced by his frequent musical collaborator Mischa Spoliansky (see Chapter 6), possibly provide the best examples of this. Schiffer, as noted by Alan Lareau, quickly established himself during the early 1920s as stylistic representative of the New Objectivity at Trude Hesterberg's Wild Stage.[35] Later in the decade, Schiffer occasionally went one better by spoofing his own style in musical revues such as *It's in the Air*, the vehicle which first helped a young Marlene Dietrich to gain prominence as a singing actress.[36] Even prior to that, however, Dietrich herself had performed in a 1927 Vienna production of *Die Schule von Uznach oder Neue Sachlichkeit* ("Uznach's School or New Objectivity") by comic playwright Carl Sternheim, another work in which the newfangled aesthetic wave was satirized from an Expressionist viewpoint.[37] Around this same period, Kurt Weill was breaking away from more conservative and constrictive modes of musical composition to achieve massive popular success with *Mahagonny Songspiel* (1927) and *The Threepenny Opera* (1928). This metamorphosis was accomplished in part, according to music historian Stephen Hinton, by Weill utilizing the cool detachment and emotional restraint of New Objectivity to effectively portray the dispossessed and marginal elements of society in musical stage works.[38] Some of Weill's late Berlin-period works, such as *The Lindbergh Flight* (1929), are described by biographer Foster Hirsch as having a "...dry, brittle, unlyrical tone —*neue Sachlichkeit* with a vengeance...."[39] On a more figurative level, after immigration to the U.S., it is no coincidence that Weill's partner and muse Lotte Lenya found herself first engaged as a singer at Le Ruban Bleu ("The Blue Ribbon") nightclub in New York City. Cabaret monikers of this sort, whether in the America or Europe, originally derived from the Expressionist color of choice so beloved by Kandinsky and his associates, and was later adopted by many of them almost as a sort of anti-fascist artistic symbol.

This leads us to unquestionably the best-known symbolic use of the color blue in all of cabaret music, and perhaps in all of film literature as well, namely, Dietrich's jolting portrayal of *Tingel Tangel* singer Lola Lola in Josef von Sternberg's black-and-white film masterpiece, *The Blue Angel* (1930). Before delving into this important topic, however, it is useful to remind ourselves once again that by the end of the Roaring Twenties, the bold aesthetic trend of New Objectivity had fully manifested itself in German art, architecture, literature, film, and music. In one sense, it represented the culmination (and end) of the Expressionist movement. By 1929, the stock market had crashed and Germany, like so many other western societies, was tail-spinning into another Depression from which it (unlike America) had hardly emerged to begin with. Consequently, extremist political elements were soon embraced by the majority of German citizens, most of whom could be well-described as angry, resentful, and hard-pressed. One tragic backlash from this vicious counter-revolution was that tremendous artistic innovation in the aftermath of the Great War was officially condemned, censored, and proscribed. All of the best innovators, with almost no exceptions, were accordingly hounded, deported, killed, or if allowed, forced to recant their previous opinions. Such was the highly-charged political and economic atmosphere in which film history was about to be made and a new international movie star dramatically created.

10. Josef von Sternberg Captures It All on Film

"I don't 'admire' anyone." — Josef von Sternberg[1]

Given that there are no known documentary film records of 1920 Berlin cabarets (nor any known live recordings), we are left with whatever poetic reconstructions or re-imaginations skilled movie directors felt obliged to create for the big screen. Fortunately, there are some outstanding cinematic examples in this regard. Foremost among these (from 1930) is Josef von Sternberg's *Der Blaue Engel* ("The Blue Angel"), starring then-relative newcomer to the ranks of international stardom, Marlene Dietrich. If Sternberg's infamous quote from the header of this chapter strikes some readers as mean-spirited or self-centered, bear in mind that late–1920s Weimar Germany was a time of artistic emotional detachment and cool, truthful candor, regardless of any attending unpleasantness or sharpness. The New Objectivity movement in visual and performing arts stressed these qualities (see Chapter 9); just as Christopher Isherwood would emphasize them in his real-life snapshots barely cloaked as literary fiction (see Chapter 7), so would film directors like Josef von Sternberg stress them in their movies from the same period. For these artists, there was simply no time for hero-worship or glorification of hackneyed stereotypes. Consequently, as Ian Buruma has written, *The Blue Angel* is a cinematic example of characters "...reduced to nothing but their lowest appetites...."[2] In this respect, the film has much in common with the paintings of New Objectivity proponents such as George Grosz, Otto Dix, and Max Beckmann.

The literary origins of Sternberg's shocking, sordid material for *The Blue Angel* are surprisingly distinguished, reaching reach back to the Überbrettl period of the early 20th century (see Chapter 1). Two German authors are mainly drawn upon. The first is the 1905 novel *Professor Unrat* ("Professor Garbage") by Heinrich Mann (1871–1950), elder brother to the more famous Thomas Mann (1875–1955), both of whom later found themselves banned from Germany (with their books burned) by the Nazis. If Kurt Weill attempted to elevate low-brow cabaret singing into high art with works such as *The Threepenny Opera*, Sternberg upped the ante one by visually stylizing German *Tingel Tangel*, generally considered the lowest of the low. The book itself is set in Lübeck, a remote harbor town located on the Baltic Sea coast, thus removed from the actual cabaret scene then burgeoning in Berlin. Sternberg saw fit to keep the setting of his movie provincial, possibly to placate Berlin authorities where filming was taking place. In his fascinating memoir *Fun in a Chinese Laundry*, Sternberg delightfully informs readers of the novelist confiding to the director that his story was based on personal experience.[3] The second major literary source drawn upon in *The Blue Angel* is the highly-influential series of "Lulu" plays by Frank Wedekind (1864–1918), culminating in *Der Büchse der Pandora* ("Pandora's Box") from 1904. Based in Munich, the boundary-pushing Wedekind had himself been a pioneer in the early cabaret movement as a member of Die elf Scharfrichter ("The Eleven Executioners"), making a big impression on the young Bertolt Brecht, among many others.[4] In addition to being a kind of posthumous, presiding spirit over the Weimar cabaret scene, Wedekind inspired high-brow art music such as the 1935 opera *Lulu* by Alban Berg.[5] Sternberg unequivocally states in his book that the character name of "Lola Lola" (a departure from the original Mann novel), was direct homage to Wedekind's femme fatale.[6]

Josef von Sternberg (1894–1969) was a naturalized American citizen, born in Vienna. His Jewish family had fled Austria, not from the Nazis, but rather from poverty, similar to his younger contemporary, the Viennese-born Lotte Lenya (see Chapter 4). His is not a household name, at least not outside of the film industry, and even within the industry his legacy is surprisingly underappreciated. Professionally active during an age of iconoclasts, renegades, and egomaniacs, Sternberg has nonetheless been sometimes referred to, not inappropriately, as the first truly independent film director, typically working as his own cameraman and scriptwriter as well. He also established (probably with intent) a martinet reputation, but got along notably well with Dietrich, the result of her routine and surprising deferral to his wishes.[7] The claim to having no heroes was augmented by a candid admission that most of his film work was done in simple opposition to others, while acknowledging influences from non-film mediums such as painting and literature.[8] After breaking into Hollywood almost by accident, Sternberg directed a stunning series of silent masterpieces between 1925 and 1929, including *The Salvation Hunters, Underworld, The Last Command, The Docks of New York*, and *Thunderbolt*.[9] When the highly-touted Sternberg arrived at Berlin UFA Studios in 1929 to make his first sound film, he was about 35 years old.[10]

The Blue Angel project began with German movie star Emil Jannings wanting Sternberg to direct his first talking picture (also the first talkie for Sternberg), despite the two having clashed badly during the filming of their last project together, *The Last Command* (1928). Jannings was able to patch things up in part by agreeing to play a lead role based on Sternberg's chosen subject matter, the novel by Mann. Sternberg proceeded to hire the best cabaret singing actors he could get his hands on, including Rosa Valetti, Kurt Gerron, Hans Albers, and Charles Puffy.[11] For the soundtrack and pit orchestra he brought in cabaret songsmith extraordinaire Friedrich Hollaender, along with his Weintraub's Syncopators, arguably the best jazz ensemble in Germany.[12] The big lead role of Lola Lola, however, was still undecided; moreover, it was by then a well-known fact that every major actress in Germany appeared to be chasing the part. Heinrich Mann, author of the novel, wanted his then-girlfriend, the enormously talented cabaret chanteuse Trude Hesterberg, for the role. Leni Riefenstahl reportedly had keen interest. Jannings and most of Sternberg's staff insisted that a more-than-willing Lucie Mannheim, one of Germany's biggest starlets, should be cast.[13] Even the woman who in real life had allegedly inspired Mann's novel, though well advanced in years, was chasing the part, much to Sternberg's amusement. All of his associates, including Jannings, would be emphatically opposed to the comparatively lesser known performer that Sternberg was about to hand-pick for himself.[14]

In Sternberg's own words, it was "by accident" that he decided one night to attend a Berlin musical revue titled *Zwei Krawatten* ("Two Bow Ties"), written by Mischa Spoliansky, with a text by Georg Kaiser, friend and former mentor of both Kurt Weill and Lotte Lenya (see Chapter 3). His impulsive decision was prompted by Valetti and Albers being among the cast, both of whom he had already hired for the movie. It was here that Sternberg first encountered a 27-year-old Marlene Dietrich on the musical stage, albeit in a supporting role. In a flash epiphany, Sternberg was completely sold on Dietrich's unique combination of classic good looks, trilingual intelligence, raw musical talent, extensive film résumé, and above all (according to him), a poised, mature, devil-may-care indifference to all those around her.[15] Visually, the art-conscious director wrote, she reminded him of a Parisian model for the Impressionist painter Toulouse-Lautrec.[16] After making the announcement for his surprise, dark-horse choice and sticking to it over everyone else's objections, Sternberg recalled with pleasure how a startled, embarrassed Max Reinhardt learned for the first time that Dietrich had once attended (and failed an audition for) his drama school. Apparently, Reinhardt had previously not even been aware of her existence.[17]

Filming for *The Blue Angel* ran from November 29, 1929, to January 30, 1930.[18] Sternberg, with no small amount of wonderment, remembered during the shoot how Dietrich would work all day on the set, continue performing at the theater in the evening, after the show party with friends through the night, then show up fresh and ready for work again on the movie set the following morning.[19] One may well ponder when she ever slept. That the early Dietrich was known as a highly-disciplined professional, abstemious with alcohol and carefully avoiding drugs, only provides part explanation for her incredible stamina and drive, especially as a young married mother. Whatever the reasons behind this mystery, let history record that *The Blue Angel* was a phenomenal world-wide success upon release in 1930 and has remained a benchmark of filmmaking excellence ever since. Over eight decades later, it is still not unusual to hear a pop singer covering Hollaender's *Falling in Love Again*, the song that Dietrich first made famous. It was the wisdom and genius of Sternberg, usually in the face of strident opposition, that deserves credit for bringing this particular creative team together and then immortalizing their sublime work on film. Apart from the grim storyline, the overarching message of the movie is clear and would have done Kurt Weill proud: intellectual pretense, no matter how sophisticated, stands no chance whatsoever when pitted against powerful forces of nature that even the lowest dregs of society can fully understand and appreciate.

After taking her bows at the premier to Berlin admirers and rivals, Dietrich immediately departed with Sternberg for Hollywood, where they continued their successful partnership for six more films: *Morocco* (1930); *Dishonored* (1931); *Shanghai Express* (1932); *Blonde Venus* (1932); *The Scarlet Empress* (1934); and *The Devil Is a Woman* (1935).[20] Sometimes she sang (always with stunning effect); other times she was strictly an actress, and a great one at that.[21] Excepting the bawdy, small-town *Tingel Tangel* atmosphere of *The Blue Angel*, Berlin cabaret was never directly suggested, although Sternberg always seemingly had a subtext going. For example, Sternberg recorded that he was well aware of the romantic same-sex overtones in Dietrich's scene from *Morocco* as French cabaret singer Amy Jolly, who famously sings "Quand l'amour meurt" ("When Love Dies") in top hat and tails, before kissing a female audience member on the lips. He then repeated a similar device for her in *Blonde Venus*.[22] Cabaret's 19th century French roots are frequently acknowledged in these films, and the German Dietrich would continue to embrace a French persona throughout her career, just as she had done as an unknown B-movie actress at UFA before Sternberg turned her into a world-wide celebrity.[23] In *The Devil Is a Woman,* Sternberg presents Dietrich delivering the rather silly "Three Sweethearts Have I" as an unlikely Spanish Carmen–type; yet, this unconventional conceit could have easily passed for a skit at Berlin's Catacombs, which was then in the process of being shut down by the Nazis. This performance, in its own deceptively innocent way, can be viewed without too much strain as a distant forebear of Kander and Ebb's

"Two Ladies" from *Cabaret* (see Chapter 15). Part of the constant juxtaposition between Dietrich's Berlin cabaret training with other foreign exotic settings was surely due to Sternberg's considerable knack in placating (and confusing) potential censors. In an era of rising censorship, none of his films were ever censored, and this helped Dietrich's career progress as well.[24] While Sternberg was later accused of being bitter towards Dietrich (perhaps for not hiring him as his career faded), he in fact wrote and spoke very highly of her during the final years of his life. For him to praise anyone in the film industry was unusual, but in the end he judged Dietrich to be an extraordinary talent, often providing him with better performances than he could have expected.[25]

Less widely celebrated than the partnership between Sternberg and Dietrich but still worthy of honorable mention in relation to Weimar Berlin cabaret is the film legacy of Georg Wilhelm Pabst (1885–1967). Pabst's greatest achievements in regard to preserving cinematic glimpses of the Berlin cabaret world include *Die Büchse der Pandora* ("Pandora's Box") and *Tagebuch einer Verlorenen* ("Diary of a Lost Girl")—both 1929 silent features starring iconic American actress Louise Brooks. Last but not least came the highly-litigated, sound film version of *Die 3-Groschen Oper* ("The Threepenny Opera") from 1931.[26] Like Sternberg, Pabst was Austrian-born, but unlike his younger colleague, did not immigrate and stayed in Germany during the Second World War, occasionally practicing his art under Nazi sponsorship which may or may not have been coerced, to his eternal discredit. Part of his decision not to leave Germany may have been due to possible poor treatment by the French as a civilian prisoner during World War I; in any event, his surviving work speaks for itself. The two silent films with Brooks give authentic, invaluable snippets of contemporary Berlin nightlight, always used as a backdrop for intense dramatic scenes, rather than for its own sake. In *Diary of a Lost Girl*, a long interlude involves an urban cabaret, complete with jazz band, drinking, smoking, shouting and dancing on a crowded club floor, framed by subplots of prostitution and vice, not unlike a famous Otto Dix painting on the same theme (see Chapter 9). *Pandora's Box*—the same Wedekind tale that inspired Sternberg—goes one better with a glittering sequence depicting the atmosphere of late 1920s Berlin musical revue, both on stage and backstage. This represents an authentic reconstruction of the same unique, Weimar-style of gaudy mass entertainment that brought Dietrich to Sternberg's attention in the first place.

In the immediate wake of massive commercial triumph for *The Blue Angel* came Pabst's own directorial response with *The Threepenny Opera* in 1931. Like Sternberg, he cast the best Berlin cabaret talent then available, with one debatable exception. Lotte Lenya, many years after the fact, gave a strange but true account of an intrepid and still relatively unknown Marlene Dietrich

marching into the studio to audition for the role of Pirate Jenny, a part originally written for Lenya by her husband Kurt Weill and recently made famous
by her across the stages of Europe. With supreme and consummate tact, Lenya
recalled that Dietrich was considered just too tall and beautiful for the part.[27]
Instead, Lenya herself thankfully was hired for the job. In addition to Lenya,
Pabst brought on board Valeska Gert, cabaret dancer extraordinaire, Carola
Neher, another veteran of Weill and Brecht's stage works, and, somewhat surprisingly, singing actor Ernst Busch (1900–1980), another original *Threepenny*
cast member but also a committed and outspoken Marxist.[28] Talent in this
case, however, overruled politics, as Pabst harnessed and utilized Busch's formidable declamatory skills almost like a Greek chorus at regular intervals in
the shooting.[29] In the final end, and despite the all of the litigation, delays,
and compromises, Pabst succeeded in creating a widely-acknowledged art
house masterpiece, immortalizing in sound and vision several striking appearances by these unappreciated and often forgotten performers. Lenya's rendition
of "Pirate Jenny" alone is priceless and gives some indication of the manner
in which she was able to dominate Weimar stages with her all-too-believable
character portraits.[30]

Late during her own life, Lenya reflected on the subtle differences
between authentic cabaret singing from the Weimar era and that being simultaneously presented on musical stages and movie houses of the time:

> The kind of songs that Trude Hesterberg and Rosa Valetti were singing in the
> cabarets had absolutely nothing to do with Kurt Weill. I mean take Dietrich's "Ich
> bin von Kopf bis Fuss auf iebe eingestellt." That has nothing to do with Brecht
> and Weill. That's a typical cabaret song. The standards were completely different
> in cabaret, you know?... I think *The Blue Angel* and *The Threepenny Opera* were
> very close, true to life.[31]

Interestingly, after distinguishing carefully between Dietrich's style and
her own, Lenya emphasizes their commonality in terms of gritty realism, a
reality that Lenya knew all too well from the unpleasant experiences of her
own childhood and young adulthood. This same uncompromising realism,
one so fiercely embraced by proponents of the New Objectivity in Germany,
also cast its powerful spell to varying degrees over fully Americanized film
directors such as Sternberg who dared to cross its path. Curiously, when Weill
came to the America in 1935, the first step he took towards successfully bringing music to a broader English-speaking was to distance himself from his
tough Berlin style of the recent past. This proved initially hard on Lenya,
since it was the tough Berlin style which had made her famous in the first
place. In the case of Dietrich and Sternberg, after 1935 they parted artistic
company, with Dietrich going on to levels of fame hardly imaginable only
half a decade previous. Sternberg, unfortunately, seemed no longer capable

of working with anyone after working with Dietrich. In 1937 came his highly-publicized fiasco (and major commercial misstep) with an expensive, abortive attempt at filming the Robert Graves novel *I, Claudius*. His career never recovered. Like Erich von Stroheim before him, Sternberg became anachronistic. By 1959, he was gratefully taking any odd job available while teaching film classes at UCLA. Among his students during the early 1960s was a young aspiring poet and rock singer named Jim Morrison, who before the decade was out would re-introduce millions of pop music listeners to Weill and Brecht's "Alabama Song," a number premiered by Lenya to enthusiastic audiences at Baden-Baden back in 1927. Thus by the mid–1930s, anyone believing that *Kabarett* was dead just because the Nazis had taken over Germany would be in for quite a shock and surprise within a few short years.

PART II —*AMERIKA* AND BEYOND

11— From the Kurfürstendamm
to Broadway

*"But how great Kurt Weill was as a composer of music, the world will
slowly discover—for he was a much greater musician than anyone now
imagines."*— Maxwell Anderson[1]

As Josef von Sternberg's film *The Blue Angel* gained rapid international
circulation and fame for Marlene Dietrich during the early 1930s, American
popular music was beginning its own cross-fertilization process, continuing
unabated for the rest of the century. This accelerating development was thanks
mainly to new, multiple technologies hitting mainstream consumer society,
combined with a wealth of infiltrating foreign influences, beginning with the
German cabaret style itself. Initial origins beyond Dietrich's Hollywood film
career, however, were not auspicious. In April 1933, a hastily and poorly
mounted English-language version of Weill and Brecht's *The Threepenny Opera*
opened and quickly flopped at the Empire Theatre on Broadway, with no
participation from any of its original creators.[2] Of the many miscalculations
made during this failed production, perhaps the biggest was that most Broadway audiences typically run for cover at any mention of the word "opera."
Another was that the show was placed on Broadway itself, whereas the Berlin
original was decidedly located off that city's main entertainment strip, the
Kurfürstendamm. Not by chance would *Threepenny* be a rousing American
success two decades later at a much smaller, off–Broadway venue sporting a
considerably lower profile (see Chapter 3). Nevertheless, this long process was
in truth part of a wider trend involving the musical cabaret style of Berlin's
Kurfürstendamm, as distilled by musical genius of Kurt Weill, slowly being
translated for wider American audiences via Broadway during the 1950s and
1960s (see Chapter 15).

By the time that Kurt Weill first landed on U.S. soil in late 1935, the
American music scene had been segregated into two more or less opposing
camps, one "popular" (led by Broadway and Hollywood) and one more "seri-

ous," with ambitious, talented composers from the latter group working hard to close the gap. Arriving in New York, Weill was immediately invited by George Gershwin (1898–1937) to attend rehearsals for his *Porgy and Bess*, the most ambitious American musical since Kern and Hammerstein's *Show Boat* of 1927.[3] The 1935 premiere of *Porgy*, however (despite its now-classic status), proved to be a failure with most critics and audiences, some of whom still object to the premise of a white composer writing theater music for an all-black cast. Two years later in 1937, when Gershwin died young at age 38, Aaron Copland (1900–1990) succeeded him as America's leading home-grown composer.[4] Though maintaining a cool attitude toward Weill's German socialist-imported brand of music drama, Copland had in fact attended early performances of *Mahagonny Songspiele* and *The Threepenny Opera* during his European travels, and could not help but be impressed, if not influenced, by Weill's accomplishments.[5] Early Copland works such as his one-act children's opera *The Second Hurricane* (1936) reflect a debt to Weill's *Der Jasager* ("The Yes-Sayer") from 1930, as well as a genuine attempt to create an Americanized version of Weill's *Gebrauchsmusik* ("Utilitarian Music").[6] Copland's huge impact on modern American music over the next two decades cannot be understated; however, this aspect of his work acting as a conduit for ideas first taking shape in Germany during the 1920s has been relatively un-remarked upon to date. Above all, Aaron Copland circa 1935–1945 was striving to reach as broad an audience as possible using indigenous materials; moreover, there can be little question that Copland's sense of rivalry with Weill during this same period factored into his simultaneous creation of a lasting populist legacy.[7]

The American "serious" or "classical" musical landscape encountered by Weill in 1935 (soon to be dominated by Copland and other like-minded composers) had its beginnings with an unlikely combination of iconoclastic academic theory and federal government intervention. As part of Roosevelt's New Deal administration, the short-lived Works Progress Administration (WPA) was launched in early 1935, including one of its lesser known offshoots, the Federal Music Project (FMP), whose goal was to bring "classics" to the masses.[8] Predictably, the FMP floundered due to lack of competent personnel. In typical roundabout government fashion, however, another new agency, the Resettlement Administration (RA) was also introduced in 1935 to help soften the blow of widespread displacement caused by the Great Depression. Surprisingly, one of its myriad branches included a Music Unit. In an act of pure serendipity, RA hired Charles Seeger (1886–1979), father of future folk-singer Pete Seeger (see Chapter 18), as technical advisor. Seeger the elder proceeded to energetically implement everything that he had preached for years as an academic, including a firm belief that interaction between serious and popular cultures should be a two-way street. Only then, he argued, could music become a true instrument of positive social change.[9] By early 1936, with son Pete and composer wife Ruth Crawford Seeger, he was in Asheville, North Carolina, attending the Ninth Annual Mountain Dance and Folk Festival in a pioneering effort to federally promote events of this kind throughout the country.[10] During his two-year tenure with the RA, Seeger continued to advocate that "serious" American music should draw upon American folk traditions rather than European models.[11] This forceful view would in turn be adopted by an entire generation of American composers (including Copland). It would also encourage Weill to heavily depart from his former, hard-edged Berlin style.[12] Alex Ross noted that American intellectual hostility to central European traditions sprang in part from language barriers plus a basic misunderstanding of Weimar music; nevertheless, these prejudices were not to be dissuaded, especially since there were plenty of readily available domestic sources to draw upon.[13]

When Weill first arrived in New York during the fall of 1935, his American Broadway musical competitors included the likes of George Gershwin, Irving Berlin, Jerome Kern, Richard Rodgers, and Cole Porter. After being welcomed by Gershwin, Weill was referred to pioneering producer Cheryl Crawford and her Group Theatre collective in Connecticut, whose members could already sing some of Weill's German songs.[14] Although Weill's current project involved working with Max Reinhardt for the delayed 1937 premier of his oratorio *The Eternal Road*, Crawford steered Weill towards the playwright Paul Green (1894–1981), who was interested in having his experimental anti-war drama *Johnny Johnson* set to music. Since the same theme resonated with Weill, having just escaped from a European continent ready to explode into world war, he agreed to meet with Green in May of 1936.[15] Arriving near Green's home in Chapel Hill, North Carolina, Weill shared his first impressions of the American South in a letter to Lenya, taking note of the country's oldest university and declaring the atmosphere to be "wonderful" despite a rustic, Depression-era setting: "When I got off the train, there was no car, no village, no telephone, only a few dilapidated Negro shanties." After hitching a ride, Weill's initial reaction to the playwright was favorable but then a few days later concluded that "Paul Green is a strange fellow...."[16] Soon, Lenya was having her first American romantic affair with Green, but it proved short-lived.[17] On January 19, 1937, she and Weill were remarried in a Westchester County civil ceremony, and by the following year (1938), she was complaining openly about Green: "He's so idiotic that he gets on your nerves.... He really is a hopeless case."[18] Nevertheless, Weill proceeded with the commission and his first Broadway musical, *Johnny Johnson*, directed by the venerable Lee Strasberg, opened in late 1936 to modest acclaim.[19]

Having gotten his American feet wet with *Johnny Johnson* and *The Eternal Road*, Weill turned to Hollywood, another major potential source for income. There in early 1937 he encountered fellow refugees from the old country, most of whom he was none too pleased to see. Writing Lenya while visiting one soundstage, Weill observed "In the greenroom with [Otto] Klemperer was the wunderkind [Erich Wolfgang] Korngold grown old. I put on my haughtiest face and stayed for only two minutes. All of them are abundantly disgusting."[20] The fact is that Weill could get no traction in Hollywood. As soundtrack historian Gary Marmorstein noted, Hollywood producers of that era gave lip service to more modern-styled composers such as Weill but in reality shared a "prevailing industry scorn toward independent composers who worked in a contemporary, unromantic idiom."[21] Serious American composers such as Weill, Aaron Copland, and Virgil Thomson tended to have more success operating outside of the film studio system.[22] Weill's main accomplishment during his time spent in southern California was to strengthen ties with the Gershwin family, particularly with George's younger brother (and lyricist) Ira, who would collaborate successfully with Weill in the near future. In another letter to Lenya, Weill wrote that while visiting the Gershwin Hollywood mansion, the entire clan was at first cool towards him as a potential competitor for movie deals, but warmed up considerably after beholding his brand new automobile, purchased especially to impress for the occasion.[23] By this time, Weill was also noting with alarm George Gershwin's erratic personal behavior, a harbinger of the great artist's premature death later that same year.[24]

Weill's fortunes in America started to prosper when he began collaboration with the American playwright Maxwell Anderson (1888–1959). The German composer had seen and admired Anderson's play *What Price Glory?* in Berlin; and one of the first dramas he attended after arriving in the U.S. was Anderson's *Winterset*, also making a big impression.[25] Through actor Burgess Meredith, a cast member in both *Winterset* and the failed American premier of *Threepenny*, Weill was introduced to Anderson in 1937. Within a year they were close friends and working together on a new musical, *Knickerbocker Holiday*.[26] The German socialist immigrant Weill and American proto-libertarian Anderson made a very unlikely creative couple, but somehow it clicked, just as Weill's earlier partnership with the Marxist Bertolt Brecht had been productive. *Knickerbocker Holiday* opened on Broadway in 1938 and was Weill's first American hit, featuring the timeless "September Song" as its centerpiece. A notable incident in the initial run involved the attendance of one performance by President Franklin Delano Roosevelt and First Lady Eleanor. The New Deal-hating Anderson had created a Roosevelt parody in the plot, even daring to portray one of Roosevelt's Dutch ancestors on stage as a corrupt buffoon. FDR saw it and reportedly laughed his head off. No doubt it occurred to Weill that Hitler would not have reacted in the same manner to a similar stage satire. After the unqualified success of *Knickerbocker Holiday*, Weill resolved to work exclusively with top-notch playwrights and lyricists, a conscious goal to which he adhered to for the remainder of his career.[27]

Beginning full force with his Maxwell Anderson association, Weill forged a new American style of musical that somehow translated the edginess and astringency of Berlin's Kurfürstendamm scene to the Broadway stage. This was accomplished in part by watering it down with more palatable outside influences, which few composers other than Weill were capable of doing. As music historian Michael Morley has noted, in approaching Broadway "Weill reacted by returning not to the German cabaret song for a model, but to a style midway between the French ballad and the German lied."[28] Kim Kowalke made a similar observation: "Weill remained ... at once European and American, 'serious' and popular, German and Jewish, abstruse and accessible."[29] Above all, Weill avoided use of the term "opera" in public (until after World War II), considering it to be box office poison in America.[30] This was from one who only five years previous had been Germany's leading operatic composer. The results were tangible. Of Weill's last seven American stage works (over the next 11 years), six would be financially successful.[31] Weill and Anderson followed up their triumph with the patriotic 1940 radio cantata *The Ballad of Magna Carta*, again featuring Burgess Meredith and culminating with Anderson's exhortation "Resistance unto tyrants is obedience to God"—for him signifying Roosevelt but for Weill meaning Hitler. The declamatory, moralistic style of this work could have easily been delivered by Gertrude Lawrence's Anna from *The King and I*, and indeed the British-born Lawrence would, within a year, play a very important role in Weill's American artistic advancement. 1940 also saw Weill and Lenya welcome their friends and fellow European refugees, the French cabaret-influenced composer Darius Milhaud and his wife Madeleine, newly arrived in New York.[32]

The successful 1938–1939 run of *Knickerbocker Holiday* made Weill more financially secure. It also helped to attract his next working lyricist, Ira Gershwin, whose brother George had recently died, and whose good graces Weill had carefully cultivated during his first two years in America.[33] The blockbuster result in early 1941 was *Lady in the Dark*, based on a book by playwright-director Moss Hart (1904–1961), produced by the legendary Sam Harris (1872–1941), and not inaptly described as Weill's American *Threepenny Opera*.[34] A stellar cast led by Gertrude Lawrence included a young Danny Kaye (emerging from the production as a new star in his own right), operatic veteran Davis Cunningham, and a 27-year-old Victor Mature, then on the cusp of Hollywood stardom himself.[35] This massive hit netted for Weill a whopping (for then) $42,500 in profits, part of which he used to purchase Brook House in Rockland County, New York, making him and Lenya next door neighbors to Maxwell Anderson and his wife Mab.[36] The music of *Lady in the Dark* featured a number of notable songs later becoming part of the standard repertoire, including "The Saga of Jenny," "Tschaikowsky (and Other Russians)," and "My Ship." The high artistic quality of the work and unequivocal commercial success of the production temporarily silenced Weill's critics, and the composer was known to hold a particularly high opinion of *Lady in the Dark*.[37] Thus on the eve of U.S. entry into World War II, Weill found himself placed squarely within the vanguard of American Broadway composers.

After Pearl Harbor, Weill also found himself, as a German-Jewish expatriot, nearly overnight becoming a leading musical symbol of resistance to fascism. During the early war years Weill was occupied with various musical fundraisers and patriotic activities while simultaneously preparing his next major Broadway show (see Chapter 12). Teaming up with American poet Ogden Nash (1902–1971), humorist S.J. Perelman (1904–1979), and choreographer Agnes de Mille (1905–1993), Weill selected for his subject matter the British comic novel *The Tinted Venus* by Thomas Anstey Guthrie, loosely based on the Pygmalion myth from Ovid.[38] *One Touch of Venus* opened in late 1943 and was another rousing commercial smash, yielding one of Weill's most famous and widely-covered songs, "Speak Low (When You Speak Love)." The show featured a breakthrough performance by the then-unknown Mary Martin, thus paving the way for her later famous premiering roles for Rodgers and Hammerstein in *South Pacific* (1949) and *The Sound of Music* (1959).[39] Although both *Lady in the Dark* and *One Touch of Venus* were made into mediocre Hollywood movies before the decade was out (1944 and 1948, respectively), Weill had little reason to complain financially by this point.[40] He celebrated his affluence in 1943 by officially becoming an American citizen. Within the space of eight years, Weill had gone from penniless German-Jewish émigré to one of the most prestigious and profitable composer brand names on Broadway.

From such dazzling heights of achievement, Weill was due for a setback and it came in early 1945 with his next big project, *The Firebrand of Florence*, designed as a vehicle for reviving the stalled career of his wife. Unlike her husband, Lotte Lenya had not enjoyed the same level of fame since their immigration to the U.S., but rather admiration from a small group of discerning connoisseurs (see Chapter 4). Using *The Autobiography of Benvenuto Cellini* for inspiration, *Firebrand* attempted to emphasize the comedic elements from Cellini's classic tale of ribaldry and intrigue (drawing upon a 1934 stage adaptation by Edwin Justin Mayer), once again harnessing the talents of Ira Gershwin as lyricist. This time, however, nothing clicked, nothing seemed to come together. Despite Weill's reliably engaging music, everyone seemed uncomfortably miscast, especially Lenya, who was attempting to segue herself into light American comedy from some of the most daring roles ever conceived for European music drama only a few years previous. Now, as the war in Europe wound down during the spring of that year, *Firebrand* was bombing on Broadway. After a short run, the production was mercifully closed down. Lenya blamed herself and resolved never to perform again, surely unable to imagine that within a decade she would be honored by the Tony Awards for almost single-handedly inventing the off–Broadway music industry with her pace-setting performance in the English-language revival of *The Threepenny Opera*.

Furious at the shoddy treatment his wife received from critics and audiences as a result of the failed *Firebrand* production, Weill came roaring back during the second postwar era in 1946–1947 with *Street Scene*, a great progressive masterpiece of the musical stage. Collaborating with African American lyricist Langston Hughes (1902–1967) and American German-Jewish playwright Elmer Rice, aka Elmer Leopold Reizenstein (1892–1967), upon whose 1929 Pulitzer Prize–winning drama the musical was based, Weill was back in his element composing path-breaking, cabaret-inflected music designed for the mass consumption. Weill had admired Rice's work since first seeing the play in Germany circa 1930. When the two finally met in 1936, Weill proposed setting it to music but Rice declined. Later, in 1939, Weill wrote incidental music for Rice's drama *Two on an Island*, and after Weill's Broadway triumphs in 1941–1943, Rice finally agreed to Weill's original proposal for *Street Scene*. In his striking, atmospheric portrayal of lower-class urban life in Manhattan (albeit from a white, immigrant point of view), Weill had considerable help from Hughes, who took trouble to give the composer a personal tour of Harlem nightclubs and bring into the artistic mix a more radical political sensibility.[41] The stylistic result was a unique combination of Gershwin and Puccini, emboldening Weill to call it an "American opera" — a remarkable departure in terminology for him — and the work proved to be a great forerunner of similar-themed Broadway hits such as Leonard Bernstein's *West Side Story* (1957).[42] Most importantly, *Street Scene* had a good commercial run and, perhaps even more impressively, won Weill a Tony Award in 1947 for Best Original Score, the first of its kind ever bestowed.[43]

The last three years of Weill's short life saw acceleration in his activity rather than any break in stride. In 1948–1949 came *Love Life*, a clever throwback to cabaret's vaudeville roots, simultaneously retaining the edgy sensibility of the Weimar Kurfürstendamm while pointing forward stylistically to 1960s concept musicals such as Kander and Ebb's *Cabaret* (see Chapter 15).[44] Once again, Weill seemed to gravitate towards working with top-notch young talent, including director Elia Kazan, choreographer Michael Kidd, and lyricist Alan Jay Lerner (1918–1986). Lerner, in tandem with his regular working partner Frederick Loewe, had recently produced his first big Broadway hit, the musical *Brigadoon* (1947), but still jumped at the chance to work with Weill.[45] The result for both was another commercial and artistic triumph. That same year (1948), seemingly working off the cuff, Weill found time to write a student folk opera, *Down in the Valley*, for Indiana University in Bloomington.[46] That, too, was a smash success, and rather amazingly, remains Weill's second most-often performed stage work after *The Threepenny Opera*.[47] Shrewdly and brilliantly, Weill was somehow able in this commission to combine then popular American western idioms with challenging moral themes explored by the composer during the Weimar era two decades previous (see Chapter 3). The piece still comes across like a casual (yet serious) *Kleinkunst* melding of Rodgers and Hammerstein's *Oklahoma!* (1943) with Weill and Brecht's German school opera *The Yes-Sayer* (1930).[48]

In 1949 Weill reunited with friend and neighbor Maxwell Anderson for his final Broadway masterwork, *Lost in the Stars*, adapted from the 1948 novel *Cry, the Beloved Country* by Alan Paton, showcasing the ubiquitous title track composed by Weill (and recorded by Lenya) during the war. Although Weill, as a German-Jewish refugee, was keen to give the explosive topic of race relations full treatment on the American musical stage ever since witnessing Gershwin's *Porgy and Bess* upon his U.S. arrival, he knew better than to confront the issue directly. Instead Weill opted to draw upon Paton's tragic depiction of South Africa at the dawn of the Apartheid era. Years before, he had been intrigued by Bertolt Brecht's idea of doing an all-black American production of *The Threepenny Opera* featuring Paul Robeson, but in the end balked at the unpleasant prospect of working again with Brecht.[49] In the mean time, Broadway had continued to experiment with African American and bi-racial casting after *Porgy*'s rejection by critics in 1935. Not including Scott Joplin's early foray into ragtime opera with *Treemonisha* (1915), the real breakthrough had come in 1927 with Kern and Hammerstein's *Show Boat*, also starring Robeson. In the wake of *Porgy* came various similar attempts either rejected or accepted by the musical establishment, with limited or no commercial impact, including Vernon Duke's *Cabin in the Sky* (1940), Duke Ellington's *Jump for Joy* (1941), and Hammerstein's *Carmen Jones* (1943), a retooling of the Georges Bizet opera.[50] *Lost in the Stars*, however, boasted an exquisite, eclectic score anchored by a hit song routinely covered by popular artists into the present day. It confronted the racial divide of a society head on, while still managing to fill theater seats: the original production outlived Weill by almost three months into 1950. At the dawn of the Civil Rights era in America during the late 1940s, Kurt Weill was once again in the cultural forefront of events and somehow managed to earn a good living while doing it.

The short but extraordinary life of Kurt Weill came to a premature end on April 3, 1950, with the great composer dying at age 50 from heart failure following a brief, sudden illness, possibly exacerbated by overwork. At the time he was enthusiastically setting to music texts by Maxwell Anderson inspired by Mark Twain's *Huckleberry Finn*. Weill had also recently expressed interest in taking on Herman Melville's *Moby Dick* as an operatic subject.[51] Had he been given the long lifespan of a Verdi or a Wagner there is no telling what he would have accomplished. Privately, Lotte Lenya admitted to feelings of guilt over not having been a good wife, which later motivated her sustained devotion to his musical legacy. Because Lenya's artistic forte was interpretation of Weill's German works, it would be the earlier Weimar-era music dramas of the late 1920s and early 1930s that would dominate revival of interest in his music over the next three decades.[52] As for his American stage works and popular songs that had been so successful between 1935 and 1950, these would be temporarily forgotten until their many merits would come to be widely recognized during the tail end of the century. Part of this shift in taste had to do with economics, since Weill died at a moment in Broadway history in which the more extravagant, independently-produced musicals dominating the first half of the century were being quickly replaced by less expensive, corporate-sponsored productions.[53] Had Weill lived to write more musicals, they would have been different in style and scope, but he had already proved several times over that he was quite capable of adapting to changes such as this.

Weill would not live to see the influence of his style spread. At the time of his passing in 1950 it would be fair to say that (thanks mainly to him) the American musical form had been permanently affected with a subtle infusion of Weimar sensibility. Weill's short but sturdy catalogue of Broadway songs rivals anything produced by home-grown composers; moreover, these songs tend to stand apart because of their unique brand of dark, moody atmosphere combined with a highly complex, purely adult-like take on romantic love. Younger American songwriters such as Frank Loesser, Leonard Bernstein, Alan Jay Lerner, and Marc Blitzstein were clearly influenced by him, while close contemporaries like Virgil Thomson, Aaron Copland, and Ira Gershwin either willingly or unwillingly felt the sway of Weill's musical impact.[54] Even Weill's biggest Broadway rivals, Rodgers and Hammerstein, though completely different in style, could not escape the fascinating allure of the German interloper's unique approach to the musical stage. In the successful wake of Weill and Gershwin's *Lady in the Dark* from 1941, Rodgers and Hammerstein created their own benchmark in American musical history with *Oklahoma!* (1943). This exuberant wartime work had more to do with Copland's effective incorporation of western folk tunes into larger scaled pieces than, say, a more authentic, vernacular portrayal of Oklahoma in Woody Guthrie's *Dust Bowl Ballads*, dating from about the same period. *Oklahoma!* was quickly followed in turn by *Carousel* (1945), another commercial smash for its creators also managing to provide an almost operatic scope to its somewhat more serious, spiritually-oriented material.

As *Carousel* was playing to sold-out houses in 1945, Weill's *Firebrand of Florence* was tanking. In a letter to Lenya during that period, Weill made no secret of his feeling a sense of direct competition with Rodgers, as well as his being miffed at the contrasting fortunes of their current productions.[55] In another letter to Lenya, Weill admits that he and Ira Gershwin both had a low opinion of Rodgers and Hammerstein's soundtrack for *State Fair* (1945), and that both naturally preferred their own relatively modest score for the obscure film *Where Do We Go from Here?* (1945).[56] After the war, Rodgers and Hammerstein attempted a more moralistic, sophisticated type of musical in *Allegro* (1947), which flopped badly; at the same time, Weill's *Street Scene* (1947) was winning a Tony and earning profits. Not until *South Pacific* (1949) and *The King and I* (1951), both productions featuring alumni stars from Weill hit musicals (Mary Martin and Gertrude Lawrence, respectively), did Rodgers and Hammerstein finally achieve a totally effective combination of serious social commentary with more popular, commercially-oriented music. By this time, Weill was gone from the scene; however, in retrospect, even his artistic failures and throw-offs — of which there were very few — still sound interesting and tend to get better with repeated listening.

Perhaps another way to appreciate Weill's artistic legacy is to contrast his American career with that of another gifted German-Jewish composer who came to the U.S. during the 1930s, Hanns Eisler (1898–1962). Like Weill, Eisler had a stellar formal background in music, rubbed shoulders with the likes of Arnold Schoenberg, worked with Bertolt Brecht, and had contacts with the *Kabarett* scene, setting texts by Kurt Tucholsky. Unlike Weill, however, Eisler became a Marxist after World War I and remained that way for the rest of his life; paradoxically, in spite of his political beliefs, Eisler did not have Weill's talent for writing hit tunes or much of a sense for musical theater of the proletariat.[57] After immigrating to America in 1933, Eisler tried his hand in Hollywood with modest success while continuing to write serious music. After World War II, however, he became one of the first high-profile victims of McCarthyism, being blacklisted and then forcibly deported back to East Germany in 1948. Afterwards, an anxious Woody Guthrie wrote his poignant song lyric "Eisler on the Go" to mark the unfortunate event.[58] If nothing else, the disappointing trajectory of Eisler's career demonstrates that Weill's phenomenal acceptance (and adaptability) in the U.S. between 1935 and 1950 were far from being automatic or pre-ordained, despite his tremendous talent. Indeed, when compared to those of his musical contemporaries, Weill's many accomplishments despite so many obstacles and in such a short space of time, come across as only slightly less than miraculous.

During his breakthrough period of the 1920s in Weimar Germany, Weill was known to have remarked (in the context of compositional history), "Once musicians obtained everything they had imagined in their most daring dreams, they started again from scratch."[59] Later he added, "There is nobody like me when it comes to discovering new grounds."[60] Indeed, it would be difficult to give another example of a composer making a more breathtaking, full transition than the one Weill made between Weimar Berlin to New York Broadway within the span a decade. This may partly explain why the revival of Weill's music since the 1950s has focused mainly on his German-language works. The impact of his American works has been nearly universal, but has never needed "revival" in the same sense because it was so thoroughly and quickly integrated into the American popular tradition. Baffling stylistic comparisons between *The Threepenny Opera* and *Lady in the Dark* are not unlike trying to explain the popular metamorphosis of a 18th century Bach cantata into the 20th century "Sheep May Safely Graze." How a German Lutheran secular text set to music eventually became a modern standard of the light classical repertoire requires a book unto itself, but then again, even Fats Waller considered himself an aficionado of Bach, despite a wide gulf in time and culture. The same could be said for Weill's songs, whose arrangements always retained a remnant of Bach's danceable, tuneful morality tales — the same inescapable music that surely influenced his youth in Saxony. How strange that this particular facet of the *Kabarett* tradition eventually led to an ill-timed collision course between its greatest composer and greatest performer during the height of World War II, an encounter which yielded little creatively and surely resulted in plenty of regrets for both of these strong artistic personalities.

12. *Kabarett* Helps
to Win the War

"Her name begins tenderly and ends with the sound of a cracking whip—Marlene Dietrich."— Jean Marais[1]

Comedian-songwriter Mel Brooks once reminisced how during World War II he (then known as Corporal Melvin Kaminsky) and other American soldiers, following the Battle of the Bulge, would effectively demoralize their nearby German counterparts by taking turns doing Hitler imitations on a megaphone. As Brooks explained, the Germans had the Führer, but the Americans had Ethel Merman, who was just as loud and strident, plus she could dance. Coming from the man who created "Springtime for Hitler" and *The Producers* (1968/2001), the flippant veneer of Brooks' remark (and typically for him) disguises a very perceptive observation. The fact is that the Allies had much superior front line entertainment than the Germans, and this held true even before they began winning the shooting war; moreover, Allied troop entertainment tended to incorporate all the best elements from Germany and then go at least one better. If first-rate German comedians such as Werner Finck were conscripted into performing for the *Wehrmacht* (see Chapter 8), the Marx Brothers made the U.S. Army laugh voluntarily and probably did it better.[2] Thus, not long after Kurt Weill had infused Broadway with a permanent dose of Weimar cabaret sensibility, Marlene Dietrich would bring her own inimitable brand of *Tingle Tangel* sass and verve directly to the front lines, often acting as her own *conférencier* in between songs.[3]

As one would expect, the artistic level of wartime entertainment did not usually rise to the sophisticated level of prewar literary *Kabarett* or that typically experienced by Weimar era patrons of the Kadeko or Catacombs in Berlin. Instead, a more innocuous, non-political style of show tended to prevail, one which in many ways was derived from the old traditions of vaudeville and light operetta. In Germany, perhaps the best example of this genre (or at least the most popular) was Austrian-set *Im Weißen Rößl* ("The White Horse Inn") from 1930, a distant forebear to Rodgers and Hammerstein's *The Sound of Music* (1959). This potpourri collaborative work was mainly the brainchild of producer Erik Charell, the same man who earlier had discovered the Comedian Harmonists (see Chapter 8), and during the 1920s had worked with some of the best *Kabarett* talent in Berlin, including Claire Waldoff and Friedrich Hollaender.[4] In many ways, the type of straightforward, sentimental love songs featured in *The White Horse Inn* were a carryover from the Überbrettl fad of the early 20th century, as well as the highly successful German operettas of Franz Lehár. Given that Lehár was one of Hitler's favorite composers, it comes as no surprise that the Nazis frequently tried to appropriate and "Aryanize" this particular format for their own propaganda purposes. Not only were *Wehrmacht* and SS personnel typically entertained with this brand of lighter fare, but Jewish prisoners in the concentration camps as well, that is, whenever entertainment was allowed in these places of horror (see Chapter 6). It is no coincidence that the talented singing actress Camilla Spira, one of the original production stars in *The White Horse Inn*, later found herself performing before appreciative audiences at Westerbork concentration camp in 1943–1944, and soon afterwards securing her release by fooling Nazi authorities into believing that she was not really in fact Jewish.[5]

Among the musical personalities traversing the boundaries between German cabaret, light operetta and film soundtracks, probably the two most prominent were Ralph Benatzky (1884–1957) and Werner Richard Heymann (1896–1961). Benatzky was a Moravian-born composer who studied under Antonin Dvořák in his youth and later migrated to Munich where he first made his professional name. After World War I, he worked in Berlin with Charell on a successful series of revue operettas, culminating in *The White Horse Inn*, for which he wrote many of the best-known songs in tandem with lyricist Robert Gilbert. Benatzky and his Jewish wife escaped the Nazis in 1932 by immigrating first to Switzerland, where he continued to write memorable music for German-language films produced by UFA. Later the couple escaped to the U.S. (thanks to a short-lived contract with MGM) but Benatzky was never really able to give up his first love of light operetta. After World War II, he returned to Switzerland and spent the rest of his career trying unsuccessfully to recapture his pre-war glory days.[6] Werner Richard Heymann began his musical career in the Berlin cabarets of Max Reinhardt and Rosa Valetti, working along side of Friedrich Hollaender and Mischa Spoliansky, until 1925 when he landed a job as music director at UFA.[7] This prolific stint ended in 1933 when Heymann, a Christianized Jew (and like thousands of others) was forced to flee Germany, but landed on his feet in Hollywood where, between 1936 and 1950, he churned out no fewer than 44 film soundtracks, receiving four Oscar nominations in the process.[8] During the 1950s, he surprisingly opted (like Hollaender) to return to his native Germany, dividing his professional time between Salzburg and Munich.[9]

As leading exponents of the light operatic tradition were either appropriated by wartime authorities, hounded out of the Germany, or relegated to the death camps, in America cabaret's more militant and aggressive sensibilities were finally finding an audience. At the forefront once again was Kurt Weill and Lotte Lenya. Weill and Lenya's performance for the fundraising show "We Fight Back" at Hunter College on April 3, 1943, showcased a blistering new Weill and Brecht composition, "Und was Bekam des Soldaten Weib?" ("Ballad of a Soldier's Wife"), perhaps the first and greatest song written in reaction to recent *Wehrmacht* disaster on the Eastern Front.[10] "Ballad of a Soldier's Wife" combined cautionary tale with a bit of gloating *Schadenfreude*, not normally part of *Kabarett* vocabulary, but coming from Weill and Brecht, two artists who had suffered grievously at the hands of fascism, understandable nonetheless.[11] Later that same year, Weill celebrated his newly acquired American citizenship.[12] Along similar lines, the same melody that Weill had written in 1934 for "Je ne t'aime pas" ("I Don't Love You") was in 1944 used by the Office of War Information in D.C. for "Wie lange noch?" ("How Much Longer?"), a propaganda piece designed to help break German morale. Another Weill-penned French song, "J'attends un navire" ("I'm Waiting for a Ship"), became the unofficial anthem of the *Resistance*. As early as 1942, Weill had collaborated with Broadway lyricist Howard Dietz (1896–1983) for the anti–Nazi satire, *Schickelgruber*, also performed at Hunter College.[13] Throughout the war years, Weill made repeated but unsuccessful efforts to recruit Paul Robeson (1898–1976) as an interpreter of his Walt Whitman songs, since Robeson, as an African American, had been prominent in the aftermath of Pearl Harbor both as a patriotic singer and recording artist.[14] In short, few (if any) American composers did as much to commit their full artistic energies to the Allied war effort as did Kurt Weill.

If Weill's unrealized partnering with Paul Robeson represented a disappointing near-miss, then his very real but short-lived association with Marlene Dietrich in 1942–1943 was ultimately an ill-fated mismatch. Weill had written French songs for Dietrich while both were in Paris circa 1933 after leaving Germany, although these songs were never performed.[15] Throughout the 1930s, Dietrich had understandably attracted some of the world's best songwriting talent, and Weill was no exception in this regard; both had admired each other's talents since their Berlin days when *The Threepenny Opera* and *The Blue Angel* made their respective smash debuts. Correspondence between Weill and Lotte Lenya between 1933 and 1938 clearly reflect Weill's keen interest in working together with the German starlet, and the interest was reportedly mutual.[16] As Dietrich and Josef von Sternberg produced their classic series of movies together during this period (see Chapter 10), Weill negotiated tenaciously with Sternberg for a piece of the action, but these talks broke down over Weill's insistently high fees.[17] Nevertheless, Weill and Dietrich continued seeking opportunities to work with each other, especially after Dietrich's partnership with Sternberg ended in 1935.[18]

After World War II broke out, it finally appeared that German cabaret's two most famous defectors to the Allies would come together for a major musical project, Weill and Nash's *One Touch of Venus*. Weill wrote the lead role of Venus with Dietrich specifically in mind, and she initially showed keen interest, soliciting the studio, praising Weill's music, and making suggestions on how to improve the script. She stopped short of signing a contract, however, at which point Weill sensed trouble. Finally, in July 1943, the bottom fell out. Complaining to Weill's creative team that the story was too profane and that she was trying to tone down her image as a sex goddess — nothing could have been further from the truth, as time would prove — the stressed-out Weill exploded with exasperation, and that was the end of their highly-touted collaboration.[19] Notoriously, Weill wrote to Lenya that "...Marlene is out. She is a stupid cow, conceited like all those Germans. I wouldn't want her if she asked to play it."[20] Instead, the coveted role of Venus was given to a young Mary Martin, who was just beginning to make a name for herself as a stage singer.[21] The move proved to be shrewd, as *One Touch of Venus* was another triumph for Weill on Broadway in 1943, in no small part thanks to Martin's brilliant performance.[22] As for Dietrich, her extravagant, over-the-top appearance in the movie version of *Kismet* (1944) drew mostly barbs and hoots of laughter from critics, although the film has since become somewhat of a kitsch classic.

In the end, Dietrich's heightened sense of celebrity and privilege understandably infuriated Weill, a great genius who nevertheless had been forced to claw and scratch for everything he ever accomplished in life. In Dietrich's defense, she seems to have been going through a rough personal patch at the time of her dealings with Weill. Though then at the height of her celebrity, Dietrich's long-time affair with matinee idol Jean Gabin was then in the process of breaking down, and he would soon depart for North Africa and Europe to join the French free forces in their struggle against the German occupation. Despite the altercation between Dietrich and Weill, one is still struck by the many similarities between them. Both were great musical stage artists with cabaret roots in Weimar Berlin, both were hounded out of Germany by the Nazis and found naturalized citizenship elsewhere, both continued to thrive in their careers even after this traumatic experience, both lived Bohemian lifestyles, both were highly-disciplined artists noted for their dedicated work ethics, and both admired each other's talent. In retrospect, their altercation and Dietrich's exit from Weill's project may represent a textbook case of star-power celebrity being initially brought in to boost a stage musical's prestige, but at a steep price in terms of technical virtuosity and ensemble working harmony. One interesting footnote to the post mortem of these events is that four years after Weill's early death in 1950, Dietrich was present in the audience at the off–Broadway revival for *The Threepenny Opera*, lending her celebrity to the considerable prestige of that event (see Chapter 4), just as she had earlier supported Lotte Lenya's solo cabaret career in New York long before it had been fashionable to do so.

Although Dietrich had been helping to sell tons of war bonds as earlier as 1942, by 1944 it was obvious that she wanted to do far more for the Allied war effort, though she was by that time 42 years old. Following in the footsteps of Gabin, she decamped for Europe and North Africa where she was foremost among the pioneering female troop entertainers for the USO, often putting herself at physical risk near the front lines, notably during the Battle of the Bulge. Almost needless to say, she quickly became a favorite of the American military, including with General George S. Patton, who gave Dietrich clearance to go more or less wherever she pleased.[23] During the fighting, she found time to make a hit recording of "Lili Marlene," a German love poem from World War I (later set to music) that became popular with both Allied and Axis soldiers. She also possibly made the recording just to annoy her old hated nemesis, Joseph Goebbels, who was known to dislike the song. In short, Marlene Dietrich was an inescapable presence in Europe as the war wound down, and surely did as much as anyone to bolster Allied combat morale while having the opposite, desired effect on their enemies.[24] In later recognition for her wartime services, Dietrich was awarded the Legion of Honor by France — itself a coveted distinction —*and* the Medal of Freedom by the United States, a very rare combination, to say the least.[25]

In terms of female star power, the Nazis had nothing that could compete with the likes of Marlene Dietrich. Trude Hesterberg, Dietrich's former colleague and rival for the screen role of Lola Lola in *The Blue Angel* (see Chapter 10), was nine years older than her more famous German-born film and singing star. During the 1920s, Hesterberg had been a leading light on the Berlin *Kabarett* scene as an actress, recording artist, and impresario for the Wild Stage (see Chapter 2), nurturing up-and-coming talent that in retrospect reads like a who's who list of Weimar artists later most influential in popular music. In 1930, Hesterberg played Madame Begbick alongside Lotte Lenya as Jenny in the Leipzig premier of Weill and Brecht's *The Rise and Fall of the City of Mahagonny*, even as Nazis demonstrators disrupted the performance. Many of her best friends, protégées, and former lovers had been blacklisted by the

Nazis for their liberal political beliefs, or were simply outlawed as Jews. When 1933 came, (at age 41) she chose her country right or wrong and remained in Germany, joining the Nazis Party like most of her countrymen.[26] Rather than being held up as a prized status symbol, however, Hesterberg was treated with suspicion and mistrust by authorities, being constantly forced to re-prove her loyalty by denouncing or distancing herself from past associations, not unlike the manner in which McCarthyism forced many Americans to turn on each other after the war. By the time that disaster had fully engulfed Germany during the early 1940s, she had been reduced to intermittent German film work and performing at the remnants of the Kadeko club in Berlin, before that too was closed in 1944. In terms of using her celebrity to assist a major war effort or to do any good in general, though, there can be no comparison of Hesterberg to what Dietrich accomplished for the Allies.

To the 21st century reader, the distant events of World War II may seem remote and irrelevant to modern day life until one repeatedly stumbles into its contemporary remnants, even in the remotest geographic areas. During recent work-related travels throughout northern Wisconsin, it has been my pleasure to become acquainted with Richard and Marlene Hogue of Clam Lake. Marlene devotes a good part of her spare time between serving as cantor for the Episcopal Church of the Ascension in Hayward and playing viola for Chequamegon Symphony Orchestra at Northland College in Ashland. She is also named after Marlene Dietrich. Marlene Hogue's late father, U.S. Army Sgt. Keith Harshfield, was a member of the 405th Anti-Aircraft Artillery Gun Battalion active in France, Germany, and the Low Countries, and long after the war ended decided to name his daughter after the great German-born artist. Although no one remembers how exactly Sgt. Harshfield came into contact with Dietrich, one possible theory is that it occurred in Belgium, where the 405th participated in the liberation of Antwerp in November 1944. It was in Antwerp where Dietrich, in typical fashion for her, rushed near the scene of fighting to perform and then later was famously photographed while autographing the leg cast of wounded U.S. soldier Earl E. McFarland on November 24.[27] In any event, it is remarkable to find one of Dietrich's honorary namesakes still making an impact on musical life in the north woods of Wisconsin — even more so perhaps than repeated revivals of Kander and Ebb's musical *Cabaret* in nearby Duluth (see Introduction).

Jean Marais' joke about the double edge in Dietrich's erotic public image also points to a more serious (but less frequently remarked upon) aspect of cabaret's reputation: namely, its leading exponents who managed to escape from the Nazis were later more than happy to assist in the war against their own native land any way they could. There were very few, if any, exceptions in this regard. The stars of the of the 1920s Weimar era in Berlin were by 1941 too old (typically in their 40s) to do any actual fighting, but most worked tirelessly to raise money, morale, and public awareness. Most considered compromises to their own physical safety and comfort a cheap price to pay for being part of the Allied civilian effort. In the final analysis, cabaret, despite its pacifist inclinations, was an active participant in the great world war against fascism. After this war had been won, however, fortune offered an interesting twist, as it often does. Marlene Dietrich may not have been able to work harmoniously with Kurt Weill during wartime, but after his death in 1950 she embarked on a new enterprise that seemingly evoked everything that Weill had strove to accomplish on Broadway. Only this project would not be on Broadway; rather, it would begin in a Nevada desert postwar boom town that curiously recalled a certain Weill opera that Dietrich had never been given a chance to star in, at least during the composer's lifetime.

13. The Resurrection
of Mahagonny

"He was the most important man in my life after I decided to dedicate myself completely to the stage [and] my highest goal until the day he left was to please him.... I lived only for the performances and for him.... With the force of a volcano erupting, Bacharach had reshaped my songs and changed my act into a real show."— Marlene Dietrich on Burt Bacharach[1]

With Allied victory in World War II and American ascendancy onto the stage of international affairs came a steep price. The same military industrial complex (President Eisenhower's term) that had first pulled the U.S. out of economic depression and then awarded transcontinental dominance was now deliberately maintained during peacetime in hopes that these earlier achievements would become long-term and perhaps even permanent. This elaborate strategy included fighting a Cold War of "defense" against Marxism as justification for continued military expenditures and subsidies on a massive, unprecedented scale. Another unfortunate corollary of this decision was the unwelcome specter of McCarthyism in domestic political affairs, which terrorized both innocent and guilty alike for nearly a decade following the war — far longer than it took to defeat fascism abroad, it should be added. Lastly (and most relevant to this study), maintenance of such a continuously mobilized society also necessitated more entertainment for both troops and the civilian population that supported them. The war itself had proven the value of this intangible factor, both as a morale builder and distraction (see Chapter 12). Perhaps the most conspicuous exponent of this new big form of show business was the spectacular postwar rise of modern Las Vegas.

Like most American teenagers during the late 1960s, I first came into contact with Weill and Brecht's "Alabama Song" through Jim Morrison and the Doors' first album (1967), having little notion of the work's complex origins until much later in life. At the time of its creation half a century earlier for *Mahagonny Songspiele* (see Chapter 3) and subsequent operatic incarnation in *The Rise and Fall of the City of Mahagonny* (1930), the "Alabama Song" had been authored by two Germans who had never personally traveled to *Amerika*. Predictably, their geography and topography in the opera are somewhat vague and confused, with Alabama and the Florida Panhandle (Pensacola) being gateway to the American west and Pacific coast, the latter adjacent to a desert and the territory of Alaska not too far away. Weill and Brecht's conceptualization and vision of how a Vegas-like metropolis (Mahagonny) would originate, develop, and eventually dominate its landscape, however, are all dead on target, some two decades before the actual events occurred. The basic plotline tells of how good-hearted men and women can be engulfed, corrupted, and eventually swallowed up by such an environment, today still a resonant theme in reference to the great Sin City of the West. In retrospect, its seems incredible that a song which premiered on the festival stage of Baden-Baden during the Weimar era should many years later become part of the standard repertoire for entire generations of Anglo-America pop stars. Even more incredible is the stark fact that a radical Weimar operatic vision from 1930 — one nearly booed off the stage at the time by Nazi demonstrators — should accurately prophesize what much later became an inescapable reality in the desert sands of Nevada.

How in America did this artistic process begin? — two words: Marlene Dietrich. During the late 1940s she opted not to return to Germany for the sensible reason that the vast majority of her former countrymen, including several members of her own immediate family, had supported the Nazi regime (see Chapter 5). She also studiously and sensibly avoided Broadway, despite the commercial ascendancy within that specialized realm of fellow German émigré, Kurt Weill (see Chapter 12). After Dietrich delivered a brilliant screen performance in Alfred Hitchcock's *Stage Fright*, by the early 1950s, for most show business movers and shakers, she was little more than a 50-something-year-old fading movie star. On the plus side, her extraordinary talents and abilities were still fully intact and in search of an outlet; moreover, she still needed to earn money and likely harbored unfilled professional ambitions. For example, memories of her projected starring role in Max Reinhardt's cancelled 1930 Berlin production of Weill's *Mahagonny* may have provided incentive for her to seek new frontiers.[2] Unlike many of her contemporaries, she seemed impervious to McCarthyism, probably due in part to her unimpeachably heroic record during the war. In any event, she was not yet ready to retire from the public eye as Garbo had done the previous decade. Instead, the restless Dietrich somehow found herself circa 1953 in Las Vegas (then still a comparative backwater) watching Hollywood colleague Tullulah Bankhead — a genuine native of Alabama with whom Dietrich was rumored to have had been involved with — perform during the twilight of her noteworthy career. In Vegas she also saw on stage a young Eddie Fisher, fresh out of the military, and had a short affair with him as well. Then she decided to try it herself, despite protestations from some of her closest friends (including Noël Coward and Maurice Chavalier), that Las Vegas was well beneath the dignity of her considerable greatness.[3] Where others saw compromise and diminishment, however, Dietrich saw possibilities.

Once word got out, offers were not slow in coming in. On December 15, 1953, Marlene Dietrich made her Vegas debut at the 500-seat Congo Room of the Sahara Hotel. She was paid a then astronomical $90,000 to perform a six-song set for three weeks, making her the highest earning entertainer in America. As during the war, she acted as her own *conférencier*. For her play list, Dietrich stayed with material that she had always been most comfortable with — "Falling in Love Again," "See What the Boys in the Back Room Will Have," "Jonny" (all three written by Friedrich Hollaender), "The Laziest Gal in Town" (Cole Porter), "La Vie en rose," and "Lili Marlene."[4] For a memorable fashion statement, Dietrich turned to all-star designer Jean Louis, who concocted for her an illusory see-through dress later be adopted by numerous other starlets, including Marilyn Monroe. Later, she accentuated the affect of the dress by employing a wind machine. Recalling her earlier thwarted appearance in Kurt Weill's musical *One Touch of Venus*, biographer Donald Spoto observed that in Vegas Dietrich presented the "image of a heavenly Aphrodite, or of Venus rising none too demurely from the waves."[5] When others expressed concern at the boldness of such a presentation during the McCarthy era, Dietrich replied: "This is Las Vegas. If not here, then where?"[6] In short, *Mahagonny* had finally arrived on U.S. soil. The Vegas show was a smash sensation, and was promptly converted into a lucrative international cabaret tour.[7] Biographer Steven Bach observed that "Within six months she [Dietrich] was the most highly paid, most highly publicized nightclub performer in the world."[8] As for Las Vegas, after Dietrich's sensational debut, the city became the land of opportunity for big name performers, and remains so to this very day.[9]

Having taken her old songs to the bank in ways previously unimaginable, Dietrich proceeded to seek still newer modes of self-reinvention. The key component in the next stage of this extraordinary evolution was her seven-year association with Burt Bacharach, who acted as her accompanist, arranger, conductor, artistic advisor, and occasional consort between 1957 and 1964. Dietrich hired the then-unknown Bacharach while shuffling musical personnel with Noël Coward, as the 30-year-old future Gershwin Award winner (see Chapter 15) was enlisted to conduct impromptu Dietrich's backup orchestra.[10] Bacharach later remembered vividly the intimidation he felt during their first meeting at the Beverly Hills Hotel, but the aging superstar took an immediate fancy to the young artist (26 years her junior), later heaping extravagant and repeated praise on him (see opening quote).[11] Before long she was browbeating the likes of Frank Sinatra for not giving her protégé more work. Then, with absolute authoritativeness akin to an Elizabethan monarch, she forbade Bacharach to have an outside personal life: "Nobody marry you Burt, over my dead body."[12] As for Bacharach, it was he who encouraged Dietrich to add contemporary popular material to her repertoire, such as Peter, Paul, and Mary's "Puff the Magic Dragon," Bob Dylan's "Blowin' in the Wind," and Pete Seeger's "Where Have All the Flowers Gone?" — all performed with inimitable Dietrich style.[13] It was also Bacharach who encouraged her to break postwar taboo and emotionally sing in German to a surprised and deeply moved Israeli audience during the early 1960s, not long after her disappointing tour of Germany (see Chapter 5).[14]

Bacharach was born on May 12, 1928, in Kansas City, Missouri, around the same time a young Marlene Dietrich was first becoming a star on the revue stages of Weimar Berlin. His Jewish parents were both artistically inclined (father a writer, mother a painter), provided him with a happy childhood, and encouraged his considerable talents.[15] Attendance at McGill University in Montreal was short-lived, but while in Quebec Bacharach indulge his Francophile tendencies and was exposed to jazz players, the high caliber of which included Oscar Peterson and Maynard Ferguson.[16] He also fell under the spell of Impressionist composers such Claude Debussy and Maurice Ravel, as well as the offbeat music of Erik Satie and Les Six, exponents of the closest French equivalent to German *Kleinkunst* having been embraced by Weimar's *Kabarett* scene.[17] Later continuing his formal studies, Bacharach's teachers included Darius Milhaud, a friend and colleague of the late Kurt Weill, cabaret enthusiast, and arguably the most prominent member of Les Six, who strongly impressed upon Bacharach the importance of good melody in finding a wide audience, recalling Ferruccio Busoni's sage advice to Weill in Berlin some three decades before (see Chapter 3).[18] Simultaneously, he was profoundly influenced by the adventurous bebop jazz movement in New York City then being led by Charlie Parker and Dizzy Gillespie. Thus Bacharach's musical training stressed an unusual combination of anti–Wagnerian European classicism and progressive American jazz, (again) not unlike that of Kurt Weill a generation earlier.[19]

Tellingly, Bacharach's early interest in the German classical tradition took a wide detour around the then prevalent repertoire dominated by Beethoven, Wagner, and Strauss. Between 1950 and 1952, military induction found him stationed in Germany near Munich, where his talent was quickly put to use in providing army entertainment at the nightclub Casa Carioca in Garmisch, similar to the experience of Friedrich Hollaender during World War I (see

Chapter 6).[20] Bacharach also found time to explore his ancestral family roots by visiting his grandparent's nearby namesake village, one which had not so long before been violently purged of its Jewish heritage during the Holocaust. No doubt Bacharach later encouraged Dietrich to return to her native Germany in 1960 in part because, if he could as a Jew, then so could she as a non–Jew.[21] The result, however, was best described as a noble failure since many Germans despised Dietrich even more as one of their own who had turned against them, as opposed to any Jew belonging to an occupying military force. After his service discharge, Bacharach cast about the American music industry to earn a living, right about the same time that Weill and Brecht's *Threepenny Opera* revival was being jet-propelled to franchise hit status largely by Lotte Lenya's incredible lead performance (see Chapter 4).[22]

Bacharach's sophisticated and ever-evolving style cannot be pigeon-holed into any single category; however, the component owing its influence to French and German cabaret has been relatively un-remarked upon to date. The very fact that his style is impossible to define itself recalls cabaret (see Introduction). In addition to his formal background — an unusual blend of European and American traditions — Bacharach's musical philosophy developed along independent lines as well. Thanks to his love for the music of Satie, Les Six, and the Impressionists, Bacharach's preference for small-scaled musical forms — the American pop version of *Kleinkunst*, if you will — lent itself perfectly to cabaret arrangements, early on fitting Dietrich's idiosyncratic song presentation like a glove. He loved to experiment with forms and did not feel constrained by rules or conventions. Bacharach's compositions were marked by occasional indeterminate keys or unlikely chord shifts, recalling the "borderland" quality so distinctive in German *Kabarett* from the 1920s.[23] The poetic content of his songs, usually supplied by Hal David or similar-inclined lyricists, was strictly adult in its mature, objective look at the vicissitudes of love and the human heart. All of these qualities were hallmarks of the cabaret style as well, translated into an accessible pop language for postwar American and British audiences. It is no wonder that Dietrich acted as if she had struck gold with Bacharach; she clearly recognized and fully appreciated his value long before others did. It should also come as no surprise that Bacharach's own performing career as a singer-songwriter eventually found a natural home in Las Vegas, the real-life American equivalent of the imaginary Mahagonny.

Before leaving this interesting topic, it would be remiss not to briefly comment upon the short, variable life and fortunes of Elvis Aaron Presley (1935–1977), another cultural icon in his own right. Presley's omnipresent impact on American popular music culminated during the final years of his life with a seven-year residency on the stages of Las Vegas. Presley had first played Vegas in 1956 during his initial rise to world-wide fame, but did not become closely associated with the city until 1963–1964 when his film *Viva Las Vegas* (with Ann-Margret) became a huge sensation and the title track since becoming Sin City's unofficial anthem.[24] In between these early Vegas sightings, however, the biggest event in Presley's personal life was a two-year army stint in Germany, where he first met future wife (and mother of his daughter) Priscilla Beaulieu, while spending a good part of his military time entertaining fellow troops, just as Bacharach had done before him. After a long and complicated courtship, Elvis and Priscilla opted for a Las Vegas wedding in 1967, a time in which the commercial appeal of the 32-year-old Presley seemed to be waning. Then in 1968, Elvis made a dramatic comeback sporting a series of live shows and studio recordings, culminating in 1969 with a triumphant return to the nightclub stages of Vegas. Present that opening night at The International hotel was Bacharach himself, among many other show business luminaries attending this noteworthy extravaganza.[25]

The unlikely excitement of Presley's late 1960s comeback shows was epitomized by these first appearances in Las Vegas.[26] Featuring a backup band showcasing guitarist and future Rock and Roll Hall of Famer James Burton, Presley's underrated late period sound and image have since become part of shared American pop culture. Writer and critic Greil Marcus at the time summarized his impressions of the legend in live concert:

> Elvis gives us a massive road-show musical of opulent American mastery; his version of the winner-take-all fantasies that have kept the world lined up outside the theaters that show American movies ever since the movies began. And of course we respond: a self-made man is rather boring, but a self-made king is something else. Dressed in blue, red, white, ultimately gold, with a Superman cape and covered with jewels no one can be sure are fake, Elvis might epitomize the worst of our culture — he is bragging, selfish, narcissistic, condescending, materialistic to the point of insanity. But there is no need to take that seriously, no need to take anything seriously.[27]

The astute observation by Marcus that late Elvis in performance refused to take much of anything very seriously harkens back to the Great War heyday of the Dadaist Movement in Zurich (see Chapter 2), which delighted in making a mockery of the crumbling world around it. While it seems unlikely that Presley consciously incorporated elements of German cabaret into his own act, connections (even if coincidental) multiply upon closer examination. For instance, his grand entry fanfare quoting from Strauss' *Also Sprach Zarathustra*, while lifted directly from Stanley Kubrick's 1968 film *2001: A Space Odyssey*, also naturally calls to mind the Nietzschean Superman ideal playing such a central role in the early 20th century creation of Überbrettl cabaret (see Chapter 1). Marcus noted the Superman connection as well in Presley's road show — updated for the American desert metropolis of Mahagonny. All in all, the aesthetic values and elements from *Kabarett* and *Kleinkunst* appear strongly manifested in Presley's later work, either consciously or unconsciously. Indeed, the Elvis legacy has since become synonymous with the nightclub spectacles of Vegas. In a very real sense, what Marlene Dietrich began in Las Vegas during the early 1950s was taken to its absurdly magnificent conclusion by Elvis some two decades later, and continues strong into the present day.

In hindsight, what Dietrich accomplished for Vegas far excelled anything she would have ever achieved for the cancelled Max Reinhardt Berlin production of *Mahagonny* in 1930.[28] Weill and Brecht's masterwork stands on its own as a work of musical theater, and always will.[29] Las Vegas, on the other hand, has become a symbol a symbol of far more than mere musical theater; it now represents the very incarnation of everything that is both grandiose and overblown in American entertainment, which in turn has become entertainment for the world. It has come to epitomize a place in which anything can be purchased but also where absolutely everything is fake. Whereas 1920s Berlin impresarios such as Erik Charell had taken the pioneering follies and reviews of Florenz Ziegfeld and raised the bar in terms of lavish splendor, Las Vegas of the post–Dietrich era took these to even greater heights or depths, or both at once, depending on one's point of view. An even more striking contrast appears when one considers that Dietirch, a true daughter of the Prussian bourgeois, eventually became a film idol and Vegas icon, while her great counterpart Lotte Lenya, a product of the Viennese slums if there ever was one, simultaneously became symbol of cabaret high culture. The startling rise of great American Sin city during the 1950s, however, was not the only significant development of that period in relation to German cabaret's deep infiltration of American pop culture. Around the same time that Dietrich was enjoying the first fruits of her latest triumph, another peerless performer — one coming from a completely different place and tradition — was busy instinctively incorporating an old Weimar classic into the contemporary musical vernacular of his own times.

14. Louis Armstrong
Connects the Dots

"I knew cats like that in New Orleans."— Louis Armstrong on "Mack the Knife"[1]

As the whole world knows or should know, Louis "Pops" Armstrong (1901–1971) was born in New Orleans, his birth almost coinciding with the exact same moment in time during which the Überbrettl cabaret fad was first taking hold in Berlin. Armstrong was gifted with a sunny personal disposition, sturdy physical constitution, and unrivaled, raw musical talent. Other than these qualities, however, he could hardly have been dealt a worse hand in life. Aside from being black and poor in one of America's worst urban ghettos, the young Armstrong had no consistent family support, but did possess a definite penchant for getting into trouble. Had he died young or become permanently incarcerated, Louis Armstrong would hardly have been the first or last enormously talented person whose life ended in wasted obscurity, either through no fault of his own or because of the destructive nature that often accompanies genius. Then at age six, the vulnerable, underprivileged child hit the proverbial jackpot. He came into contact with the Jewish Karnofsky family of New Orleans, who operated a local scavenger business. The Karnofskys took the young street waif into their home, gave him paying work, recognized his special attributes, nurtured him, and pointed him in the right directions for future accomplishment in life. Some 15 years later, Armstrong arrived in Chicago, beginning his breathtaking ascent as the world's greatest jazz musician. For the rest of his life, Armstrong wore the Star of David around his neck as a memorial to the family who probably saved his life and preserved his talent for the world. Armstrong also experienced (by his own later admission) an epiphany that blacks were not the only demographic in America encountering ugly racial discrimination.

Although one does not usually associate Armstrong's venerable name with German cabaret, a number of notable connections appear during his long, impressive trek through 20th century popular music. As early as 1931, during the first flush his international fame, he recorded for RCA a poignant version of the Irving Caesar English translation for Casucci and Bramer's German-Austrian hit "Just a Gigolo." Although the number had been recently covered by numerous artists (including Bing Crosby), Armstrong was the first African American jazz musician to interpret the work, and probably the most prominent one as well. It was certainly unusual and bold for a black American pop figure — more so perhaps for one of his stature and visibility — to record a serious cover of a European cabaret standard.[2] At that early stage in jazz history, there were still many listeners on both sides of the Atlantic who strongly felt that it could not and should not be done. Nevertheless, Armstrong pulled it off with flying colors, as he had done most everything else musically that he set his mind to. More impressive still is that Armstrong opted to record this song during the early Depression era at a time when the German Weimar Republic was still in existence (though faltering) and long before any exiled German artists had landed on American soil. More likely, the decision was made to cover the tune in the immediate wake of Marlene Dietrich's phenomenal trans–Atlantic stardom after 1930. Dietrich herself would much later record "Just a Gigolo" in 1978 while making her final screen appearance (see Chapter 5), but by 1933 the Nazis had taken over Germany and by 1935, like many of her former cabaret colleagues, Dietrich was officially or unofficially a German exile living in the U.S.

Two decades later in 1955, as Dietrich entered a fabulous new phase of her career, Armstrong was leading his group of All-Stars, a small, scrappy, versatile combo of crack Dixieland veterans capable of effectively navigating the rapidly shifting currents of commercial studio recording and live public performance. His producer and chief creative advisor at Columbia Records was living legend and Armenian émigré George Avakian, whose jazz production credits came to include the likes of Miles Davis, Benny Goodman, and Dave Brubeck, among many others. Under Avakian's guidance, Armstrong had recently recorded tribute albums to W.C. Handy (1954) and Fats Waller (1955). In part because of his dual background in both classical and popular music, Avakian was keenly aware of the burgeoning off–Broadway success of Weill and Brecht's *Threepenny Opera* in the English translation by Marc Blitzstein (see Chapter 4). He tried urging all of the best musicians under his production banner to transform the "Moritat" (aka "Mack the Knife") into a jazz standard, but all resisted the German operatic associations with the piece, despite its on-going stateside hit status.[3] Some of those who rejected Avakian's suggestion included Brubeck, Gerry Mulligan, John Lewis, and Erroll Garner.[4] The song itself had been banned from the radio in some quarters because DJs had occasionally taken to playing it after visible incidents of gang violence.[5] Then in 1955, Dixieland revival trombonist Turk Murphy, seeing the wisdom of the idea, wrote a swing arrangement, cut a demo, and recommended to a skeptical Avakian that he personally present it to Armstrong himself. Armstrong, whom no one had considered even asking given his musically conservative, traditionalist reputation, heard Murphy's demo and immediately agreed to tackle the arrangement, noting that the mood and lyric of "Mack the Knife" reminded him of his shady (and sometimes) violent adolescent acquaintances from the slums of New Orleans.[6]

Before delving further into Armstrong's historic recording of "Mack the Knife" and its wide aftereffects, it is useful to briefly survey that particular moment in jazz history and the context in which the sessions were held. By the mid–1950s, American jazz had evolved from the most disreputable form of low-life entertainment to a revered cultural status somewhat approaching respectability, but at a price of lesser commercial appeal. 1955 would represent the year in which rock and roll would begin its irrepressible ascent to commercial dominance, with adolescent-themed lyrics specially-geared for appealing to a growing youth market. Jazz, on the other hand (like cabaret before it), tended to be very adult in content and complexity, though like rock and roll's blues and country roots, far less respectable in image and origins. Most of the best still-active jazz pioneers were combating this perceived problem, albeit with smaller instrumental forces necessitated by postwar economics of the music industry. Perhaps the leader in this regard was Duke Ellington, who through his own special brand of genius had managed to transform himself from Cotton Club house bandleader into a national treasure, assuming the mantel of a serious American classical composer over the course of some four decades.[7] At the same time, any controversial political topicality in the face of McCarthyism could be problematic for artists. Younger innovators such as Charlie Parker and Dizzy Gillespie — so admired by the young Burt Bacharach — were taking the complex improvisation of jazz to new heights, ones which also seemed to preclude widespread popular acceptance. Concurrent with the rise of bebop and cool jazz came the Beat Poetry Movement, especially in New York City where the avant-garde nightclub scene began in some ways to resemble the adventurousness of Weimar Berlin *Kabarett* during the 1920s (see Chapter 2). Thus by 1955, jazz had become far more serious and dignified in its demeanor; the only major figure who seemed to occasionally resist the dominant trend (despite his old-fashioned reputation) was Louis Armstrong.

At the other end of the musical spectrum, after the death of Kurt Weill in 1950, and perhaps the most respected representative of the European cabaret style in the classical sphere (but one still sympathetic to jazz) was Darius Milhaud (1892–1974). The French-Jewish Milhaud, a highly-visible and prolific surviving member of Les Six, had established himself in America as an academic at Mills College in California before World War II, and proceeded to influence almost everyone coming into contact with him, including Bacharach and Brubeck.[8] Milhaud had been captivated by jazz as early as 1922 when traveling in Harlem, then wonderfully incorporated the new music into his own written compositions by 1923.[9] By the mid–1950s, Milhaud was dividing his teaching time between the U.S. and France, but the full impact of his ideas would not be felt until a few years later when his numerous, talented students came of age. The first artist, however, to truly cross the seemingly impassable bridge between 20th century European classicism and the rough-and-tumble commercialism of American popular song for the masses, had by that time very little left to learn musically from anyone. Nor would this unusual breakthrough be the result of any intellectual treatise or deliberative process; instead, it would follow an instinctive, snap decision made by a veteran mega-talent possessing an open ear and open mind.

Just as the singular, intuitive genius of Louis Armstrong had recorded "Just a Gigolo" in 1931, so he also came to reinterpret "Mack the Knife" in 1955. The recording sessions took place on September 28, 1955, at Columbia Studios in New York City under Avakian's direction.[10] The clever decision was made to invite Lotte Lenya into the studio for her participation, and she happily showed. Several versions were recorded, both instrumental and vocal, with and without Lenya. Later during an interview Lenya shared on her astonishment at Armstrong's boundless musicality.[11] It had been possibly her first close personal encounter with a world-class jazz player. Avakian, for his part, later recalled that Lenya was a bit out of her element, with swing tempo being an alien concept to her: "Lenya just had no sense of jazz rhythm...." Gallantly, Armstrong tried to teach her on the spot, but in the editing room the wise choice was made to release Armstrong's solo version, with Lenya's rendition not appearing on disc until many years later.[12] There were, however, still several major benefits to Lenya's presence in the studio. First, Armstrong and his All-Stars were obviously excited by her being there, and this kept the performance inspired. Second, Lenya's then-husband George Davis, the man who had done so much to resurrect her singing career (see Chapter 4), was present as well. Right before the second take, Davis whispered something to Armstrong and then during the recording he ad-libbed Lenya's name into the lyric, where it pretty much remained in many a subsequent recording. Thus "Lotte Lenya" has rightfully become synonymous with the song. After the session, Armstrong and his All-Stars departed for a three-month European tour with "Mack the Knife" becoming, in the words of biographer Ricky Riccardi, "one of the biggest hits of his career."[13] As for Lenya, she afterwards reflected that Weill, who had died five years previous, would have loved the whole thing because his original melody had stayed in tact and because (as she put it) "A taxi driver whistling his tunes would have pleased him more than winning the Pulitzer Prize."[14]

Initially, Armstrong's revolutionary single was banned by CBS Radio for the same reasons the song had been previously censored, but Columbia shrewdly released his instrumental version first, which promptly sold over a million copies. Then (as often happens) greed trumped alleged moral scruples, the ban was lifted, and Armstrong's "Mack the Knife"—this time complete with lyrics — moved even more units than the instrumental take.[15] After this, everyone wanted a piece of the action, and many got it. Bobby Darin's classic late 1958 recording with full big-band swing arrangement tore up the pop charts in early 1959 and won a Grammy Award; then in 1960, Ella Fitzgerald also took home a Grammy for her live Berlin recording in which she improvised her own lyrics after forgetting the opaque verses which had so terrified American censors only a few years before. Other notable singers associated with the tune over the years include Frank Sinatra, Bing Crosby, Tony Bennett, Anita O'Day, Eartha Kitt, Peggy Lee, Sting, Roger Daltry, Ute Lemper, Max Raabe, Michael Bublé, Jimmy Buffett, and Lyle Lovett, whose odd, dark cover of "Mack" graced the closing credits of Robert Redford's 1994 film *Quiz Show*.[16] Last but certainly not least, Lenya had been able to record her own more Germanic and less jazzy (but no less captivating) version in Hamburg circa 1955, a few months before teaming up with Armstrong's All-Stars in New York City.[17]

After 1955, floodgates seemed to open for recording interest in Kurt Weill's music, although some of his isolated American-era standards such as "September Song" and "Speak Low" had never really gone out of fashion (Frank Sinatra, for instance, recorded both songs). By 1960, however, Weill's music, both Weimar-era and post–Weimar, was being commercially released to a new, unprecedented extent, and this trend has more or less continued unabated for the last half century. Other songs that had been originally German language from the same bygone era also began to appear during the late 1950s and early 1960s. Perhaps the most well-known piece in this regard was Friedrich Hollaender's "Falling in Love Again," recorded in short order by both Doris Day (1961) and Sammy Davis, Jr. (1962), and after a postwar hiatus of two decades, has remained part of standard repertoire ever since. Hard on the heels of Armstrong's "Mack the Knife," a rousing version of "Just a Gigolo" was waxed by Louis Prima in 1956 and has also continued to reappear at regular intervals.[18] For example, who can forget the energetic 1978 reading by the Village People or David Lee Roth's exuberant and deliberately silly 1985 cover version (and video) which, for many listeners who came of age during that period, remains definitive? The Weimar influence in American popular music began to exert itself in a more diffuse, indirect manner as well. A smash hit such as Peggy Lee's "Is That All There Is?" (1969), though written by Leiber and Stoller and arranged by Randy Newman (see Chapter 18), aside from perfectly conveying the same jaded mood as a Berlin cabaret number, had in fact been inspired by an early Thomas Mann short story ("Disillusionment").[19] The song itself has sometimes been rightfully described as existentialist in outlook, another descendent of, or throwback to, German philosophy from an earlier era (see Chapter 17).

Taken within a larger context, the surge in popularity for more realistic, darker-themed hit parade songs during this period admittedly may not have been the sole result of Armstrong's "Mack the Knife" recording, but rather larger social and economic forces which brought greater visibility to all music of this type. Examples from the late 1950s and early 1960s are seemingly limitless. Leonard Bernstein, who directed the first revival performance of Weill's *Threepenny Opera* in 1952 (see Chapter 4), soon afterwards wrote the music for *West Side Story*, conquering Broadway in 1957 and then becoming a lauded feature film in 1961.[20] At the other extreme end of the music spectrum was Top-40 radio. Apart from Bill Haley and the Comets jarring instrumental version of "Mack" from 1959, a good case study for this particular trend is North Carolina–born Fred Lincoln "Link" Wray, the iconoclastic electric guitarist who, in the words of Bob Dylan, invented heavy-metal music but never receives credit for it. Wray's highly innovative, mostly-instrumental work from the late 1950s through the late 1970s consistently suggested a violent, underworld persona, eschewing titles such as "Switchblade," "Jack the Ripper," "The Shadow Knows," "Big City After Dark," and "Rumble"—the last one directly inspired by gang violence portrayed in *West Side Story*. While it would be too much of a stretch to claim that Wray and his heavy-metal descendants resulted from Louis Armstrong's "Mack" sessions, there can be little doubt that all of these pop recordings capitalized on similar, related social impulses driving the American record industry of those times. In a very broad sense, all of these records are Weimar cultural offspring, drawing their inspiration from darker emotional impulses that had very little prior visibility on the American scene.

Meanwhile, the by now advanced and fabled careers of Armstrong, Lenya, and Dietrich continued apace as if no end were in sight. Armstrong and Dietrich, who were almost the same age (61), appeared together live in 1962 at the Riviera Hotel in Las Vegas—a city that Dietrich had helped to build—where, when not singing and playing, the two vamped together for a series of still treasured photo ops. Four years later, after the shock of the musical British Invasion had somewhat subsided, Lotte Lenya scored her last great triumph on the musical stage with Kander and Ebb's *Cabaret* in 1966 (see Chapter 16). Wasting no time, Armstrong recorded the ubiquitous title track from *Cabaret* for Columbia Records that same year, then in 1967 he debuted the song on the Ed Sullivan Show, the same night that the Rolling Stones were allowed to perform "Let's Spend the Night Together" only by changing the lyrics to "Let's Spend Some Time Together."[21] In retrospect, it seems somewhat odd that Sullivan should allegedly have objected so strenuously to the suggested sexuality of the Jagger-Richards composition while giving a free pass to "Cabaret," a song whose creative roots (both immediate and distant) could not have been more questionable. Surely this was largely due to Armstrong's stature and skill as an arbiter (and ambassador) of good taste and manners. In any event, "Cabaret" and "Mack the Knife" continued to be staples in Armstrong's performing repertoire for the remainder of his career.[22] Thus the former street waif from turn-of-the-century New Orleans had effectively tapped into the underappreciated talent of the former street waif from turn-of-the-century Vienna (Lenya) and amplified these gifts for the sake of a wider audience. This unusual feat, it would seem, could have been accomplished only by Louis Armstrong and no one else.

The entire jazz community suddenly took notice as well. Weill's music, sans lyrics, was pleasantly subjected to an improvisational echo chamber of sound by some of the world's leading players. Weill himself had made numerous dance arrangements from his own compositions and most popular melodies, but his material that began to appear in the decades following his death seemed as much designed for the concert hall (or home entertainment system) as for the ballroom. Immediately following Armstrong's breakthrough, electric guitar pioneer Les Paul rendered a tasteful instrumental version of "Mack the Knife," several years before Link Wray created his own sinister musical persona in the rock and roll sphere using similar technology.[23] On far more sophisticated level, the late arranger-composer Gil Evans frequently drew upon Weill's music for inspiration and showcasing his own talents. These recordings included the first of his historic collaborations with Miles Davis on the groundbreaking *Miles Ahead* LP (1957), featuring a haunting cover of "My Ship" (from Weill and Gershwin's *Lady in the Dark*). Later, more Weill standards were covered on Evans' own solo albums: "The Bilbao Song" from *Out of the Cool* (1961) and "The Barbara Song" from *The Individualism of Gil Evans* (1964). These arrangements proved once again that Weill's music firmly stood the test of time, quite apart from Bertolt Brecht's bracing original lyrics. Apart from this new, widespread enthusiasm for Weill's music, the old Weimar warhorse "Just a Gigolo" (as in the vocal field) became favorite recording fodder for top-notch jazz pianists, including Thelonious Monk (1962) and Erroll Garner (1965). These represent just a few, selected examples from half a century ago. Today, one need not look far to find even more in a similar genre.

Strictly speaking, Armstrong may not have been the first talented, American-born musician to contemporize Weimar material, but he was surely the first one to sell it effectively for mass consumption. To accomplish this, he had to make creative snap connections not unlike those made by the ancients when linking heavenly clusters into personified star constellations, ones that the average person can recognize and remember. Even the great Marlene Dietrich, with the lone exception of her totally Americanized Weimar hit "Falling in Love Again"— a song that American movie audiences already knew — did not dare to draw upon German material (let alone operatic) after she began recording in Hollywood, unless it had been first carefully retrofitted by a trusted old collaborator such as Hollaender or Mischa Spoliansky (see Chapter 6). As for Lotte Lenya, a far more specialized talent, her U.S. singing career suffered for decades before off–Broadway revival of *The Threepenny Opera* (and later *Cabaret* on Broadway) finally gave her a viable commercial outlet for performing. In spite of her apparently never learning true swing rhythm, the genius of Armstrong was able to look beyond that, and all of this makes his breakthrough appear even more impressive in hindsight. It also paved the way for American popular songwriting to undergo its own striking metamorphosis, one led not too surprisingly by a young Dietrich protégé.

15. Bacharach and David Redefine the Brill Building

"None of my songs were considered R&B. They were borderline pop. Nobody really understood or knew how to categorize it, which was the wonderful part of recording their music.... We were so different musically from anything that was being recorded and/or written in that period of time that we kind of carved our own little niche out."— Dionne Warwick[1]

At a White House ceremony on May 9, 2012, Burt Bacharach and Hal David became the fourth annual recipients of the prestigious Library of Congress Gershwin Prize for Popular Song, acknowledging their considerable lifetime achievements in a competitive field that many enter but in which few prosper.[2] Performers honoring the distinguished duo included Stevie Wonder, Diana Krall, Lyle Lovett, Sheryl Crow, Michael Feinstein, Arturo Sandoval, Mike Myers, rising pop star Sheléa (Frazier), and British-Pakistani singer-songwriter Rumer (aka Sarah Joyce).[3] In addition to the tremendous eclecticism of the music, it somehow seemed quite fitting that the honorees should be awarded with a prize named after two artists who, during their own time, had both been closely associated with Kurt Weill. It was George Gershwin who had invited Weill and Lotte Lenya to sit beside him during the premier of his *Porgy and Bess* in 1935, almost immediately after the two had first arrived in America. It had been George's brother Ira who later collaborated with the German-Jewish émigré to produce Weill's first blockbuster American show, *Lady in the Dark* (see Chapter 11). For that matter, it had been a 1926 Berlin performance of George Gershwin's *Rhapsody in Blue* attended by Weill that had helped re-shape his classically-trained attitude favorably towards American jazz (see Chapter 3). Half a century later, what went around came around. The sublime "borderline pop" of Bacharach and David that Dionne Warwick was so proud to have been involved with, owed a significant part of its origins to the close interaction between these extraordinary composers many years before.

Rarely mentioned nowadays is the impressive fact that before Burt Bacharach established himself as a premier American songwriter, he had presided over the spectacular Indian summer of Marlene Dietrich's singing career during the late 1950s and early 1960s, acting as her close musical collaborator, accompanist, arranger, bandleader and advisor. Despite an age difference of some 26 years, Dietrich instantly appreciated the talents of a then-unknown, 28-year-old Bacharach upon their first meeting in 1957, hired him full-time in 1958, and retained his professional services for the next seven years, much of which was spent on international tour. As Bacharach later reminisced, "She [Dietrich] probably believed in me more as a writer at the time than I believed in myself."[4] When Bacharach's own star began to rise during the 1960s, it became inevitable that the partnership would soon dissolve, but not before leaving its permanent mark on all parties involved. When Bacharach severed the connection 1965 (by marrying Angie Dickenson), Dietrich later complained that she felt like "a robot" and, in so far as anyone knows, never again had a close romantic relationship after decades of intense affairs with members of both sexes.[5] Suffering a steady decline in health, Dietrich was out of the game completely by 1975, although she did succeed in winning a 1968 Tony Award for performing on Broadway (a risky gig previously avoided) and made a final 1978 appearance singing on film (see Chapter 5). As for Bacharach, his musical art was forever enhanced, incorporating a pop sensibility that was strictly adult in its outlook (and cabaret in feel) — this during an era of dominant teenage consumerism — all no doubt influenced by his long association with one of cabaret's greatest exponents. Dietrich, for her part, in 1964 perhaps paid Bacharach the ultimate compliment for a tunesmith by performing live his timeless melody for *Kentucky Bluebird* with a German language lyric (*"Kleine Treue Nachtigall"*).[6]

Like Kurt Weill before him, Bacharach over the course of his long career has worked with many fine lyricists. Just as Weill's name will be forever linked with Bertolt Brecht, however, so will that of Bacharach's be with Hal David, who penned most of his best-known song lyrics during their 1960s heyday while the two worked together in Manhattan's legendary Brill Building. A Jewish native of New York City (Brooklyn) and somewhat older (born 1921), David, like so many other artists of his generation, first seriously began his trade while serving in the military — in his individual case, writing for USO performances given in the Pacific theater during World War II.[7] After the war, he found on-and-off work with prestigious bandleaders such as Sammy Kaye and Guy Lombardo, but it was not until 1957 when he started working with Bacharach that his visibility and fortunes truly began to rise. In short order, they wrote catchy, consecutive hits for country singer Marty Robbins ("The Story of My Life") and pop crooner Perry Como ("Magic Moments"), and thus a successful songwriting partnership was off and running for the next half century or so. For the next seven years, as Bacharach toured and worked with Dietrich, his artistic collaboration with David simultaneously came to full fruition. Though intensely private in his personal life, David's song lyrics over the last five plus decades have consistently reflected a fully mature and exclusively adult outlook in all matters of life and love; hence, these have usually provided a perfect fit for Bacharach's deceptively simple and subtle "borderline pop" arrangements. The somewhat unusual fact that both men have also frequently worked independently of each other over the years to produce quality material only serves to underscore the very special nature of those songs which they have completed working together.

After Dietrich and David, the third most important professional relationship in Bacharach's career would be with Dionne Warwick, born Marie Dionne Warrick in 1940, East Orange, New Jersey. Armed with formal training, Warwick, through sheer talent and force of will, by the early 1960s had turned herself into a veteran studio back-up singer in New York's then-thriving pop music industry, appearing without credit on numerous well-known recordings by other big-name stars. In 1961, she caught the ear and eye of Bacharach while singing in the chorus for his hit song "Mexican Divorce" being recorded by the Drifters. She immediately accepted Bacharach's offer to record solo demos (again, for other artists), and by 1962 had signed a solo contract with Scepter Records (also recording home to superstar girl-group, the Shirelles). Thinking that she was recording Bacharach and David's classic "Make It Easy on Yourself" for her own release, Warwick watched in dismay as the same song was given to Jerry Butler, for whom it was a huge commercial success. According to the story, Warwick angrily accused the two songwriters with "Don't make me over!" — thus herself providing the song title which subsequently became her first big solo hit. Between 1963 and 1969 came a continuing string of Warwick-sung Bacharach and David standards, including "Anyone Who Had a Heart," "Walk On By," "Reach Out for Me," "You'll Never Get to Heaven (If You Break My Heart)," "Are You There (with Another Girl)," "Do You Know the Way to San Jose?," "Alfie," "Promises, Promises," "I Say a Little Prayer," "I'll Never Fall in Love Again," "Trains and Boats and Planes," "(There's) Always Something There to Remind Me," and "Message to Michael," — the last an effective repackaging of "Kentucky Bluebird (Message to Martha)" which had also been a hit for Lou Johnson in 1964.[8] The first pinnacle of Warwick's early celebrity came in 1966 when she was invited to perform at the modern-day shrine of French cabaret, the Paris Olympia, and was introduced to the audience by none other than Marlene Dietrich.[9] Indeed, it is hardly a stretch to note that Warwick's definitive 1960s readings of Bacharach and David classics are much in the same emotional and intellectual spirit as Dietrich's own earlier work with Bacharach and her even earlier Weimar partnerships with German-born cabaret songwriters of the previous generation (see Chapter 5). For example, a Bacharach and David gem like Warwick's stunning performance of "I'll Never Fall in Love Again" comes across almost as a direct response to the Friedrich Hollaender–Sammy Lerner classic originally made famous by Dietrich, "Falling in Love Again."

Warwick, like the other outstanding musical personalities discussed herein, went on to enjoy a long career quite apart and independent from the magnificent body of 1960s adult pop with which she is most typically associated. Meanwhile, Burt Bacharach, with seemingly infallible commercial instincts, excelled at everything he attempted during the late 1960s and early 1970s, both with and without David and Warwick. The Beatles ("Baby It's You") and Elvis Presley ("Any Day Now") covered his material, as did most every other popular performing artist of stature. Diverse names like Aretha Franklin, Rod Stewart, Gene Pitney, Barbra Streisand, Jack Jones, Dusty Springfield, Neil Diamond, Roberta Flack, Elvis Costello, Dr. Dre, and Patti LaBelle represent the mere tip of the iceberg in this regard. Few songwriters have enjoyed a similar range of stylistic appeal. Many feel the apotheosis of their craft found full expression in Jackie DeShannon's timeless 1965 rendition of "What the World Needs Now Is Love," a pacifist masterpiece in the same grand tradition as many Berlin anti-war songs from the Weimar period. In a lighter vein, the extroverted 1965 soundtrack rendition of "What's New Pussycat?" by Tom Jones (aka Sir John Thomas Woodward) can without much effort be imagined performed on the fictional stage of Berlin's Kit Kat Klub from *Cabaret* (see Chapter 16). In 1968, Bacharach and David won a Tony Award for their Broadway musical *Promises, Promises*, produced by David Merrick with a book by Neil Simon, based on the 1960 Billy Wilder film, *The Apartment*. In 1969, B.J. Thomas' Dylanesque reading of "Raindrops Keep Falling on My Head" from the anti-western film *Butch Cassidy and the Sundance Kid* won an Oscar Award for best song.[10] The tune could have easily been an anthem for German *Kabarett* singers a generation earlier (see Chapter 6). Another massive Bacharach and David hit was the late Karen Carpenter's revelatory take on "Close to You," a straightforward, adolescent-like love song, seemingly out of character for its creators until one considers that Weimar operetta (harkening back to turn-of-the-century Überbrettl cabaret) would often take similar, nostalgic detours (see Chapter 12). In 1971, Bacharach finally released his first true solo album, successfully positioning himself as a polished singer-songwriter-performer quite capable of playing almost any kind of live venue, including Las Vegas, a city which he had personally witnessed conquered by Elvis Presley's comeback shows in 1969 (see Chapter 13).[11]

This rare kind of sustained commercial and critical success deserves a brief detour of stylistic analysis, though coming strictly from a non-professional viewpoint. Other commentators, however, have offered some insights intelligible to most laymen or casual listeners. Bacharach's interim biography Michael Brocken, along with many other critics, has noted that many of best his compositions generously mix major and minor keys, which "creates a deliberate mood of indistinctness" in his work.[12] Here, Warwick's classification of Bacharach's art as "borderline pop" and Kevin McMullin's cabaret descriptor of "borderland music" (see Introduction) are yet again evoked. Odd, unpredictable key progressions, rhythm changes, and harmony combinations define Bacharach's American version of *Kleinkunst*, just as these same qualities often graced Kurt Weill's best compositions and, for that matter, Darius Milhaud's as well. Similar to Weimar cabaret, which frequently quoted Argentine tango rhythms, Bacharach's style has always had a close affinity with Latin jazz, and throughout his career he has maintained working relationships with musicians such as Herb Albert and the Tijuana Brass. All of these characteristics are surely the cumulative product of Bacharach's wide-ranging, sophisticated background in both classical and popular idioms, but always geared towards broad mass appeal. A difficult trick to pull off, certainly, but a very select group of composers — often those affiliated directly or indirectly with cabaret — have managed to pull it off over the course of the last century.

To further highlight this remarkable achievement, perhaps a good mini-case study is Bacharach and David's "Kentucky Bluebird," an unequivocally great song that has been memorably covered by many singers, both male and female. In early recordings by Jerry Butler, Lou Johnson, and Dionne Warwick, regardless of the arrangement or gender point of view, certain qualities remain constant.[13] The melody can hardly be described as catchy or easily humable, yet is both striking and poignant. The variable rhythm and structure of the piece (with a slight syncopation and Latin inflexion) grabs and holds the attention of listeners without being hackneyed or predictable. Instrumentation is big but not overwhelming. Above all, the music seems to be in perfect sync with Hal David's lyrics; no operatic music drama was ever more effective. The singer-narrator asks a bluebird to send a pleading missive to a distant lover — a fictional cousin of Sally Bowles from *Cabaret*— who is trying (probably in vain) to make a music career in the cabaret-cafes of New Orleans. Even David's choice of the symbolic bluebird is suggestive. Apart from flexible rhyming possibilities, the word obviously has multiple connotations, some with the indigenous American music form by the same name, others with a simple English adjective meaning sad or lonely. Another association, however, stretches back to the German Expressionist movement of the early 20th century, in which blue — suggestive of both deep spirituality and cool emotional detachment — became the express symbolic color of painters such as Wassily

Kandinsky and Franz Marc, while the "New Objectivity" was in turn occasionally adopted by Weimar filmmakers, designers, and cabaret songsmiths (see Chapter 9). Bacharach's subtle, understated musical structure for "Kentucky Bluebird" certainly seems to hark back to this earlier time and place.[14]

Around the approximate time that "Kentucky Bluebird" was written (circa 1962), Bacharach and David were in process leading a transformation and rejuvenation of their resident working address at 1619 Broadway (the Brill Building) from an old-fashioned, out-of-date tune factory into a modern, sophisticated hit parade machine for adults both young and old. Led by Elvis Presley, the commercial ascendancy of rock and roll during the late 1950s seemed to spell demise for the old Tin Pan Alley system mastered decades before by the Gershwin brothers and later manifested within the complex business apparatus of the Brill Building.[15] By 1956, highly-simplified adolescent and teenage-oriented music appeared to be the order of the day, with no end in sight; moreover, the song material being generated by traditional Broadway sources looked to be on the way out, and permanently. Into this large breach stepped a young but not-too-young songwriting team unusually well-equipped to turn the situation around, although it is very unlikely that they ever thought of themselves that way. They wildly succeeded in introducing a whole new kind of viable commercial song, one that had strong adult and international appeal, drawing upon (not too surprisingly) an incredible wide range of influences, one of which was the German-Jewish and European cabaret tradition. In effect, Burt Bacharach and Hal David artistically reinvented the prestigious Brill Building, important vestiges of which survive into its present day incarnation.

After nearly two decades without a commercial misstep, Bacharach and David finally stumbled in 1973 by committing to a musical score for a disastrous attempted remake of Frank Capra's 1937 classic film *Lost Horizon*.[16] The end product was rejected by audiences and critics alike, lawsuits proliferated between all involved parties, and the Bacharach-David-Warwick partnership that had seemed so invincible over the previous 10 years crumbled with startling rapidity. The three collaborators had actually begun to drift apart at the beginning of the 1970s as Bacharach began his solo career, and when serious financial adversity first hit, it seemed to be the signal for everyone to go on hiatus. For years the former songwriting partners communicated only through lawyers. Bacharach and Warwick (along with notable friends Stevie Wonder, Gladys Knight, and Elton John) reunited magnificently in 1985 under the banner of AIDS research charity for "That's What Friends Are For," a celebratory song co-written with Bacharach's then wife, Carol Bayer Sager. Finally, by 1993 (after legal affairs between the two had been settled), Warwick decided that enough was enough and brought the long-estranged Bacharach and David back together again to write for her a new song, "Sunny Weather Lover." The two elder statesmen of American popular song have reportedly been cordial ever since, even while journeying down their now mostly separate artistic paths.[17]

The influence of the so-called Brill Building "sound" as reshaped by Bacharach and David during the early 1960s has since fanned out like a tidal shock wave in all directions. Other notable songwriters from the Brill Building of that era, such as Carole King, certainly felt their impact as well, eventually turning to a successful solo career performing more mature, adult-oriented material with which she is now most associated. Beach Boys resident genius Brian Wilson has emphatically called Bacharach his favorite songwriter, and the compliment is especially self-evident when examining Wilson's more serious and introspective musical forays of the mid–1960s, from the early "In My Room" (1963) to *Pet Sounds* (1966) and his later collaboration with Van Dyke Parks on the long-germinating *Smile* project (1966–2004). Unlikely, iconoclastic contemporaries from the 1960s such as the late Frank Zappa (see Chapter 18) have heaped praise on Bacharach as well.[18] The wide stylistic spectrum of admiration coming from the likes of Wilson and Zappa, both of whom were direct music competitors with Bacharach, is especially revealing. Only a composer with a nearly indefinable range of musical language could appeal to both a stalwart of Top-40 radio and a free spirit who deliberately rebelled against it. Perhaps the most visible barometer of Bacharach's influence has been the continuing use of his music for films. Beginning with the comedy *What's New Pussycat?* (1965) and the James Bond thriller *Casino Royale* (1967), in which Dusty Springfield splendidly debuted "The Look of Love," the Bacharach songbook has really never gone out of fashion as an ornament for the big screen. Possibly the best-known of these many movie appropriations was the routine appearance of Bacharach's music (and sometimes of Bacharach himself) in Mike Myers' *Austin Powers* trilogy between 1997 and 2002. By this time, tributes, compilations, and revivals were to be found everywhere. Few (if any) of Bacharach's countless admirers, however, ever mention his early tutelage under Darius Milhaud, or his army years in Germany, or those spent with Marlene Dietrich.[19] Then again, the crucial formative periods for most artistic geniuses tend all too often to be ignored or downplayed by critical commentary.

For a composer whose venerable name can be linked with just about every other prominent musical artist of his era, Bacharach has been surprisingly individualistic and consistent in his overall creative approach. The mantra we have come to expect from him is a simple one: pushing of boundaries, avoiding monotony, and constant, delightful surprise. The proof is that his has become a brand name unto itself. Among his countless collaborators, however, a relatively early and obscure one that stands out is singing actor Joel Grey (aka Joel David Katz), who recorded his own version of "What's New Pussycat?" as a guest artist (along with Tony Middleton) on *Burt Bacharach Plays His Hits* (1965), a tentative forerunner to Bacharach's first proper solo LP for a major label five years later.[20] This was only one year before Grey would go on to create the Broadway role of the Emcee in *Cabaret*, a role for which he won a Tony Award and for most American audiences, has since become the dramatic embodiment of Weimar decadence (see Chapter 16). Grey's achievement, of course, owed no small debt to the creators of this landmark 1966 musical, including its own stellar songwriting team who first came into public prominence almost immediately after Bacharach and David had established their own considerable reputations. In terms of bringing the excitement of Weimar cabaret straight and permanently into the American public consciousness, few artists have done more than John Kander and Fred Ebb. It is to their remarkable story that we now turn. Meanwhile, we can all be grateful for Burt Bacharach's relentless exploration of margins, those both technical and emotional, within the field of American popular song.

16. *Cabaret* on Stage and Film

"...it was clear that Cabaret was a production that made deep, dark connections between Weimar and the present day because much of current popular culture has its roots in a peculiar brand of German aestheticism."— Keith Garebian[1]

Remarkably, and perhaps coincidentally, John Harold Kander was born on March 18, 1927, in Kansas City, Missouri, approximately one year before Burt Bacharach in the very same city. Both composers came from artistically inclined, non-orthodox, German-Jewish families.[2] Both went on to have immeasurable impacts on American popular music, utilizing the remaining vestiges of Weimar-era cabaret music which had arguably reached its zenith during the time in which both artists were born into a completely different society on the other side of the Atlantic Ocean. While the young Bacharach departed relatively soon afterwards for a more cosmopolitan lifestyle in New York City, Kander spent most of his early formative years enjoying what future songwriting partner Fred Ebb once frustratingly described as a "Norman Rockwell" childhood in the historic music capital of the lower Midwest. Nothing perceived as elitist could be said against either of their upbringings. It is therefore tempting to draw at least one conclusion from this unusual correlation between the backgrounds of Kander and Bacharach: both composers, despite their legendary sophistication of musical range, always remained highly focused on reaching as broad an audience as possible with their respective arts, both for personal and professional reasons.

By contrast, Fred Ebb (1928–2004), the finest song lyricist of his generation, could hardly have come from a more different realm of experience. Like Kander's, Ebb's heritage was German-Jewish, but similarities ended there. Born and raised in New York City, Ebb was the product of a merchant-class family who had little time or inclination for the arts. As he later reminisced, "I never saw my father pick up a book."[3] Rebelling against parental expectations, the unhappy child listened to records and sought theater as an escape.[4] At age 15, he informed his incredulous parents that he wanted to be taken to a musical; his wish was granted and the repercussions were permanent.[5] Later graduating valedictorian from DeWitt Clinton High School and then earning a B.A. in English from New York University, Ebb became a huge fan of Frank Loesser (*Guys and Dolls*), a Broadway songwriter heavily influenced by Kurt Weill (see Chapter 11), and one who later advised Ebb never to meet his own heroes.[6] Ebb loved to sing and perform on stage, but like Lotte Lenya, never learned to read music.[7] He began writing song lyrics during the early 1950s with other tunesmiths, and some of these were recorded by the likes of Judy Garland, aka Frances Ethel Gumm ("Heartbroken"), and Carmen McRae ("I Never Loved Him Anyhow").[8] Biographer James Leve observes that Ebb "...was, by most accounts, complicated, occasionally misanthropic, often overwhelmingly generous, and eternally devoted to his friends."[9] While earning his master's degree at Columbia University, Ebb initially met fellow graduate student John Kander, by that time an alumnus of Oberlin College (in Ohio) and fully steeped in the western classical music tradition. Upon their graduation from Columbia in 1957 — the same period in which Bacharach met Marlene Dietrich and Hal David — no one at the time could have foreseen a future working relationship that would continue almost non-stop for over 40 years.

Kander's first big break on Broadway after graduating from Columbia came when he was literally hustled out of a barroom crowd to play substitute piano in rehearsals for the original production of *West Side Story* in 1958. This in turn led to a similar gig plus composing dance arrangements for Styne and Sondheim's *Gypsy* in 1959, then doing the same for David Merrick's production of the French musical *Irma la Douce* in 1960.[10] Kander's first complete musical (without Ebb) was *A Family Affair*, which briefly ran on Broadway in early 1962 and where he met Hal Prince, then directing his first show. Later that same year, Kander was re-introduced to Ebb by music publisher Tommy Valando, and one of their earliest song efforts, "My Coloring Book," became a hit for Sandy Stewart (after being introduced on the Perry Como Show by Kay Ballard). The recording was nominated for a Grammy Award, and the song later became closely associated with the young Barbra Streisand.[11] Then the team was commissioned to write a full stage musical on short notice for legendary producer George Abbott (1887–1995), then 73 years old and whose 1927 international hit *Broadway* had included in its Vienna cast a yet-to-be-famous Marlene Dietrich (see Chapter 5).[12] The result, *Golden Gate*, was never produced (and is the only Kander and Ebb musical still waiting to be produced), but its auditions impressed Abbott enough to hire the new songwriting duo again for his next big project.[13]

Kander, Ebb, and Abbott reunited for the 1965 production of *Flora, the Red Menace*, a satirical stick-in-the-eye for McCarthyism portraying Marxists more as pathetic, boring losers and duped, innocent victims, rather than any real threat to national security, not unlike the manner in which novelist Christopher Isherwood had portrayed them in Berlin three decades earlier (see Chapter 7).[14] The new project also reunited Prince with Kander (this time partnering with Ebb), and was originally intended as a vehicle for Edyie Gormé. When the star singer made the mistake, however, of standing up Abbott for dinner, Liza Minnelli, the eager, untested, 19-year-old daughter of Vincente Minnelli and Judy Garland, was brought in over Abbott's initial reservations but with Kander and Ebb's enthusiastic coaching and strong endorsements.[15] Although a limited run of *Flora* (at the Alvin Theatre, today known as the Neil Simon Theatre) did not turn a profit, Minnelli won a Tony Award for her energetic lead performance. Once again Abbott, who by this point in his long career was interested in other things besides mere monetary profit, soothed his discouraged collaborators by insisting that they work together on yet another venture. Thus the stage was set for creation of what has often been called the most influential Broadway musical of the 20th century.

The idea of a musical version for Christopher Isherwood's *Berlin Stories* had been bounced around by a number of people over the course of many years, following a successful stage adaptation in 1951 and less successful film version in 1955. The project began in earnest with Hal Prince, who had the longest working relationship with Abbott.[16] Like Burt Bacharach, Prince had a military duty station in Germany during the early 1950s and vividly remembered attending cabaret performances in Stuttgart.[17] Keith Garebian noted that, in terms of motivation, Prince "found 'a reason for telling the story parallel to contemporary problems' in the United States...."[18] Prince himself famously remarked upon "the parallel between the spiritual bankruptcy of Germany in the 1920s and [the United States] in the 1960s."[19] First off, he hired recently Tony-nominated playwright Joe Masteroff to collaborate on writing a new book musical with a more authentic Weimar Berlin feel to it, yet one that would not succumb to nostalgia, pastiche, or fail to be anything less than contemporary.[20] Revamping the 1951 play and 1955 film (neither of which had a cabaret stage), Prince and Masteroff opted for a Shakespearean play-within-a-play structure, with the Berlin Kit Kat Klub becoming a metaphor for Weimar society.[21] Borrowing from John Van Druten's dramatization of the Isherwood short stories, the decision was made to focus on the character of Sally Bowles, with Isherwood's British William Bradshaw narrator transformed into the American Clifford Bradshaw, but remaining emotionally distant like his original model. In a similar manner, Fräuline Schroeder's change to Schneider was retained, but Masteroff added a doomed romance with the Jewish street peddler Shultz. Masteroff also brought back Sally's abortion episode from Isherwood.[22] Abbott chimed in by suggesting two acts instead of three, a wise decision that stuck.[23] The result was a book for the first modern "concept" musical, credit for which usually goes to Prince.[24]

At this crucial juncture entered Kander and Ebb as songwriters. Although Kander, like thousands of others, had seen Lotte Lenya perform in the off–Broadway revival of *The Threepenny Opera* in 1954, by his own admission, "Weill's American work had a greater impact on me."[25] In preparation for his assignment, Kander immersed himself in lesser known Weimar-era recordings of Friedrich Hollaender and German jazz pianist Pater Kreuger, intentionally avoiding Weill's music for fear of being labeled an imitator.[26] Like Prince, Kander associated cabaret music with a strong lead role for the *conférencier*, based on his own personal experiences watching Marlene Dietrich in live performance, and the work opens with a long vamping introduction by the emcee.[27] Above all, in the great tradition of cabaret, both Kander and Ebb strove to make their music and words appeal to as broad an audience as possible. Ebb later reflected that

> I think there are a lot of guys writing for the theatre who write in an elitist way. They write to please a small group who come the first three months or the first three weeks. They're content to write that way, and I think everybody has to do his own thing. As for me, I always wanted to be popular, and I always want to be well liked.[28]

Utilizing this populist approach, combining good homework, solid formal training, and vast personal experience, the duo began pounding out their "Berlin Songs" with amazingly fluency. Several of their earliest compositions eventually became some of the best known songs from the show, including "If You Could See Her Through My Eyes," "The Money Song," "Tomorrow Belongs to Me," "Two Ladies," and "Willkommen."[29]

Prince then proceeded to round out his a creative team with supporting personnel that, in retrospect, could not have been more shrewdly selected. Many had past experience working with Weill when he was alive. Set designer Boris Aronson and lighting designer Jean Rosenthal had both worked with the WPA Theater Project in 1935 when Weill and Lenya first arrived in America and were invited to perform there (see Chapter 11). Aronson went on to become a member of Weill's production team for the groundbreaking *Love Life* in 1948.[30] Choreographer Ron Field had been an eight-year-old dancing cast member in Weill's *Lady in the Dark* from 1941, and it was he who successfully lobbied to have "Willkommen" as the show's opening number.[31] Costume designer Patricia Zipprodt, though not having known Weill personally, worked hard screening old films by Sternberg and Pabst (see chapter 10) and by studying the artwork of George Grosz (see Chapter 9).[32] In a stroke of genius, Prince cast a young and relatively unknown Joel Grey in the key role of the Emcee. The real casting coupe, however, was Prince inviting a 68-year-old Lotte Lenya to play Fräuline Schneider when not acting as senior mentor of the overall production as the former Mrs. Kurt Weill. Two of her biggest numbers, "So What" and "What Would You Do," were appropriately stylized by Kander and Ebb more in the spirit of her late husband's music.[33] The only misstep was rejecting Liza Minnelli for the stage version of the musical because Prince thought the rising American star was too talented to play an English Sally Bowles of decidedly limited stage talent.[34] Instead, British-born Jill Hayworth was brought on board and proved to be the weak link in the cast, though not nearly enough to offset the production's other myriad virtues.

After a brief trial run in Boston, Kander and Ebb's *Cabaret* opened at the Broadhurst Theatre in November 1966, and the rest is history: 1,165 performances with eight Tony Awards (11 nominations), including best musical and best original score, with Grey, Field, Aronson, Zipprodt, Prince, and even supporting actress Peg Murray all winning individual awards.[35] The show has since enjoyed six major stage revivals in New York (1987, 1998) and London (1986, 1993, 2006, 2012) alone. With success came controversy, which may have helped box office. Some Jewish audience members not prepared for the objective realism being served up on stage were offended by perceived anti–Semitism in "If You Could See Her Through My Eyes," while others swore that "Tomorrow Belongs to Me" was an actual Nazi anthem from the Weimar era. Both claims were preposterous, but at the time had the mostly Jewish production team (including the songwriters) running scared.[36] In the long run, these protests only proved further testament to the creators' tremendous artistic achievement. As Foster Hirsch later wrote, "The spirit of Kurt Weill, musical-theatre reformer, hovers over the show...."[37] John Kander himself observed that a major theme in the work was survival in a hostile environment, much the same as in Weimar cabaret itself. Fred Ebb chimed in that the title song was not intended to be a happy one, especially given its context, even though it is often mistakenly interpreted that way.[38]

Given the magnitude of such a triumph, *Cabaret* "the movie" was inevitable; fortunately, the 1972 film version was hardly less spectacular, again mainly thanks to the good judgment of Prince and the versatility of its composers. The first lynchpin to this success involved Prince (who had a scheduling conflict) bringing in Bob Fosse (1927–1987) as director, despite his risky reputation and infamous temperament.[39] Producer Cy Feuer, a fan of German Expressionism, gave Fosse license to rework the stage musical as he saw fit for the big screen, and Fosse immediately elected to film in Germany.[40] The second masterstroke was casting Liza Minnelli as Sally Bowles, since she had been waiting (and preparing) over six years to play the role. British star Michael York was brought in to play the narrator, renamed Brian Roberts and finally, after four decades, accurately playing a British bi-sexual adventurer close to Isherwood's original literary model.[41] Joel Grey was wisely retained as the Emcee, and had considerably refined his performance over the years, including the addition of a believable German accent to his character.[42] As art critic Ian Buruma has accurately observed: "For those of us born after World War II there is one face that best conjures up the spirit of Berlin about 1930, and that belongs to a man who was born in 1932 ... Joel Grey, master of ceremonies and androgynous host of the Kit Kat Club in the 1972 film *Cabaret*.... He is the sum of everything we find repellent yet deeply intriguing about Berlin at the dawn of the Third Reich."[43]

Storylines were tweaked as well. The Schneider-Schutz romance was jettisoned and replaced with a Fritz-Natalia courtship (harkening back to the 1951 play), both as a foil to Brian and Sally's falling out, as well as a poignant commentary on the anti–Semitism of the Holocaust.[44] Lastly, Kander and Ebb happily added three new magnificent songs, the Marlene Dietrich–tribute "Mein Herr" (eventually becoming the visual symbol of the film), the raucous "Money, Money" (a fantastic duet for Minnelli and Grey), and "Maybe This Time"—the last number originally written a decade earlier for singer Kay Ballard but never previously recorded.

Overall critical and popular reception of the film upon its release was (and still is) perhaps best summarized with those remarks made by Pauline Kael (1919–2001), arguably the most eloquent reviewer of her generation. She begins with "*Cabaret* is a great movie musical, made, miraculously, without compromises. It's miraculous because the material is hard and unsentimental, and until now there has never been a diamond-hard big American movie musical."[45] Kael adds that "*Cabaret* is the only expensive American movie musical (actually, it was shot in West Germany) that takes its form from political cabaret."[46] Repeatedly noting the consciously Expressionist look of the film, Kael catalogues the many Weimar reference points which give the movie its illusion of authenticity, even more so than the earlier Broadway show: "*Cabaret* turns the conventions of recent big-musical movies inside out: the floor show at the Kit Kat Klub is used as a prism through which we see the characters' lives.... With this prismatic approach, *Cabaret* totally escapes grandiosity; it's a big musical that doesn't feel like one, and the first really innovative movie musical in many years. Not only is the subject not wholesome but the tone is detached and objective."[47]

Kael's observations recall the *neue Sachlichkeit* ("New Objectivity") movement which played such a central role both in Weimar culture (see Chapter 9) and Isherwood's novels (see Chapter 7); moreover, the gripping performances of Minnelli and Grey often recall the respective musical styles of Dietrich and Weill.[48] In terms of "big" musicals, Kael saw *Cabaret* almost as an antithesis to Rodgers and Hammerstein's *Oklahoma!*, its older and only American rival in terms of widespread contemporary influence.[49] Summarizing, the dean of American movie critics marvels that "The grotesque amorality in *Cabaret* is frightening, not because it's weak but because it's intensely, obscenely alive."[50] The film was nominated for 10 Oscars by the Academy and won eight, including individual awards for Fosse, Minnelli, and Grey. Finally, on a personal note, it should be added that this writer, like millions of other viewers at the time, was first consciously introduced to the subject of Weimar cabaret as an adolescent through this film, after having been initially exposed (unconsciously) to its music through Bobby Darin's hit version of "Mack the Knife" in 1959 (see Chapter 14).

For multiple reasons that are beyond the scope of this study, Kander and Ebb struggled over the next several decades to write a comparable blockbuster, although the quality of their work remained consistently outstanding. Suffice it here to say that *Cabaret* proved to be a once-in-a-lifetime event by almost anyone's standards. After their first three major works, 14 more full-length Kander and Ebb musicals and revues would appear over the next 46 years, two being produced (thus far) after Ebb's death in 2004: *The Happy Time* (1968); *Zorbá* (1968); *70, Girls, 70* (1971); *Chicago* (1975); *The Act* (1977); *Woman of the Year* (1981); *The Rink* (1984); *And the World Goes 'Round* (1991); *Kiss of the Spider Woman* (1993); *Steel Pier* (1997); *Over and Over* (1999); *The Visit* (2001); *Curtains* (2007); and *The Scottsboro Boys* (2011). During their long partnership, it would not be overstatement to say that they typically worked with some of the biggest names in American musical theater while in the process being bestowed a truckload of Tony, Oscar, Golden Globe, and Drama Desk awards from their peers. Ebb and Kander also worked independent of each other, but never with different songwriting partners; professionally, they were like married couple (though not personal partners). They tended to be most fond of their commercial failures, usually with good artistic justification. Kander became an accomplished soundtrack composer, with *Kramer vs. Kramer* (1979), *Still of the Night* (1982), and *Places in the Heart* (1984) among his many distinguished credits. Together, Kander and Ebb supplied songs for films as well, including *Funny Lady* (1975), *A Matter of Time* (1976), and most famously, Martin Scorsese's *New York, New York* (1977). The latter work showcased the title track, the duo's biggest commercial hit single after Frank Sinatra recorded it in 1980.[51] Ebb always continued to work with his old protégée Liza Minnelli for *Liza with a Z* (1972), *Goldie* [Hawn] *and Liza Together* (1980); and *Liza's Back* (2002), among many other notable projects.[52] Perhaps the ultimate compliment came from an elderly, retired Lotte Lenya, who told one interviewer that she only went out "when Fred Ebb is doing something...."[53]

Although Kander and Ebb enjoyed several big commercial hits on Broadway after *Cabaret*, their only other stage work similar in monumental impact and influence to date has been *Chicago* from 1975, but it took a major revival over two decades later to really bring the show to a wide audience. Originally another Fosse collaboration, *Chicago* opened to mixed reviews and was overshadowed at the box office that same year by the ephemeral success of Hamlisch and Kleban's *A Chorus Line*. Interestingly, *Chicago* was based on the true story of two aspiring Chicago cabaret singers from the 1920s acquitted during a sensational murder trial, soon afterwards turned into a 1926 play by Chicago Tribune reporter Maurine Dallas Watkins, herself later becoming a model for the gullible Mary Sunshine character in the musical.[54] The popular play became first a silent movie in 1927, then a talkie in 1942 (*Roxie Hart*), starring a game but severely miscast Ginger Rogers. Fosse talked the songwriters into doing an update as a showcase for his wife Gwen Verdon, but suffered from a heart attack during production, one of many bad breaks suffered by the show. Later Fosse featured much of the same music and turbulent back stage history in his semi-autobiographical film *All That Jazz* from 1979.[55] Finally in 1996, in wake of seemingly endless public and personal scandals of the Clinton era, a revamped and retooled *Chicago* featuring Fosse-like choreography by original cast member Ann Reinking became the surprise smash sensation of the decade. Even the critics changed their minds, inventing a litany of excuses for themselves, although the real reason for the slow acceptance was probably best summarized by James Leve: "*Chicago* is one of the most unsympathetic musicals ever written, second only to *The Threepenny Opera* in its cynical view of humanity."[56] By 2002, Miramax Films had turned *Chicago* into a major motion picture event directed by the brilliant Rob Marshall, who had worked with Kander and Ebb on their first important revival, *Zorbá* in 1983, *Kiss of the Spider Woman* in 1993, and the Sam Mendes revival of *Cabaret* in 1998.[57] The film took home six Academy Awards, including Best Picture, and to the composers' pleasant surprise, generated a best-selling soundtrack as well.

Certainly it would be misleading to suggest that *Chicago*, like *Cabaret*, takes its main inspiration from the Weimar musical tradition; on the other hand, it would also be a distortion to deny its presence completely. The songwriters themselves always rightfully maintained that the show had its primary roots in an older vaudeville tradition, and the Rob Marshall film version accentuated this aspect of the musical with great success. The story setting and points of reference are purely American; the closest thing to a political threat facing the characters is the threat of Irish policemen half-heartedly enforcing Prohibition. In spite of these marked differences, however, there is no escaping the aesthetic values that left such a deep impression on the composers earlier in their careers. For one, 1920s Chicago and 1920s Berlin, as societies, are both severely lacking a moral compass. Roxie and Sally will stop at nothing to get what they want. In this, they are aided and abetted by nearly everyone around them, which makes for wonderful musical theater, but also disturbing implications for the world in which we all live. Musically, the hot jazz-inflected numbers of *Chicago* draw upon turn-of-the-century vaudevillian traditions, but then again, so did Weimar *Kabarett* and Überbrettl, a borrowing which often manifested itself in the larger-scaled revues and light opera works for which 1920s Berlin was so famous. Producer-director Hal Prince, who in the past had worked with Kander, Ebb, and Fosse on *Cabaret*, was later known to have privately criticized *Chicago* for being too much of a *Cabaret* redux.[58]

The same can be said to varying degrees for nearly all of Kander and Ebb's musicals, especially those coming after *Cabaret*. When Prince helped to turn the duo's dark take on Manuel Puig's *Kiss of the Spider Woman* into a Broadway hit in 1993 (and thus setting the stage for a serious revival of *Chicago*), he insisted that facets of the lead role (in the words of James Leve) "...called for an iconic Dietrich figure...."[59] This requirement was magnificently filled by the casting of Kander and Ebb veteran Chita Rivera, who won a Tony Award for her efforts.[60] Latter-day Dietrich influence makes itself felt as well in *The Act* (1977), a story set in Las Vegas (see Chapter 13) and another special vehicle designed by the songwriters for Liza Minnelli. Also winning a Tony for her lead in the Kander and Ebb hit musical *Woman of the Year* (1981) was a 57-year-old Lauren Bacall, despite a constricted voice range and limited experience on Broadway. Her secret, as she later explained, was allowing herself to be guided by the sound of Lotte Lenya's voice from *Cabaret*.[61] Older French cabaret roots are frequently acknowledged as well. *Zorbá* (1968) includes a touching tribute to the archetypal Parisian *chanteuse* in the character of Madame Hortense. For that matter, even in *Cabaret*, the Emcee politely addresses the audience in bilingual English and French, thus subtly acknowledging the art form's original French origins (see Chapter 1). *Steel Pier* (1997) takes its cue from the same Orpheus myth that so fascinated a young Kurt Weill, and has an Atlantic City (east coast Las Vegas) setting that was actually visited by John Kander as a child in 1933, the fateful year of Nazi takeover in Germany.[62] *The Visit* (2001) is based on the 1956 Friedrich Dürrenmatt play (seen by Kander) and features a song ("Love and Love Alone") that Leve describes as "...evocative of Weill's Berlin theater music."[63] Kander and Ebb's most recent Broadway production, *The Scottsboro Boys* (2011), has been called "their most unsettling work" (Leve), a minstrel show exploring the disturbing overlap in early 1930s American racist attitudes both towards blacks and Jews, one that cannot help but evoke parallel events in Germany from the same time period.[64] Taken as a whole, it is safe to say that Kander and Ebb's stage works owe as much to Weimar *Kabarett* as to any single time and place in musical history.

Kander and Ebb's pervasive influence on Broadway over the last five decades needs little elaboration within these pages. This influence, however, has also carried over into film, probably with even bigger impact. In addition to *Cabaret* (1972) and *Chicago* (2002), a steady stream of similarly distinctive movie musicals has continued to entertain and often shock Cineplex audiences. The outstanding work of Wisconsin-native Rob Marshall, director of *Chicago*, represents one of the best exemplars in this regard. Other previous Marshall films reflecting the cabaret ethos in one form or another include *Victor/Victoria* (1995), a story based on the original 1933 German film *Viktor und Viktoria*; the 1997 Fred Ebb adaptation of Richard Rodgers' *Cinderella* (1997); the night-club documentary *Tony Bennett: An American Classic* (2006); and most recently, *Nine* (2009), a visual extravaganza recalling the heyday of lavish Weimar musical stage revues. At the other end of the stylistic spectrum, the film version of Mel Brook's delightfully vulgar film musical version of *The Producers* (2005) was directed by, and developed in its 2001 stage incarnation by Kander and Ebb protégé Susan Stroman. One could go further and say that Brooks' notorious "Springtime for Hitler" — originally taken from his 1968 film version — could not have been foisted on an unwary movie-going public until Kander and Ebb had first paved the way with the controversial "Tomorrow Belongs to Me" from *Cabaret* in 1966. Another outrageous Brooks number from the same show such as "When You Got It, Flaunt It" today sounds like a direct descendant of Hollaender and Tucholsky's "Take It Off, Petronella!" from the Weimar period. This is not to cast any doubts on Brook's biting originality, but rather to underscore the many since forgotten ways in which Weimar culture has since infiltrated the American movie industry. Above all, Kander and Ebb, as modern day practitioners of that art, deserve full credit for perfecting and introducing to a wide audience the so-called "concept musical" in which songs performed on a stage-within-a-stage also reflect dramatic events portrayed in the character's lives — a format first introduced in the theater works of Weill and Brecht during the late 1920s in Weimar Germany.[65]

When Kander and Ebb first came forcefully into the public eye circa 1966 with *Cabaret*, American popular music (as we all now know) was going through seismic changes; in fact, it would accurate to assert that Kander and Ebb helped to preserve Broadway theater as a viable and socially relevant art form during a time in which it was in danger of being completely superceded. The high risks and costs of mounting a big show were, by the mid–1960s, being scaled back in favor of more modest and efficient economic models such as small group combos and touring performance units. As John Kander himself has repeatedly noted over the years with wise perceptiveness, financial failure is no longer tolerated on Broadway as it once was, and aspiring artists today better have a steady day job even while pursuing their passion. Just as *Cabaret* once introduced a more intimate kind of aesthetic to theater-goers previously conditioned strictly to a bigger is better approach, so did the British Invasion of the mid–1960s clearly demonstrate that a leaner and meaner performance style had its own advantages as well, both economically and artistically. Once again, however, all of this seems to have begun in Germany, both before and after the war.

17. The British Importation of *Kleinkunst*

"It was Hamburg that did it. That's where we really developed. To get the Germans going and keep it up for twelve hours at a time we really had to hammer. We would never have developed as much if we'd stayed at home."— John Lennon[1]

In July of 1960, Lotte Lenya left the city of Hamburg, where she had intermittently spent the last five years successfully performing, recording, and making personal peace of sorts with the country from which she had fled in 1935, not to return again until 20 years later. After her latest departure, it would be another six years before she helped to push the music of Kander and Ebb into the public spotlight with her portrayal of Fräuline Schneider in *Cabaret*, but in 1960 both Ebb and Kander were still struggling songwriters who had yet even begun working together. By that time, Elvis Presley had returned to the U.S. from Germany following his two-year military stint (see Chapter 13); however, it may be safely said that American popular music was at a crossroads during that summer season. The early excitement of 1950s rock and roll had begun to subside, and many of its original exponents were now retrenched into respectability, completely out of public favor, or dead. Earlier that spring, Marlene Dietrich, with a young Burt Bacharach in tow as bandleader on tour, had nearly been booed out of an unforgiving Germany for her heroics against the land of her birth during World War II. As for Bacharach, his brilliant songwriting partnership with Hal David had yet to really hit its stride as they gradually reinvented the Brill Building sound (see Chapter 15).

Top-40 hit parade was, at that moment, dominated by the likes of Paul Anka. Then, by some strange confluence of fate, a few weeks after Lenya left Hamburg, a group of five very young, relatively inexperienced, art school dropouts-turned-musicians from Liverpool, England, would arrive in that same city and begin to make pop music history. Their names of course were

John Lennon, Paul McCartney, George Harrison, John's best friend Stuart Sutcliffe, and drummer Pete Best.

Analysis of the Beatles' music typically does not begin with a discussion of Existentialist philosophy, but within this particular context a brief overview seems appropriate, if not essential. In reference to German culture, Existentialism is usually traced to the 19th century writings of Friedrich Nietzsche, the same philosopher who played such an inspirational role for the founders of Berlin Überbrettl at the dawn of the 20th century (see Chapter 1).[2] In terms of post–World War II Germany, however, the leading Existentialist writers for most Germans were in the French language, namely, Jean-Paul Sartre (1905–1980) and Albert Camus (1905–1960), the latter having died in January of the same year that John Julian Lennon (1940–1980) brought over his small entourage of adolescent misfits to entertain the rough-neck clientele of Hamburg's notorious Reeperbahn district. At the time, neither the Beatles, nor most of their prospective German audience, had any clue about Existentialist philosophic principles, although some of the educated students they were about to meet certainly knew of Sartre and Camus. More importantly, intelligent German and English youth of the time needed to rebel against their own immediate surroundings, and French intellectual writers were one way to fit the bill. Another was what eventually became known as the Existentialist fashion look — dark, moody, introspective, dangerous, and above all, photogenic. Hamburg, an inland port city, had always been especially receptive to foreign trends, and during the late 1930s had been home to the ill-fated *Swingjugend* counterculture movement (see Chapter 8). It was here that an ambitious, 19-year-old Lennon landed with his (mostly) even younger, intrepid band of aspiring rock and roll stars on August 8, 1960.[3]

The two men most responsible for bringing the Beatles to Hamburg had tough reputations and questionable backgrounds, to put it mildly. The far more benign of the two was Welsh hustler and businessman Allan Williams, the group's first manager, and owner of several music clubs in Liverpool, including the Wyvern Social Club, later known as the Blue Angel, named after the ubiquitous Marlene Dietrich film (see Chapter 10).[4] After auditioning Lennon's then rag-tag ensemble in early 1960 for a projected Scottish tour, Williams subsequently persuaded the band to cross over the channel and brave the seedy dives of Hamburg's St. Pauli Reeperbahn strip with promises of steady paychecks and possible future glory. Williams' business contact in Germany was another club owner, a crippled *Wehrmacht* war veteran, Bruno Koschmider, who had a genuine knack for frightening his employees and club patrons into strict obedience, backed by force if necessary.[5] Two months after installing Lennon's Beatles at the second-rate, low-visibility Indra Club, Koschmider hedged his bets by bringing over another Liverpudlian group,

Rory Storm and the Hurricanes, as resident band for his marquee operation, the Kaiserkeller Club. The Hurricanes lineup at that time included a 19-year-old drummer, Ringo Starr (aka Richard Starkey), who when not performing himself, enjoyed demanding song requests from the Beatles as he sat in the audience.[6] By late 1960, the Beatles and the Hurricanes were alternating their rowdy, ear-splitting acts at the Kaiserkeller, sometimes together playing 12-hour sets straight through the night, often propelled by easy-to-obtain performance-enhancing narcotics such as Preludin, used both to keep themselves going and to stave off hunger.[7]

Into this sordid working environment stepped the first and perhaps most positive influence the group would encounter during its professional life. Astrid Kirchherr, Klaus Voormann, and Jürgen Vollmer were three similar-aged art students attending Hamburg's Meisterschule für Gestaltung when they stumbled upon the recently arrived Beatles and Hurricanes at the Kaiser-keller in late 1960. It was the first time they had ever heard authentic, live rock and roll, and were left speechless, not unlike the manner in which their parent's generation had been thunderstruck by the arrival of Josephine Baker in 1920s Berlin (see Chapter 2). Despite Lennon's routine brusqueness, lifelong friendships were soon forged between the English ruffians and the German "Exis"— short for "Existentialists"— as the student trio came to be known to their British counterparts.[8] Kirchherr and the James Dean–like Sutcliffe became romantically involved, then later engaged. Crucially, the Beatles' look changed, with new haircuts, hipper clothes, snazzier instruments, more confidence on stage, and even more attitude than they previously possessed. Kirch-herr and Vollmer were talented photographers, and their early images of the Hamburg Beatles have since become classics of the genre.[9] Voorman was a painter and musician, and it was his intellectual connection with Sutcliffe (also a painter) that soon brought the chronically skeptical Lennon around to civility. The unlikely and often touching story of youthful bonding between these two opposite circles was later poignantly dramatized in the 1994 British-German film *Backbeat*.

From all accounts, the first Beatles Hamburg shows were inauspicious. As Lennon later explained, they were intimidated by the claustrophobic cabaret atmosphere: "...it was a little nightclub and it was a bit frightening because it wasn't a dance hall, and all these people were sitting down, expecting something."[10] McCartney remembered transvestites, prostitutes, and gangsters amongst the crowds.[11] After receiving a tepid reception on opening night from an audience that could have stepped right out of *The Threepenny Opera*, the Beatles were ordered in pigeon English by an impatient Koschmider to "*mach shau*" ("make show"). Consequently, they played louder, faster, and above all, with more theatricality. Lennon and McCartney began dividing up duties as *conférencier* in between songs, making jokes and regaling the audience or, in the case of Lennon, trying to rile them up ("Heil Hitler!"). Gradually, the seats filled. Just as the group hit its performing stride on stage, however, Koschmider had them evicted from Germany before the end of the calendar year, first blowing the whistle on Harrison's 17-year-old underage status, then reporting a minor act of vandalism by McCartney and Best; in reality, he was angry because the Beatles had breached their contract by playing at a rival venue, the Top Ten Club. Thus for the second time in a single lifetime, Bruno Koschmider found himself on the wrong side of history: first by fighting for the Nazis and then by firing the Beatles from his employ. All departed from Germany except Sutcliffe, who stayed behind with his new fiancé Kirchherr. Nevertheless, it would not be long before the Beatles returned triumphantly as professional performers. Many years later, Lennon well summarized the experience: "...I grew up in Hamburg."[12]

The fabled Lennon and McCartney songwriting partnership was born in Hamburg as well. With freedom to be outrageous, a desperate need to fill long sets, and little left to lose, they began to try out their own original material. Lennon's aggressive rock and roll leanings were tempered by McCartney's interests in branching out into other musical styles. As McCartney himself explained long after the fact:

> I could never see the difference between a beautiful melody and a cool rock 'n' roll song...—"Till There Was You," "My Funny Valentine"—I thought those were good tunes. The fact that we weren't ashamed of those leanings meant that the band *could* be a bit more varied. And there was a need for that, because we played cabaret a lot. Songs like "Till There Was You" and "Ain't She Sweet" would be the late-night cabaret material. They showed that we weren't just another rock 'n' roll group. The Lennon-McCartney song-writing collaboration was forming during that period.[13]

Their visual image also softened by degrees, even as their sound grew harder and more disciplined. Kirchherr photographed them in suits, and they discovered that a less scruffy appearance often translated into better paychecks.[14] They purchased higher quality instruments sporting respectable German and German-American brand names such as Rickenbacker, Höfner, and Ludwig, all later becoming associated with their iconic stage appearance.[15] In his diary at the time, Sutcliffe wrote how their musicianship was improving, with an aside that they were even playing "a German number"—possibly the Friedrich Hollaender classic, "Falling in Love Again" (see Chapter 6) which they would record live the following year.[16]

In 1961, the undiscouraged Williams arranged for the Beatles to return to Hamburg's Reeperbahn for an extended engagement at (appropriately enough) the Top Ten Club. Although this gig soon led to a falling out between

Williams and the group over commissions, it was also during this second stay in Germany that the Beatles made their first professional recordings as backup for singer Tony Sheridan, with German songwriter and bandleader Bert Kaempfert (1923–1980) producing.[17] Throughout 1962, this time with Brian Epstein as their new manager and (by mid-year) Ringo Starr as their new drummer, the Beatles returned to Hamburg for series of high-profile shows at the newly-opened Star-Club. Epstein was Jewish, gay, theatrical, and a skillful promoter; from day one he recognized the value of the German connection, encouraging the group to continue polishing their act as originally suggested by their "Exis" friends. Just before their arrival in April, however, the 21-year-old Stuart Sutcliffe — the person co-credited with Lennon for coming up with the Beatles brand name — had collapsed in school during painting class and died suddenly of a brain hemorrhage, leaving all those who knew him shocked and grief-stricken.[18] The Hamburg Star-Club performances of 1962 were poorly recorded, artificially re-mastered, and later released in 1977 as a Beatles artifact from about a year before they became world-famous.[19] The diversity of the play list anticipates the eclecticism that marked their heyday. Alongside original material and covers of Chuck Berry, Little Richard, and Carl Perkins, are several standards from a bygone era, including McCartney singing "Falling in Love Again," the song that made Marlene Dietrich famous back in 1930.

When they had first left Liverpool in 1960, the group formerly known as John Lennon's Quarrymen were little different from hundreds of other aspiring English bands; after returning from Hamburg, however, they had become The Beatles, both in name and sound. They had, in the popular slang amongst musicians, "gone to the crossroads."[20] In a less mythological sense, it would not be inaccurate to say that the German cabaret tradition played a crucial role in this development process. As early as 1960, after they had been initially deported from Germany, the change was evident. Thinking of themselves as failures, the group instead immediately found work and never had trouble finding it again.[21] Harrison later remarked, "And we probably looked German, too; very different from all the other groups, with our leather jackets. We looked funny and we played differently."[22] After being infamously rejected by the Decca label in 1962, Epstein obtained an audition for the band before George Martin of EMI, and though not overwhelmed by their early crude sound, signed the Beatles after being wowed (as was Epstein) with their rapid fire, stand-up wit — skills originally honed in the nightclubs of Hamburg with each group member acting as his own *conférencier* in between songs. After replacing Best with Starr as drummer — thus finally uniting the formidable Hamburg sound of the Beatles and the Hurricanes — the group was off to the races and inevitable domination of the pop charts. To sustain their popularity, Martin tapped into the group's resourcefulness and willingness to experiment with non-rock and roll forms — again, a trait that first manifested itself in Hamburg. Under his early guidance, the Beatles confidently and smoothly recorded pop tunes such as Burt Bacharach's "Baby It's You," previously a hit for the Shirelles.[23] One of the first Beatles shows after having hit the big time in 1963 was their November Command Performance at the Prince of Wales Theatre in London, where the group excitedly shared the stage with Marlene Dietrich and later giddily mugged photo ops with her. As Dietrich's biographer Donald Spoto wrote, "the quartet agreed with reporters that Dietrich was indeed one of the most elegant women in town."[24] Two years later in 1965, even as the group became more artsy and pretentious under Martin's direction, Lennon began to deliver song lyrics with a decidedly Existentialist flavor, such as "Norwegian Wood" and "In My Life" for their masterful, path-breaking LP, *Rubber Soul*.

Favoritism towards the German language continue to manifest itself in surprising ways during the Beatles' group and later individual performing careers. In 1964, they famously re-recorded two of their biggest hit songs for the German market, "Komm gib mir deine Hand" ("I Want to Hold Your Hand") and "Sie liebt Dich" ("She Loves You"). In 1966, during the Beatles' final German tour and trip to Hamburg, Harrison delighted fans by singing "Am Sonntag will mein Süßer mit mir segeln geh'n" ("On Sunday My Sweetheart Wants to Sail with Me"), originally recorded in 1929 by Dajos Béla, the same bandleader who originally helped to make "Just a Gigolo" famous (see Chapter 5). This was during the same era of the group's *Revolver* LP (with distinctive cover art by Klaus Voorman), in which Lennon continued his dalliance with Existential lyrics, epitomized by the Lennon and McCartney masterpiece "Nowhere Man." Three years later in 1969, as the group was beginning to fall apart, McCartney sang a spirited pigeon German-language version of "Get Back" ("Geh raus") during the same live, rooftop recording sessions that brought traffic to a halt on Abbey Road.[25] When Lennon broke solo with the Plastic Ono Band in 1970, he hired Voorman as his bassist, playing on most of Lennon's classic recordings from that period, one marked by more personal and politicized material such as "Working Class Hero."[26] Finally, during undated and unreleased recording sessions from the late 1970s (and not long before his tragic murder in 1980), Lennon returned to "Falling in Love Again," beginning as an acoustic German folk ballad but ending (in typical Hamburg fashion) with a Hitler voice parody in the coda.[27] It seems that, towards the end of his unexpectedly short life, Lennon's thoughts returned once again to Hamburg's Reeperbahn district, the geographic place on the map where he always claimed having grown up, despite being born in Liverpool.

As the Beatles went, so went the entire British Invasion. Of the myriad English, Aussie, and Canadian groups coming in their wake, however, few if any had a comparable German experience on their résumé. The Rolling Stones, despite the amazing longevity of the Jagger and Richards songwriting partnership, have always maintained a much closer adherence to the traditions of indigenous American blues and country music, and tended to emulate the Beatles only when they were direct professional competitors with each other. An early example of this tendency was the Jagger and Richards ballad "As Tears Go By" from late 1964, written as a response to Lennon and McCartney's "Yesterday," with both songs achieving hit status despite their breaking away from a strict rock and roll stylistic mode. The loss of innocence theme prevalent in these numbers is, for lack of a better description, far more adult and serious in tone than one is used to hearing on commercial radio from that era. While German *Kabarett* never claimed a monopoly on this sort of thing, it certainly embraced it, and there can be no denying that the Beatles' early forays into musical diversification were facilitated and bolstered by their youthful residency in Hamburg. This confident aptitude for bold experimentation within the routine and often banal simplicity of the pop music sphere in turn filtered out to anyone else listening to the Beatles' music, an audience which, by the mid–1960s, constituted a huge worldwide demographic.

While the Rolling Stones flirted with the boundaries of cabaret style, one of their prominent English musical compatriots embraced it fully. Marianne Faithful, Jagger's then girlfriend (and fodder for the tabloids) during the swinging London era of the late sixties, at age 17 successfully recorded "As Tears Go By" (before even the Stones did), then followed it up with her own relatively obscure but effective version of the Beatles' "Yesterday" in 1965. Her maternal ancestry was German-speaking and colorful: part–Jewish with family connections to Leopold von Sacher-Masoch of *Venus in Furs* fame (see Chapter 8) and a ballerina mother who once danced for Max Reinhardt and performed the works of Kurt Weill on stage. As the 1960s came to an end, Faithful reportedly inspired or helped to compose a number of well-known songs, including the Stones' powerful "Sister Morphine," which she co-wrote with Jagger.[28] By 1979, after a long struggle with personal demons and substance abuse, Faithful re-established her solo career with the acclaimed LP *Broken English*, emphasizing edgy, adult torch ballads designed for the newly-burgeoning alternative music scene (see Chapter 19). In 1985, she recorded Weill and Brecht's eternally topical "Ballad of a Soldier's Wife" for the group project *Lost in the Stars: A Tribute to Kurt Weill*. During the 1990s, she continued to perform the works of Weill and Brecht in productions of *The Threepenny Opera* and *The Seven Deadly Sins*. In 1996, Faithful released a well-received live LP, *Twentieth Century Blues*, consisting mostly of material by Weill and Brecht (plus two songs by Friedrich Hollaender), followed by a DVD, *Marianne Faithful Sings Kurt Weill* (1997), recorded live at the Montreal Jazz Festival. Thus at the close of the century, she found herself as the unlikely, leading exponent of German cabaret music among the post–World War II generation of Anglo-Americans who grew up listening to (and playing) rock and roll during the 1950s and 1960s.

In December 1968, a moment in time considered by many as be the artistic high-water mark of late–1960s popular music, Faithful appeared in a cancelled BBC television special, *The Rolling Stones Rock and Roll Circus*, wearing a formal gown and singing Mann and Goffin's "Something Better," a ballad of oblique, wistful yearning that could not be imagined coming from the Brill Building songwriting factory before the innovations of Bacharach and David (see Chapter 15).[29] The London sound stage for this event was memorable in that it was small, enclosed, and intimate. Bands alternated literally with circus performers. The audience, which included the performers, was itself in costume, while performers took turns acting as *conférencier*. The overall effect was not unlike that of a cabaret or vaudeville show, in which anything could happen and often did. Another guest star was an enthusiastic John Lennon (minus the other Beatles) sporting an extraordinary pick-up band ("The Dirty Mac"), with personnel including Eric Clapton on lead guitar, drummer Mitch Mitchell (of the Jimi Hendrix Experience), Keith Richards (playing bass), primal scream vocalist Yoko Ono, and Israeli classical violinist Ivry Gitlis. An intense, straightforward reading of Lennon's "Yer Blues" was followed by a startling free-form jam that seemed to combine every musical element known to the western world, and then some, all anticipating Lennon's early solo work with the Plastic Ono Band less than two years later. Then came the Who, fresh off tour and by then the world's best live band. Performing a telescoped version of Pete Townsend's first so-called rock opera, irreverently titled "A Quick One While He's Away," this group, one later associated with stadium-sized venues, began by singing shoulder-to-shoulder *a cappella*, then unleashing a song delivery of *Sturm und Drang* ("storm and stress") fury within the friendly confines of Wembley's Intertel Studio that would have made the German poets Goethe and Schiller proud. Audience and camera crew were left breathless. Consequently, and according to legend, producer Mick Jagger later scrapped the entire project, realizing that the Rolling Stones (who performed last in order) had in fact been badly upstaged by the Who, and probably Lennon as well.[30]

While the Who were soon to achieve deserved, widespread fame with their extended "rock opera" *Tommy* (1969), another London group initially enjoying considerable chart success was beginning to sink into undeserved commercial oblivion. The Kinks, led by main songwriter Ray Davies and his brother Dave on lead guitar, came from a more polished, sophisticated musical background than many of their British contemporaries, one which included immersion in jazz and the music hall tradition of their parents, the rough English equivalent of American and German vaudeville. By the mid–1960s, it was clear that the Kinks were not like most other groups; their material was prolific, varied, and introspective.[31] Large-scale touring did not agree with them and, like the Beatles, they rebelled early against the prevailing industry standards in this regard.[32] They preferred intimacy and audiences who listened attentively. Even as their record sales declined, their music became richer and more durable. In 1968, the group released *The Kinks Are the Village Green Preservation Society,* one of the earliest rock "concept" LPs and arguably among the very best, although it was ignored by the record-buying public. A year later in 1969 came *Arthur (or the Decline and Fall of the British Empire),* a somewhat better received project, possibly because it was a "rock opera" similar to the Who's *Tommy,* although *Arthur* was musically excellent in its own right. These "concept" LPs with unifying lyrical themes were possibly influenced by the recent (1966) commercial success of Kander and Ebb's Broadway "concept" musical *Cabaret* (see Chapter 16), and it is certainly true that Davies' idiosyncratic, restrained, and combative style has always reflected vaudeville and cabaret instincts. Davies became, in the words of critic Greil Marcus, "...a social critic, or more appropriate for rock 'n' roll, a social complainer"— not unlike the brilliant and tragic lyricist Marcellus Schiffer, whose work epitomized the Weimar period (see Chapter 6).[33] In 1970, the Kinks finally once again enjoyed full-fledged commercial success with their hit single *Lola,* a song celebrating colorful, sexually-ambiguous characters who could have stepped straight out of a Weimar-era Berlin cabaret. This belated comeback surely helped to keep the group going as long as it did, until 1996 when the Davies brothers finally both went solo and have securely stayed that way ever since.

When the substantial and durable recorded legacy of the British Invasion struck America like lightning during the 1960s, it did more than merely to bring contemporary American popular music back to the attention of its own countrymen. It also brought contemporary European traditions along with it as well. Foremost among these was the cabaret aesthetic of Germany, thanks mainly to the Beatles and all other groups, both Anglo and American, who were influenced by them. This approach featured, among many attractive qualities, an emphasis on direct one-on-one connection with audience members, combined with a performing ethos stressing that smaller was better, even as these same artists experimented with larger forms and more eclectic, international sources. The *Kleinkunst* of the British Invasion (though the descriptor is never used) ultimately placed its heady emphasis on short songs presented by small ensembles in preferably intimate venues, thus reinforcing prevailing industry economic trends long preceding the advent of postwar rock and roll. Weimar cabaret tradition deserves, at the very least, a nod of respect in this regard. This is certainly not to take all credit away from the U.S.; in fact, during the early the 1960s, and long before the Beatles became a household name, other branches of American pop music were beginning to take notice of earlier German models, apart from, and in addition to, the dazzling achievements of Louis Armstrong, Burt Bacharach and John Kander. One of these in particular had been labeled with the misnomer "folk music," but was about to be more or less dominated by a young upstart from Duluth, Minnesota. The repercussions of this takeover would soon extend into the seemingly unrelated realms of country and African American music, and finally result in the total breakdown of popular music categorization, surely much to the approval of the then 20-year-old artist who initiated the process. By 1970, when a solo John Lennon sang vehemently that he did not "believe in Zimmerman," in point of fact he was using a mode of song expression pioneered by the very same performer (and American rival) whom he was criticizing at that particular moment.

18. Singer-Songwriters Become Bankable

"If I hadn't gone to the Theatre de Lys and heard the ballad 'Pirate Jenny,' it might not have dawned on me to write them, that songs like these could be written."— Bob Dylan[1]

Infamously, Bob Dylan is accused as being the first person to give marijuana to the Beatles; be that as it may, Dylan should more often receive credit for inspiring the British quartet, more than that of any other contemporary artist, to cast aside their potentially stifling mode of popular cuteness and harmlessness to instead venture into the risky realm of serious adult songwriting.[2] In early 1965, John Lennon wrote and recorded "You've Got to Hide Your Love Away" for the blockbuster film *Help!*, the first full manifestation of Dylanesque influence on the Beatles' music, although Lennon had been experimenting with Dylan's distinctive style throughout the previous year. By the end of the decade, this highly personal (and sometimes politicized) approach was fully integrated into Lennon's bracing solo work, so much so that it was no longer generally remarked upon.[3] Thus the working class hero from Liverpool effectively appropriated whatever he was able to learn musically from a nomadic Jewish songwriter and song-interpreter of the Upper Midwest, born Robert Allen Zimmerman (about six months after Lennon) in Duluth, Minnesota, the same city that by the turn of the new century would be hosting spirited revivals of Kander and Ebb's *Cabaret* (see Introduction). Interestingly, Lotte Lenya, the same performer who would help make the original 1966 production of *Cabaret* a smash sensation, also seems to have had made a profound impression on the young and then-unknown Bob Dylan nearly five years prior to her last major stage role.

Immediately upon his 1959 graduation from high school in nearby Hibbing, Robert Zimmerman fled the Duluth area to the Twin Cities, where he lasted less than a year at the University of Minnesota, but also where he began to call himself Bob Dylan as a performer and admirer of Dylan Thomas' poetry. On sudden impulse, Dylan then hitchhiked to New York City, where he arrived in Lower Manhattan and Greenwich Village at the beginning of 1961. Here he was able to meet his musical idol Woody Guthrie (1912–1967), then hospitalized, and intermingle with the burgeoning folk music scene then being guided mostly by Pete Seeger and his followers. In less than a year he became a fixture on the coffeehouse scene, landing his own record deal with Columbia's legendary producer John Hammond. His first, self-titled LP, consisting of mostly cover songs, appeared in 1962. Sales were slight, however, and Dylan was in real danger of being dropped by his label when he made the bold decision to go for broke and record his own original material, beginning with "Blowin' in the Wind," a mature synthesis of Negro spiritual melody and Guthrie-like lyrics. *The Freewheelin' Bob Dylan* was released in May 1963 and was a riveting commercial breakthrough. In retrospect, the album could have easily been a one-shot phenomenon (like so many others), but even before its appearance Dylan had begun a profound transformation as a songwriter. In the slang parlance of performing artists, he (like his contemporaries, the Beatles) had already been to the "crossroads" of musical development, and now there would be no getting rid of him, which over the course of the next half century would prove to be mostly a good thing for attentive listeners of popular music.

Among all the people than Dylan came to know during those early years in Greenwich Village, none exerted more a positive influence on him than the late Suze Rotolo (1943–2011), his first serious girlfriend, and famously posing with him on the album cover of *Freewheelin'*.[4] Her Italian-American parents, like Pete Seeger, had been members of the Communist Party, and Rotolo enjoyed the bohemian upbringing of an artist, reading Shakespeare and studying Kandinsky.[5] As related in her memoirs, one of her earliest vivid memories was the 1954 off–Broadway revival of *The Threepenny Opera* at the Theatre de Lys in Greenwich Village and its subsequent cast recording featuring Lotte Lenya (see Chapter 4).[6] Later Rotolo began working at the Theatre de Lys as a stage hand and set artist, which she viewed as a second home around the same time Dylan came into her life in 1961.[7] In particular, she came to admire the plays and poetry of Kurt Weill's lyricist Bertolt Brecht who, like her parents and many of their friends, had suffered grievously due to his political beliefs. Because of then-raging McCarthyism in the U.S., and because of the blacklist, Rotolo observed during her adolescence that "Many lives were ruined as result."[8] She reminisced how "Brecht became a symbol for me during the Cold War."[9] By early 1963, Rotolo was working at the Sheridan Square Playhouse in rehearsals for a new production of *Brecht on Brecht (An Improvisation)*, a spoken and sung revue popularized by Lenya's performance during the previous year at the Theatre de Lys.[10] One of the six actors in the newest version of *Brecht* was an African American singing actress (taking Lenya's previous role) named Micki Grant. Rotolo persuaded Dylan to attend one of the rehearsals where he heard, among other numbers, Grant sing "Pirate Jenny" from *The Threepenny Opera*, making a profound and lasting impression on him, especially given current events then unfolding across the country with respect to the struggle for Civil Rights.[11]

Anyone doubting the powerful impact of this event on the 21-year-old Dylan's creative trajectory need only consult his own 2004 memoir, *Chronicles: Volume One*, written over four decades after the fact. Near the end of the final chapter ("River of Ice"), Dylan goes on for nearly five pages about his first close encounter with German cabaret music and, in particular, Weill's "Pirate Jenny." Recognizing an element of stark realism not to be found in most American folk music, he commented at length upon the novelty and strength of material being presented: "You couldn't call this a play, it was more like a stream of songs by actors who sang. I went there to wait for Suze and was aroused straight away by the raw intensity of the songs.... Songs with tough language. They were erratic, un-rhythmical and herky-jerky — weird visions.... The singers were thieves, scavengers or scallywags and they all roared and snarled."[12]

The young Dylan also immediately picked up on the fact that these deceptively complex works had not been written by itinerant folk singers; rather, the numbers were highly sophisticated arrangements disguised in a popular folk idiom. As he put it, "Woody [Guthrie] had never written a song like that. It wasn't a protest song or topical song and there was no love for people in it."[13] Referring specifically to Micki Grant's unusual presentation, Dylan recalled the lasting effect that it had on him: "The song that made the strongest impression was a show-stopping ballad, "A Ship the Black Freighter." Its real title was "Pirate Jenny," but I didn't hear that in the song so I didn't know what the real title was. It was sung by some vaguely masculine woman, dressed up like a scrubbing lady who performs petty tasks, goes about making up beds in a ratty waterfront hotel."[14]

As a budding songwriter at the time, Dylan noted that "I could see that the type of songs I was leaning towards singing didn't exist and I began to play with the form, trying to grasp it — trying to make a song that transcended the information in it, the character and the plot." Impressed by the "resilience and outrageous power" of "Pirate Jenny," Dylan resolved to ramp up his own songwriting skills recently beginning so promisingly with "Blowin' in the Wind." Looking back many years later, he marveled: "My little shack in the universe was about to expand into some glorious cathedral, at least in songwriting terms."[15] In effect, this was the moment that Bob Dylan said he decided to become a songwriter in earnest, which he proceeded to do with a vengeance.

One could also say that this moment marked the true birth of the singer-songwriter in American popular music, although Dylan has always disowned (perhaps rightfully) the moniker as being too narrow and confining.[16] *Freewheelin'* may have been mostly in the can by the time that he first heard Weill and Brecht's songs performed (the album would be released shortly thereafter), but the flood of outstanding, original Dylan material coming in its wake clearly bear the stamp of the Weimar musical stage. For example, signature anthems such as "The Times They Are a-Changin'" and "When the Ship Comes In" (both from 1964) are near direct quotes from Brecht's poetry, while Dylan, as the uneasy new leader of a relatively confined folk music scene, moved into progressively more varied and flexible musical arrangements, much in the same spirit as Kurt Weill's utilitarian and rule-bending *Gebrauchsmusik* from the 1920s. With respect to Dylan's songwriting, Alex Ross wrote, "The spirit of Berlin played on."[17] This is not to say, however, that Weill and Brecht were the only serious influences on Dylan during this period; on the contrary, there can be no denying the important role of the Beat Poetry movement during his formative years, and on just about every other artist then active on the Greenwich Village folk scene.[18] Even the corrosive atmosphere of bordello scenes from *Threepenny Opera* providing a nominal setting for "Pirate Jenny" had their American counterparts, and Dylan was keenly aware of these. His 1961 recording of the anonymous prostitute's lament, "House of the Risin' Sun," was taken directly from Dave Van Ronk's folk performing arrangement, and in turn was made into a British Invasion hit single by the Animals in 1964, via English folk sources drawing upon Dylan's recording. Certainly no musical tradition, not even Weimar cabaret, can claim a monopoly on this particular subject matter, although in this case they coincide. One thing is for certain, however; for the photo cover art of Dylan's 1965 album *Bringing It All Back Home*, he surrounded himself with some of his favorite things, including the album jacket of *Lotte Lenya Sings Berlin Theatre Songs by Kurt Weill*. Thus it is clear that by the mid–1960s Dylan had become a devotee of Weimar-era music recorded in Hamburg a decade earlier by one of its leading exponents (see Chapter 4).

In providing a quick overview of Dylan's formative influences, it would be remiss not to include a brief discussion of two venerable names frequently associated with his own; namely, those of Woody Guthrie and Pete Seeger (b. 1919).[19] While the unmistakable musical styles of Guthrie and Seeger are as purely American as apple pie, neither can they be one hundred percent divorced from the Weimar cabaret tradition. In the case of Guthrie, although his songs had a political edge from the get-go, this Brechtian side of his musical personality did not fully emerge until migration to California in 1936–1937 radicalized him.[20] After dust storms had ravaged his native Oklahoma and adopted home of Pampa, Texas, in 1933–1935, Guthrie hoboed his way to KFVD radio in Los Angeles, where he teamed with Maxine "Lefty Lou" Crissman for the highly-popular "Woody and Lefty Lou Show," earning enough money for the first time in his life to pronounce that "...I don't care what other people think about me." From this period stemmed many of his earliest classics such as "Do Re Mi," originally performed as a duet with Crissman.[21] Interestingly, this was the same period that Friedrich Hollaender (see Chapter 6) and other musical Jewish refugees from Weimar Germany began to arrive in Hollywood to earn a living, although there is no evidence that Guthrie, more of a hillbilly singer than a conservatory composer, ever came into direct contact with this foreign group. At this point, however, socially conscious influences did begin to exert themselves on the fiery troubadour, including biblical imagery (which he always possessed), World War I–era "Wobblie" protest songs such as "Joe Hill," and even nominal contacts with the American Communist Party.[22] By 1939, Guthrie was keeping company with the likes of novelist John Steinbeck, at whose "Grapes of Wrath" benefit concert he was introduced to a 19-year old Pete Seeger. As musicologist Alan Lomax (1915–2002) later wrote, "You can date the renaissance of American folk song from that night."[23] Strict Americana aside, as late as 1948 Guthrie was still writing lyrics such as "Eisler on the Go," a mournful homage to the Weimar composer émigré Hanns Eisler, one of the first high-profile deportee victims of McCarthyism.[24]

Pete Seeger was the son and musical heir of Charles Seeger, the forward-thinking musical scholar who did so much during the New Deal to promote and bring respectability to indigenous American folk traditions (see Chapter 11).[25] Seeger the elder, with encouragement from Lomax, was among the first formally trained musicians to break with the elitist attitude of the classical tradition towards folk music, and was later joined in this regard by important figures such as Aaron Copland and Marc Blitzstein.[26] Seeger the younger, at age 16, had his ears transformed in 1936 by attending (with his father) the Ninth Annual Mountain Dance and Folk Festival in Asheville, North Carolina, where he first heard the five-string banjo played with aplomb by white performers such as Samantha Bumgartner and Bascom Lamar Lunsford, the latter lending to a delighted Seeger his own instrument.[27] After playing the five-string, there would be no going back for him. By some strange confluence of fate, around the same time (1936) the Seegers were in Asheville, Kurt Weill and Lotte Lenya were not far away in Chapel Hill, North Carolina, beginning their first American collaboration with playwright Paul Green, although there is no evidence that the two parties were aware of each other. Like the case of Guthrie and Hollaender both in Hollywood not long afterwards, the physical proximity of Seeger and Weill in North Carolina almost suggest that the merging of classical and popular music traditions during this time and place had some kind of magnetic geographic coordinates, but in this we digress. After adopting a Marxist political stance during the late 1930s, Seeger's career later survived the McCarthy era through some mysterious combination of luck and tenacity, with his original song "Where Have All the Flowers Gone" recorded by Marlene Dietrich.[28] By the time Dylan arrived in Greenwich Village circa 1961, Seeger was the elder statesman of the folk music scene there. Initially a powerful mentor to Dylan, Seeger was inevitability alienated by his younger colleague's embrace of rock and roll's high decibel levels and growing apolitical stance, notwithstanding Dylan's "Talkin' John Birch Society Blues," which he was barred from performing on the Ed Sullivan Show in 1963. Nevertheless, Seeger's substantial influence on Dylan eventually filtered out to the latter's innumerable artistic offspring, the more distinguished of which included the likes of Bruce Springsteen and Joan Baez. By the mid–1960s, Dylan had shied away from the earnest, self-important image of a "protest" singer-songwriter, but in the process enjoyed a bigger audience than the more controversial Seeger and Guthrie ever enjoyed individually or combined.

Meanwhile, the 1960s and 1970s rolled on, and with them, songs of "tough language" and "weird visions" first noticed by Dylan in *Brecht on Brecht* began to infiltrate the popular vernacular of hit parade radio. Dylan himself rejected the artsy pretensions of late 1960s psychedelia in favor of exploring American roots music and its related European-African folk counterparts. This arresting journey of discovery has continued more or less unabated over the last five decades, and its musical offshoots are too numerous to catalogue in a confined space such as this study. Paul Simon, 2007 recipient of the Gershwin Prize, an honor also later bestowed on Stevie Wonder, Burt Bacharach (see Chapter 15) and Paul McCartney (see Chapter 17), had his own long and distinguished career jumpstarted in 1965 when Dylan producer Tom Wilson decided to overdub "Sounds of Silence" with rock and roll instrumentation. Short-lived but widely-imitated American groups such as the Byrds and Lovin' Spoonful had success with a similar folk rock style, fusing lyrical sophistication with instrumental pizzazz. By 1966–1967, other new, distinctive voices began to appear on both coasts stateside. Lou Reed's Velvet Underground emerged from New York City with disreputable, cabaret-like song titles such as "Venus in Furs," "Heroin," and "Femme Fatale," the latter originally sung by the German-born Nico (aka Christa Päffgen), a seeming throwback to the female stage vamps of the Weimar period. In 1967, Jim Morrison of the Doors, a former USC film student of Josef von Sternberg (see Chapter 10), recorded Weill and Brecht's "Alabama Song" for the group's eponymous first LP which, for many of us, was our first express introduction to the Weimar world of *Mahagonny* (see Chapter 13).

During the same period, singer-songwriters of extraordinary talent began to appear outside of the U.S., and were honored outside of the U.S. as well. By 1968, Irish-born Van Morrison had established a still-running solo career with the landmark album *Astral Weeks*, a jazz collaboration featuring original gems such as the 10-minute "Madame George," an extended, expressionist meditation on trans-sexual love (later covered wonderfully by cabaret revivalist Marianne Faithful) that would have fit in perfectly well within the anything-goes entertainment atmosphere of 1920s Berlin. Outstanding Canadian singer-songwriters such as Leonard Cohen, Gordon Lightfoot, and Joni Mitchell (aka Roberta Joan Anderson) all owe indisputable debts to this particular facet of Dylan's art. Idiosyncratic American-born artists such as Tom Waits and John Prine have always closely aligned themselves with more intimate, informal performing venues normally associated with cabaret. Canadian-born Neil Young, though exhibiting an ongoing penchant for political and environmental concerns in his songwriting only since 1970, really began to hit his stride as a solo artist in 1968–1969 after recruiting his long-term backup group Crazy Horse (formerly the Rockets), arguably America's finest, glorified bar band, from the Whisky a Go-Go on West Hollywood's Sunset strip. Notably, several of the aforementioned performers (the Doors, the Byrds, Van Morrison) did extended stints at this American west coast version of cabaret during the mid–1960s. Perhaps the most adventurous of the Whiskey a Go-Go alumni was Frank Zappa (1940–1993) and the Mothers of Invention who by 1966, like the Dadaist art (see Chapter 1) which inspired Zappa, were taking humorous musical pot shots at anything resembling pretension, Dylan and the Beatles not excepted. It should therefore come as no surprise that before the end of the decade, Zappa and his band of provocateurs made a touring pilgrimage to Berlin, resulting in a series of memorable recordings, including the cabaret-like instrumentals "Overture to a Holiday in Berlin" and "Holiday in Berlin, Full Blown."[29] In the true spirit of cabaret, the witty and irrepressible Zappa was famous for acting as his own *conférencier* during live performances. Returning the compliment posthumously, the city of Berlin named a street frequently associated with the popular music industry after him in 2007 (Frank-Zappa-Staße), while the German city of Bad Doberan has sponsored an annual musical festival in Zappa's honor since 1990.

Among all of these accomplished performers, and perhaps second only to Dylan himself in terms of prolific, consistent quality, is Randy Newman, often seeming to combine the astringent song lyrics of Fred Ebb with the compositional versatility of John Kander into a single musical personality. Equally well-versed in the seemingly opposite worlds of classical music (nephew of film-score composer Alfred Newman) and New Orleans boogie-woogie rock and roll, Newman's professional songwriting career has spanned over half a century, successfully covering almost every popular genre, although he is still barely a household name at best.[30] Like many of his best competitors in the field (Bob Dylan, Paul Simon, Lou Reed, Leonard Cohen), Newman is Jewish; unlike most of them, however, he has been a fixture on the Hollywood movie scene for over 30 years, resulting in a very wide public exposure for his Academy Award–winning work, if not his name as a songwriter. His startling transition from eccentric, offbeat 1960s–1970s solo artist to 20 Oscar nominations (and still counting) for Best Original Song was possibly best explained by critic Greil Marcus, who noted that Newman is "...a singer whose songs contain an astonishing affection for every American ... cannot be satisfied with the attention of an elite, of critics and a few more, because a cult contradicts the best impulses of his work."[31] As for his extensive non-movie play list, its incredibly wide-ranging and fearlessly acerbic subject matter can read like a thematic catalogue of similar material appearing on cabaret stages of the late Weimar period. A brief sampling of these include nationalist martial aggression ("Political Science"); celebration of the grotesque ("Burn On" and "Davy the Fat Boy"); predatory sexual obsession ("Suzanne"); vampires, ghosts, and femme fatales ("Last Night I Had a Dream"); strip tease ("You Can Leave Your Hat On"); sympathy for anti-heroes and villains ("Lonely at the Top" and Little Criminals"); racism both blatant and proud ("Sail Away," "Yellow Man" and "Rednecks"); hostility towards conventional religion ("God's Song"); unbridled greed ("It's Money That I Love"); fascist moral decay ("In Germany Before the War"); and innocent prudishness confronted by decadence ("Mama Told Me Not to Come").[32] In general, Randy Newman has proved once again the old adage that to effectively mock something one must have a true affection for the object of satire.

One of the most remarkable aspects of this long and complicated process is that truly independent musical forms such as the blues and country music were eventually tinged by the Weimar influence as well, probably the inevitable result of cabaret's rapid assimilation into American culture during the mid–20th century plus the naturally anti-insular nature of American folk music itself. In the field of country music, one of the earliest embracers of this foreign quality was the late, great Johnny Cash (1930–2003) who, in addition to being a Dylan fan and collaborator, had, like many other musicians of his generation (Burt Bacharach, Elvis Presley), honorably completed a military stint in Germany during the early 1950s. During the 1970s, Cash made it a point to perform in Germany and record some of his hits in German, including "I Walk the Line" ("Wer kennt den Weg"). Cash also found himself to be a kindred spirit with other prominent country artists who enjoyed working with Dylan or owed to him a degree of artistic debt, including fellow future "Highwaymen" Willie Nelson, Waylon Jennings, and Kris Kristofferson. For that matter, one could easily argue that non-mainstream C&W genres with attempted categorizations of "outlaw country" and "alternative country" simply refer to those performers following Dylan into an older, partly–German tradition of playing edgier material in smaller venues. A good example of this would be the understated, introspective recordings of Emmy Lou Harris, especially over the last two decades with innovative producers such as Daniel Lanois and T-Bone Burnett. At the other end of this spectrum is the highly-publicized Dixie Chicks flap of 2003, in which the superstar group was essentially punished by former fans and its record label for making controversial political statements on stage.[33]

Alex Ross has perceptively written that during the last century "African American composers appropriated European material into self-invented forms of blues and jazz."[34] It is certainly true that African American artists ventured into the realm of political commentary via popular music long before the Weimar influence began to exert itself stateside. Prominent examples included Paul Robeson, who like Pete Seeger was pilloried for his Marxist sympathies, Louisiana bluesman Lead Belly (aka Huddie Ledbetter), thanks in part to his close association with Woody Guthrie, and of course jazz singer extraordinaire Billie Holiday, whose 1939 recording of "Strange Fruit" still retains the power to shock, offend, and inspire.[35] By the Civil Rights era of the early 1960s, it was natural that rhythm and blues, gospel, and soul music should become more politicized. Taking the lead in this respect were groups such as the Staple Singers, led by the incredible (and still active) Mavis Staples, often performing on the same stages as Dylan, Seeger, Joan Baez, and other socially-conscious songwriters from the Greenwich Village scene. As early as 1963, the Staples had recorded "Blowin' in the Wind," making them the first African American group to cover Dylan's songs, a practice they would continue throughout their career. Just as a young, impressionable Dylan witnessed Micki Grant singing Weill and Brecht, so within a few years would black pop artists be routinely covering Dylan's material, no matter how one chose to classify it. As for Dylan, he still lodges objections to any narrow definitions, especially with respect to African American performers:

> Topical songs weren't protest songs. The term "protest singer" didn't exist any more than the term "singer-songwriter." You were a performer or you weren't, that was about it — a folksinger or not one.... I tried to explain later that I didn't think I was a protest singer, that there'd been a screwup. I didn't think I was protesting anything any more than I thought Woody Guthrie songs were protesting anything. I didn't think of Woody as a protest singer. If he is one, then so is Sleepy John Estes and Jelly Roll Morton. What I was hearing pretty regularly, though, were rebellion songs and those really moved me.[36]

All definitions aside, by the late 1960s high-profile black recording artists were embracing political content in their work, both race and non-race related.[37] Some of the more prominent ones included Jimi Hendrix ("Star-Spangled Banner"), Sly and the Family Stone ("Everyday People"), and James Brown ("I Don't Want Nobody to Give Me Nothing").[38] It is now difficult to conceive that such widespread, crossover politicizing in popular music had been unimaginable only a few years previous when Dylan sat watching and listening to 1963 rehearsals of "Pirate Jenny."

Greil Marcus has thoroughly documented the meteoric rise of socially-conscious African American pop music during the early 1970s and its swift retreat immediately thereafter. After the premature death of Hendrix in 1970 and Sly Stone's defiant rejection of audience expectations in 1971 with *There's a Riot Goin' On*, the breach for heady soul music was immediately filled by a host of talented black artists.[39] Leading the pack (not too surprisingly) was Motown and Marvin Gaye, whose 1971 landmark LP *What's Goin' On* conclusively proved that a totally self-contained and politically controversial pop recording artist did not necessarily have to be white. Other Motown artists, most notably the Temptations ("Papa Was a Rolling Stone") quickly followed suit, although the Tempts had been putting objective street reality into their songs as early as 1968 with the hit single "Cloud Nine." By 1972–1973, similar works by other artists proliferated across the charts. A small sampling of these included Curtis Mayfield's "Superfly" and "Freddie's Dead" (from the *Superfly* film soundtrack); War's "Slipping into Darkness" and "The World Is a Ghetto"; the O'Jays "Backstabbers" and "Love Train"; the Undisputed Truth's "Smiling Faces Sometimes"; and, Motown's crowning achievement in this genre, the sublime 1973 album *Innervisions* by future Gershwin Prize–winner Stevie Wonder, featuring among its tracks "Too High," "Higher Ground," and "Living for the City."[40] After 1973, however, black "protest" music seemed to vanish from the mainstream airwaves practically overnight, and quickly replaced by more bankable, non-political forms of dance music (mostly disco and funk) that reached even larger commercial audiences.[41] The entire cycle was eerily reminiscent of Dylan's own repudiation of the Greenwich Village folk scene about a decade earlier.

Recently things seemed to come full circle on May 29, 2012, as a 71-year-old Dylan was presented with the Presidential Medal of Freedom for lifetime contributions to American culture, awarded to him, appropriately enough, by the nation's first African American President. At no point during the White House ceremony was there any mention of Weimar cabaret or Kurt Weill or *Kleinkunst*, and to have done so would have probably been inappropriate given the occasion. As emphasized within these pages, Dylan's formative influences have been vast and continuous, as were those of the Beatles; in the final analysis, original German components to their music constitute only a single facet of very complex artistic personalities. Nevertheless, such a component is there to be found. In Dylan's case, a misfit kid from the Iron Range of northern Minnesota discovering excitement in the 1950s rock and roll of Little Richard and Buddy Holly soon afterwards found himself entranced by introspective, adult sensibilities of cabaret. The same may be said for an entire generation of voracious music consumers coming of age during the 1960s and 1970s, although most of us were certainly less conscious of it at the time. By the mid–1970s, however, it appears that the previously unconscious nature of this source inspiration was beginning to make its way more into the cognitive forefront of musical creative efforts, particularly in America and Great Britain. As the popular music industry of that era came to fully embrace a do-it-yourself, independent approach to record making, the latter half of the baby boomer generation simultaneously began to show greater awareness of history, geography, and the pre–World War II origins of their favorite performing traditions.

19. Adoption by the Alternative Scene

"I was determined this great artist [Lotte Lenya]
should be reviewed."— Patti Smith[1]

In late 1995, as the last century began to wind down, Bob Dylan toured briefly but memorably together with Patti Smith, sometimes singing duets together on stage that have since become a bootlegger's treasurer trove (especially on YouTube), in addition to the source of numerous photo op favorites. The two artists always had mutual admiration for each other's work, and this good feeling clearly comes across in images and recordings from that period. Both also had a Lotte Lenya connection, as shall be seen in a moment. Though only five years younger than Dylan, the Chicago-born Smith probably deserves as much credit as anyone for injecting some much needed life and intelligence into the realm of popular music during the 1970s, at a time in which many recording stars from the 1950s and 1960s (Dylan was an exception) seemed to have faded from cultural relevance.[2] Smith spent a seven-year bohemian apprenticeship in New York City during the late 1960s and early 1970s, performing music, doing journalism, becoming a published poet-playwright, and famously (in retrospect), living with photographer Robert Mapplethorpe (1946–1989). After forming the Patti Smith Group in 1974, she released her first acclaimed album, *Horses* (1975), and has pretty much continued to delight or provoke audiences with her bracing, eclectic work ever since. Years before audiences had heard of her name, however, Smith (like Dylan before her), had a series of vivid and impressionable encounters with the on-going musical legacies of Kurt Weill, Bertolt Brecht, and Lotte Lenya.

Throughout her engaging and award-winning memoir *Just Kids* (2010), Smith recounts in almost loving detail her repeated exposure to Weimar music drama during her early years in New York City. After returning from a pilgrimage to the Montmartre district of Paris ("city of our dreams"), the French birthplace of cabaret, Smith met folklorist-collector Harry Everett Smith, at the time working on an experimental film inspired by Brecht, and won his friendship by reciting lines from "Pirate Jenny."[3] Soon afterwards, she was invited to screen bits from his cinematic take on Weill and Brecht's *The Rise and Fall of the City of Mahagonny*, and the experience stayed with her.[4] In 1970, she found herself posing as Robert Mapplethorpe's first photographic model along side a Lotte Lenya recording of Weill's Berlin songs, in imitation of Dylan from his *Bringing It All Back Home* (see Chapter 18).[5] In 1971, Smith arm-twisted *Rolling Stone* editor Jan Wenner into allowing her to do a glowing review of a new double LP anthology by Lotte Lenya, whom she praised as "a strong feminine presence."[6] That same year (1971) *Creem* magazine published Smith's terrific poem "Autobiography" in which she cites Lenya and Dylan in the same breath as her main musical influences. In early 1971, she celebrated the birthday (February 10) of Bertolt Brecht with an improvised performance at St. Mark's Church by reading "Mack the Knife" to guitar accompaniment from Lenny Kaye, her future bandleader.[7] This was followed up on the anniversary of Arthur Rimbaud's death (November 10), billed as "Rock and Rimbaud," with a reading of Kurt Weill's American-era standard "Speak Low."[8] By this time, Smith had Jane Friedman as a press agent, who had previously worked with the likes of Lenya, Gypsy Rose Lee, and Josephine Baker.[9] Thus Patti Smith appears to have become a cabaret disciple long before she was transformed by the media into a high priestess and godmother of the New York City alternative music scene.

In the immediate wake of Smith's exposure to a wide listening public rode the exciting (and often frightening) new wave of American punk rock groups, most of whom were alumni of New York's CBGB club scene. Unquestionably the most influential (yet commercially marginal and ultimately tragic) of these were the Ramones from Forest Hills, Queens. Bassist-songwriter Dee Dee Ramone, aka Douglas Colvin (1951–2002), in many ways represented the soul of the group, acting as a tough buffer between singer Joey Ramone, aka Jeffry Hyman (1951–2001), and guitarist Johnny Ramone, aka John Cummings (1948–2004), who were usually at loggerheads over creative, political, and personal issues. Colvin was the son of an American GI and German immigrant mother who spent a good part of his teen years in 1960s Berlin. After the Ramones exploded out of the New York City landscape in 1976 with a breakthrough album that defied all criticism, the remaining 20 years of their existence as a group saw them consistently exhibit a fixation on German points of reference when writing and recording original material. These ranged from the neo–Nazi overtones of "Blitzkrieg Bop" to the anti–Marxist sentiments of "Havana Affair." One of their final recordings, the intense "Born to Die in Berlin," has a verse sung-shouted in German language through a megaphone. Whether these devices were used out of true conviction or merely to provoke the so-called Love Generation is beside the point; this was the public image they chose to present and it was quite effective. As a group, they were to rock and roll what Trude Hesterberg (see Chapter 12) was to cabaret: an essential component but also, in retrospect, politically incorrect and outcasts. All in all, as historian Peter Gay once described the essence of Weimar culture (see Introduction), the Ramones, like most of the dynamic punk rock movement of their milieu, were the ultimate cultural outsiders become insiders for a very brief moment in time.

Meanwhile, on the U.S. West Coast (in Los Angeles), a less militant but no less interesting form of new wave popular music was taking hold during the late 1970s. Foremost among these California bands was X, still active to this date, featuring lead vocalist Excene Cervenka (aka Christene Cervenka), bassist John Doe (aka John Duchac), guitarist Billy Zoom (aka Tyson Kindell), and drummer DJ Bonebrake. The group's producer for their acclaimed first album, *Los Angeles* (1980), was Ray Manzarek, former keyboardist for the Doors and, along with his deceased band-mate Jim Morrison, a former USC film student of Josef von Sternberg (see Chapter 10). In 1967, it had been the Doors that introduced Weill and Brecht's "Alabama Song"— a work originally premiered by Lotte Lenya in 1927 for a German audience (see Chapter 3)— to whole new generation of listeners, and (it should be added), counted a young Patti Smith among their huge fan base. Manzarek successfully nurtured X into becoming the musical and spiritual successors to the Doors, as well as the new wave torchbearers for the cabaret tradition in L.A. Staples from X's play list such as "We're Desperate" could easily speak for an entire lost generation of Weimar cabaret performers.

In England similar things were happening. During the early 1970s, David Bowie had risen to prominence with a combination of versatile, chameleon-like musical excellence and outrageous, androgynous stage persona that would have been recognizable to most Weimar cabaret audiences two generations earlier. Later Bowie (like Morrison before him) would record the "Alabama Song" and participate in a film project ("Just a Gigolo") that would succeed in bringing Marlene Dietrich briefly out of retirement (see Chapter 5). Bowie's near–British contemporary Bryan Ferry of Roxy Music also found a steady commercial niche utilizing a more traditional, cabaret-like presentation both for his solo and group recordings. Among these are several albums of pre–rock and roll standards, the latest being *As Time Goes By* (1999), notable for its inclusion of Kurt Weill's "September Song" and Friedrich Hollaender's "Falling in Love Again." Like the Ramones (who came shortly after him), the politically conservative Ferry has occasionally fallen afoul of liberal fans with his profuse praise for prominent artists of the Third Reich such as Leni Riefenstahl and Albert Speer.

The real alternative music action in Great Britain, however, began in 1976 with the appearance of the Sex Pistols, the Clash, and countless other English punk groups that followed them. The do-it-yourself, devil-may-care approach and attitude of these bands were truly in the spirit and tradition of Christopher Isherwood's semi-fictional Sally Bowles (see Chapter 7). Most of them were short-lived but far from forgotten. The most notorious were the Sex Pistols, whose abrasive 1977 album *Never Mind the Bollocks, Here's the Sex Pistols* remains a benchmark for musical provocateurs everywhere. Many of their song lyrics seem to superimpose the history of Germany onto England. "Holidays in the Sun" references both the Berlin Wall and the same Bergen-Belsen concentration camp that came to haunt the Dietrich family (see Chapter 5); "Sub-Mission" compares sexual seduction to a submarine mission, vaguely U-boat in type; "Anarchy in the U.K." recalls the chaotic beginning and end of the Weimar Republic; "God Save the Queen" bashes the monarchy system retained by England but discarded by Germany after the Kaiser; "No Feelings" harks back to the German New Objectivity of the 1920s, both as a modus operandi of scorn and as a tool for survival; "Pretty Vacant" declares a firm disbelief in but also persistent need for illusions, a favorite theme among earlier cabaret songwriters. Lastly, the infamous on-stage antics of the group recalled the Dadaist movement of the early Weimar era, with its withering, relentless attack on anything considered respectable in society.

In terms of longevity and versatility, certainly the most dynamic figure to emerge from the British new wave of the 1970s has been Elvis Costello (aka Declan Patrick MacManus), whose early recordings with his group the Attractions occasionally veered towards pro-fascist or anti-fascist themes (sometimes one could never be quite sure which), especially on the bracing 1979 LP *Armed Forces*, originally titled *Emotional Fascism* ("Two Little Hitlers"). Around this same time, Costello committed a major PR gaff by privately using the "N" word in reference to James Brown and Ray Charles, and has pretty much spent the rest of his career doing penance for it. By the 1990s, Costello's status as one of his generation's leading songwriters had become readily apparent, as was his encyclopedic knowledge of past songwriting masters. In 1997, his performance of Kurt Weill's "Lost in the Stars" was featured on the exemplary tribute album *September Songs*, an interesting selection for Costello given that this number was the cornerstone of Weill's last Broadway musical, a poignant meditation on racial discrimination at the dawn of the American Civil Rights era (see Chapter 11). The following year (in 1998), Costello, a voracious collaborator in the true cabaret tradition, continued his ongoing association with Marlene Dietrich's former bandleader, Burt Bacharach, releasing an entire LP of originals, *Painted from Memory*, consisting of broken, bittersweet love songs and highly sophisticated arrangements similar to those created by

Bacharach and David for Dionne Warwick three decades before (see Chapter 15).[10]

Another great collaborator of the postwar British generation has worked with Costello, among many, many others. Brian Eno first came to prominence as Bryan Ferry's partner with Roxy Music, but by 1974 had embarked on a fruitful, lifelong journey of musical experimentation, sometimes solo but more often with other artists. During the late 1970s, Eno worked with David Bowie on three of the latter's most acclaimed LPs, *Low* (1977), *Heroes* (1977), and *Lodger* (1979), the first two recorded fully or partly in West Berlin's legendary Das Hansa Tonstudio ("Hansa Studio by the Wall") near Potsdamer Platz, while Bowie shared an apartment with fellow German traveler Iggy Pop (aka James Osterberg) in Marlene Dietrich's old Schöneberg neighborhood.[11] The German influence also rubbed off on the former Stooges front man as he worked with Bowie to record two of his most famous albums at Hansa, *The Idiot* (1977) and *Lust for Life* (1977). Many of the songs from these sessions, not unexpectedly, are sprinkled with German allusions, including themes that had been popular in Weimar cabaret. For example, Pop's "Fall in Love with Me" (from *Lust for Life*) makes direct reference to Berlin, as well as indirect reference to the lyric Marlene Dietrich first made famous. During this same period, Eno also found time to work with the American new wave group Talking Heads (led by David Byrne) on three seminal albums, *More Songs About Buildings and Food* (1978), *Fear of Music* (1979), and *Remain in Light* (1980), all of which helped to establish and secure the band's long-term reputation. The opening track from *Fear of Music* ("I Zimbra") is a musical setting of a poem by Hugo Ball, one of the founders of the Dadaist movement in Zurich during World War I (see Chapter 1).[12] Possibly more than any individual, it was Eno who helped both British and American bands from the 1970s discover their innate German cabaret instincts as they matured artistically.

Hip-hop music also emerged during the late 1970s, concurrent with punk rock.[13] Though fiercely independent and original by its very nature, African American street music had already been touched by political themes via Top-40 soul music from the late 1960s and early 1970s (see Chapter 18), and when mainstream radio began to abandon this volatile topicality after 1973, it was gradually appropriated by Bronx artists working mostly outside of the establishment system. In 1982, Grandmaster Flash and the Furious Five released "The Message," overtly combining infectious dance music with serious social commentary. The first hip-hop group to enjoy massive success by blending dance music, street poetry, and socio-economic awareness, however, was RUN DMC of Queens, whose bold and unlikely amalgamation of musical styles (R&B, hard rock, electronic) found big audiences both inside and outside of black urban ghettos.[14] Whether these artists had ever heard of names like

Weill or Dietrich is questionable, but there is not much difference between the lyric sentiment of a track like RUN DMC's "Wake Up" and Friedrich Hollaender's "Münchhausen" from the early 1930s. By the end of the 1980s, the media misnomer "gangster rap" had come into wide circulation, usually applied to innovative (and selectively obscene) purveyors of agitprop such as Public Enemy and Ice-T (aka Tracy Marrow). In point of fact, much of this music persona was a direct descendant of Mackie Messer or Mack the Knife, the great granddaddy and modern prototype for all gangster-themed popular songs.[15]

The final two decades of the 20th century saw hosts of popular artists from both sides of the Atlantic borrow and appropriate musical bits and pieces from the Weimar cabaret legacy. The impossible-to-categorize Prince (aka Prince Rogers Nelson), a Minnesota native (like Bob Dylan), came into his own during the early 1980s and has been defying audience expectations ever since, while somehow making a decent living in the process. Whether being political ala "Sign 'o' the Times" (1987), personal, or scatological, his catchy songs, covers, and live performances are often laced with a substantial dose of camp humor and subtle irony, reminiscent of cabaret revue's scandalous heyday. Another Grammy-winning artist gaining prominence during the early 1980s was Cyndi Lauper, whose exuberant debut LP (1983) included "Time After Time," a massive, much-covered hit that might as well have been written about the tenacious real-life relationship between Kurt Weill and Lotte Lenya. Lauper, who is of German and Swiss heritage, also later (in 2006) found time and inclination to debut on Broadway in Weill and Brecht's *The Threepenny Opera*. Her first group, before becoming famous, was named the Blue Angels, in partial homage to Marlene Dietrich.[16] Other female performers coming into the public eye during the late 1980s, sometimes sporting a gay or bisexual image, seemed to update the cabaret style for a new generation of listeners. Suzanne Vega's first album (1985) explicitly held up Dietrich as a role model ("Marlene on the Wall" and "Freeze Tag"), while Tracy Chapman's "Talkin' 'Bout a Revolution" (1988) continued the old Weimar tradition of blending agitprop and entertainment.[17] Arguably the most brilliant and melancholy of these late 20th century alternative figures, however, was Kurt Cobain (1967–1994) of Nirvana, whose introspective lyrics of bitter irony hit an unforeseen chord of mass appeal during the early 1990s. Remarkably, Nirvana could be effective playing loudly or softly. They seemed equally at home in quiet acoustic arrangements or ferocious, amplified attacks led by the left-handed Cobain's blistering Stratocaster barrage. Many of these songs recalled the doomed *Kabarett* genius of Marcellus Schiffer (see Chapter 6) with their disapproving view of consumer fads, as epitomized by the smash single, "Smells Like Teen Spirit" (1991).

All things considered, the group that surely best exemplifies the inescapable influence of German music on Anglo-American pop over the last four decades is Dublin's very own U2, a band taking its ambiguous name from a fictional German submarine. After establishing its superstar status with early masterpieces such as the politically-themed *War* (1983), U2 successfully branched out to expand its sound and audience by working with Brian Eno and Daniel Lanois on *The Unforgettable Fire* (1984), and later reaching the pinnacle of its initial popularity with *The Joshua Tree* (1987).[18] A series of artistic missteps during the late 1980s, however, resulted in diminished commercial status by the end of the decade, and credible rumors began to circulate that the band was on the verge of breaking up. At this crucial juncture, a seemingly eccentric decision was made by the group to visit Berlin for improvised recording sessions at Hansa, again with Eno and Lanois as producer and engineer. Like so many others before and after them, the group found themselves inspired by Berlin's eternally thriving club culture and the emotionally stripped down style of industrial music being played there — all continuing legacies of Weimar New Objectivity (see Chapter 9). In Germany (immediately after the fall of the Berlin Wall), U2 learned the fine art of reducing emotional outpouring in song to better emphasize those emotions which remained or were left unspoken. Their touchstone album *Achtung Baby* was released in late 1991 to nearly universal acclaim, and in large thanks to this Berlin rejuvenation, the band has been going strong ever since.[19]

As the last century began drawing to a close, German filmmaker Wim Wenders released *Until the End of the World* (1991), a dreary, apocalyptic glimpse into the future that mostly confused the limited audiences who screened it. The soundtrack to the movie, however, was far more commercially successful than the film, and with good reason. It featured across-the-board performances by some of the finest alternative recording artists from the previous 25 years. The lynchpin to the album was the film title track, recently recorded in Berlin by U2 and previewing their then-upcoming release of *Achtung Baby*.[20] Other artists showcased in the project included Talking Heads, Neneh Cherry, Lou Reed, R.E.M., Elvis Costello, Nick Cave, Patti Smith, Daniel Lanois, T-Bone Burnett, Jane Siberry, and k.d. lang — all artists sympathetic with the German cabaret ethos to varying degrees and comfortable with spiritual themes always having been at the heart of the genre. The soundtrack provides a good summation for the bleak but transcendent worldview of diverse independent artists making music from that era, most of whom are still active in the industry. Their cumulative mood and tone are not all that different from those found in club music coming out of Weimar-era Berlin. This was over 20 years ago. Since then, alternative pop has changed little except perhaps to intensify and become even more universal in scope than it was during the early 1990s. Cabaret, which always boasted an international, inclusive spirit as it biggest selling point, now appears to be one of the few things that most people everywhere can happily relate to in one form or another. It is no longer purely French, or German, or American; during the 21st century, cabaret has gone global.

20. A Turbulent New Century Begins

"When we think of Weimar, we think of modernity in art, literature, and thought ... we think of The Threepenny Opera ... Marlene Dietrich. And we think, above all, of the exiles who exported Weimar culture all over the world."— Peter Gay[1]

Though uncommented upon by the mass media, January 18, 2001, marked the centenary founding of Überbrettl, Berlin's first cabaret (see Chapter 1), which itself existed only a year while spawning a host of imitators and a tradition that continues into the present, seemingly stronger than ever. Less than nine months later (for many of us), the horrors of September 11 inaugurated the 21st century in a manner that could at best be described as inauspicious. Whereas the cabarets of early 20th century Berlin sprung up amidst widespread German optimism for the future, the current and ongoing transnational spread of cabaret-style entertainment is playing out surrounded by an equally understandable mood of ominous bewilderment, very similar to the post–World War I zeitgeist of Berlin literary *Kabarett* and *Kabarett-Revuen* (see Chapter 2). Is the original German cabaret style still recognizable in contemporary popular music? Of course it is. Standards associated with Kurt Weill, Lotte Lenya, Friedrich Hollaender, and Marlene Dietrich are still performed regularly, sometimes by artists completely unfamiliar with the originals. Cabaret-influenced mega-talents such as John Kander and Burt Bacharach continue to compose even as this is being written. Paul McCartney, Bob Dylan, and Patti Smith all remain active. Beyond these obvious examples, however, the biggest residual of the Weimar legacy in music tends to be more subtle and below the surface in character. Safe to say that German and French cabaret styles have become so fully integrated into American and World music styles that these are no longer even thought of as being German or French, despite their origins.

Before giving a brief survey of cabaret's international expansion over the last few decades, it is useful to recall from whence it came, long before the modern Great War of 1914–1918 began the unpleasant acceleration of civilization becoming more interactive and volatile than previously thought possible. Going back to Otto Julius Bierbaum's novel *Stilpe* (1897), a book written when Kaiser Wilhelm II was at the height of his political power, one can read of an ongoing and doomed struggle to bring quality, thoughtful entertainment to an eternally uncomprehending and unappreciative public. As historian Alan Lareau has summarized, Bierbaum's cabaret advocate and idealistic hero Stilpe has all the cards stacked against him from the very beginning: "He is ripped apart by two conflicting aims: on the one hand, he plays the game of journalism, selling lies and lacing everything with irony; on the other, he longs to be a 'real' poet and transcend the petty machinations of society, to which he has sold out his own rebellion. Torn between the two poles, the modern poet meets an ironically tragic fate."[2]

Climatically in Bierbaum's novel, Stilpe kills himself on stage out of protest and frustration. The story takes on additional resonance in that only a few years later, Bierbaum himself failed as a cabaret operator before denouncing the very concept he helped to articulate. The fictional Stilpe's fate becomes even more prophetic and disturbing considering that several prominent cabaret artists took their own lives during the 1930s out of fear and despair for the future (see Chapter 6). By the 1920s, considered by some as the "Periclean Age" of Weimar culture, *Kabarett* had become far more sophisticated and exciting, but still faced the same problem — namely, how to make ends meet without sacrificing its lofty ideals.[3] As early as 1922, Berlin critic and cabaret enthusiast Max Herrmann-Neiße identified a similar issue which still applies today: can high art really be successfully combined with mass entertainment?[4]

The rampant commercialism of the late Roaring Twenties wiped out the literary cabaret ideal in Berlin.[5] This was quickly replaced, however, by the lavish cabaret revues, many of which were little more than large-scale girlie shows, but in the hands of accomplished songwriters and performers could take on a whole new dimension — one which soon brought a young Marlene Dietrich to the attention of Josef von Sternberg (see Chapter 5). Dietrich herself was a good case in point. A great beauty with a brain whose considerable singing and acting talents (not to mention her idealistic courage) transcended her pin-up girl status, she always strove, oftentimes in futility, to give her fans something more thought-provoking than what they were expecting. Once again, Lareau effectively summed up the dilemma facing outstanding artists like Dietrich:

> Even to the most committed artists, the ambivalence of the cabaret's rebellion against modern culture was apparent: it longed to revolt but remain popular — and commercially successful. This constant tightrope act made it a particularly unstable

form. To this day, the German cabaret remains an art form in crisis, whose death is diagnosed more often than its vitality. Yet its few brilliant sparks of life continue to arrest us.[6]

By narrowly defining cabaret as the smaller-scaled literary style that briefly flourished in Berlin during the early 1920s, Lareau notes that "The stirring vision behind the cabaret's struggle to unite art and entertainment, and the frustration and resignation which resulted, make up the fascination and the misfortune of the cabaret experiment."[7] On the other hand, if one opts to view German cabaret more broadly to include revues, comedy, operetta, music drama, and other popular forms — some of which survived into the Nazi era — then cabaret becomes far more than a noble, failed experiment. In this wider context, cabaret can be seen as an ongoing interaction between elitist and populist notions of musical entertainment or, in the words of Alex Ross, "...the long-running conversation between classical and popular traditions."[8] Looking into the future, Ross speculates that "One possible destination for twenty-first-century music is a final 'great fusion'; intelligent pop artists and extro-verted composers speaking more or less the same language."[9] This, almost needless to say, is more hopeful vision but one having thus far proved (at best) difficult to sustain, although the cabaret tradition has also shown itself to be one the great musical path-breakers in this regard.[10]

During the 1980s and 1990s several commercially recorded tributes were organized whose artistic rosters confirmed the high regard in which historical figures such as Kurt Weill and Marlene Dietrich continue to be held by younger generations of performers and audiences.[11] *Lost in the Stars: The Music of Kurt Weill* appeared in 1985 on the A&M label and featured performances by Sting, Marianne Faithful, Van Dyke Parks, Lou Reed, Tom Waits, Aaron Neville, Charlie Haden and Todd Rundgren, among many others. Better still was *September Song: The Music of Kurt Weill* from 1997, which included two of the aforementioned artists (Reed and Haden) plus relatively younger names such as Elvis Costello, P.J. Harvey, Nick Cave, and Mary Margaret O'Hara. Interspersed on the same album project were interpretations by jazz veteran Betty Carter, a cappella vocal group the Persuasions, opera star and Lenya protégé Teresa Stratas, plus a Brecht *Threepenny* reading by poet William S. Burroughs. Vintage recordings by Lenya and Brecht were thrown in for good measure. The result was one of the better popular anthologies to close out the last century, appropriately setting the stage for a new one. In 2007, original *Cabaret* director Hal Prince (see Chapter 16) and Pulitzer-winning playwright Alfred Uhry collaborated for the Broadway production of *LoveMusik*, based on the personal letters of Kurt Weill and Lotte Lenya and utilizing Weill's own musical compositions.[12] Revivals of the 1972 revue *Berlin to Broadway with Kurt Weill, A Musical Voyage* continue to be mounted, including one at

Northwestern University in 2007, attended by this writer.[13] Suffice it to say that Weill's core play list has lost none of its impact or appeal over half a century after the composer's death. And of course there are Weill's own stage works, the ongoing revivals of which are too numerous to list here. In 2012, it is not unusual to watch popular TV shows such as *Smash* or *Mad Men* and hear Weill's music performed, either as part of the story or simply over end credits.

As for Marlene Dietrich, her iconography throughout popular culture has become almost as familiar as that of Marilyn Monroe. Although a widely rumored Hollywood biopic has not materialized to date, Dietrich was posthumously made an honorary citizen of Berlin in 2002.[14] It took 52 years for her native city to forgive Dietrich enough after her role in favor of the Allies during World War II in order for this honor to be bestowed. This came a year after Dietrich's grandson David Riva filmed the engaging documentary *Marlene Dietrich: Her Own Song* (2001), focusing on her extraordinary heroism as a front-line performer during the war.[15] Perhaps Dietrich's most durable, continuing legacy in music, however, is her too-often unacknowledged role in reinventing the modern nightclub act into a Las Vegas–style gala event (see Chapter 13). It was a singular accomplishment for which she was uniquely prepared, having come up through the ranks of Berlin cabaret and cabaret revue, then as a big screen film icon, and finally as a wartime morale booster. For example, as recently as 2012, during the halftime entertainment for Super Bowl XLVI held in Indianapolis, while Madonna and a long train of guest hip-hop performers staged a massive display of light and sound, it was difficult not to think of Josephine Baker in 1920s Berlin (see Chapter 1) or the lavish musical revues of Weimar Germany which first propelled a young and then-unknown Dietrich into the gaudy limelight of Hollywood.

During the waning years of last century, a number of other German-born popular recording artists also came into prominence, enjoying significant success in America and exerting a substantial influence on all those coming into contact with their work. Ute Lemper began her career as an impeccable, rock-solid interpreter of Kurt Weill's songbook (both German and American), then convincingly branched out to prove that she could adopt the mantel of Dietrich or Édith Piaf (in English, French, or German), as well as that of Lotte Lenya. Her stunning 1996 bi-lingual recordings of forgotten Weimar-era songs by Friedrich Hollaender, Mischa Spoliansky, Kurt Tucholsky, and Marcellus Schiffer (see Chapter 6) in many ways represent the crowning jewel of Decca's ambitious *entartete Musik* series. Combining film starlet appearance with a triple threat (singing, dancing, acting), major stage credits for the German *chanteuse* include Kander and Ebb's *Cabaret* and *Chicago*, as well as Weill and Brecht's *The Threepenny Opera* and *Mahagonny-Songspiel*, among many others. Since the new millennium, Lemper has collaborated with Anglo-American alternative and crossover artists interested in the cabaret style, including Elvis Costello, Tom Waits, Nick Cave, and Laurie Anderson, in addition to her often striking and ongoing solo work. A 2003 live performance at Chicago's intimate, cabaret-style Athenaeum Theatre (located in the heart of the city's old north side German neighborhood) was described by one leading critic as "a provocative, free-ranging discourse on greed, lust, politics, crime, corruption, and other comparable preoccupations."[16] In short, the spirit of Weimar Berlin once again comes to life whenever Ute Lemper sings to an audience, even though she was born a full three decades after the Weimar Republic ceased to exist.

Lemper's near contemporary and fellow German-born performer is the ineffable Max Raabe, whose professional music career stretches back to the 1980s, but before 2004 had never appeared on stage in the United States. Since then, Raabe and his Palast Orchester have routinely sold out the most prestigious American venues, including the likes of Chicago Symphony Center, Royce Hall, and Carnegie Hall. At first glance, Raabe's physical appearance is not unlike that of a blonde, Aryan poster boy from the 1930s, but closer inspection reveals a sly, tongue-in-cheek image of androgyny, quite fitting for the bygone era that his music represents.[17] It is almost as if David Bowie had been transported back in time, dressed in formal wear, and then brought back for modern audiences. Raabe's tenor-falsetto singing attack is in the classic Weimar style, standing perfectly upright and still (no matter how salacious the lyrics), rolling his eyes, and minimizing all gestures, reminiscent of Claire Waldoff's distinctive stage persona from two generations earlier (see Chapter 5). Surrounding himself with a crack ensemble of formally-trained musicians, Raabe's shows on one hand call to mind the great Weimar dance bands such as the one led by Dajos Béla, while on the other reflecting the humor and panache of the Comedian Harmonists (see Chapter 12), a group that greatly influenced him. His eclectic play list features a combination of old and new hits from both Jewish and non–Jewish composers. Fittingly in 1999, Raabe was cast opposite contemporary German cabaret star Nina Hagen in new production of *The Threepenny Opera*, subsequently recorded for commercial release on CD. Raabe has also recorded Kurt Weill's extensive dance arrangements for his own stage music, an widely unknown but still delightful body of work.

Given the more recent international stardom of performers such as Raabe and Lemper, it should come as no surprise that German cabaret as a performing style can now be found in almost every corner of the globe, albeit with modifications to accommodate local tastes. Even the musical *Cabaret* has gone global; since 2002 there have been documented revivals (outside of the U.S.

and Great Britain) in Australia, Mexico, Cuba, Peru, Spain, and France, to name a few.[18] And then of course there is the American heartland and cities like Duluth, Minnesota, which has successfully revived *Cabaret* twice since 2001 (see Introduction). This is not the provincial, semi-fictional Duluth ruthlessly satirized in Gore Vidal's 1984 comedic novel, but rather a lesser known Duluth with a deep German and Jewish cultural heritage, not to mention being the birthplace of Bob Dylan (see Chapter 18).[19] As for the clubs, specific examples (and shades of respectability) are innumerable and could well fill a book by themselves; many are ephemeral and short-lived, not unlike their original Weimar prototypes. Not only are these to be found anywhere the German or French language has traveled (an extensive geographic sweep, to be sure), but also in more remote locales such Japan, where cabaret "hostess clubs" or *Kyabakura* have become an urban fixture, or India, where the exotic cabaret dances and production numbers have become an essential ingredient of Bollywood's consistent recipe for success. In terms of festivities, the Australians have established the highly successful Adelaide Cabaret Festival, an annual alternative extravaganza since 2001 and still going strong, recently spawning a rival cabaret festival in Melbourne. Nowadays, one is at a complete loss to classify popular youth acts such as Katzenjammer Kabarett, a French alternative group paying aggressive homage to the Weimar-era aesthetic. The worldwide spread of African American hip-hop music — even into the Arab world — owes both its political edge and extensive reliance on the emcee role of a DJ or MC (pioneered by the identical, indispensable role of the cabaret *conférencier*) to much earlier Weimar models.

Perhaps the best way to appreciate the international reach of cabaret in the new millennium is to examine the rich and seemingly endless complexities of a single event. In 2004, the ephemeral, multi–Grammy Award–winning jazz vocalist Dee Dee Bridgewater (aka Denise Eileen Garrett), presented one of her typically unpredictable show at the North Sea Jazz Festival in Rotterdam, focusing on the underappreciated American material of Kurt Weill.[20] Bridgewater, earlier in 2002, had recorded an album of Weill's music, enigmatically but appropriately titled *This Is New*. As an African American artist steeped in a jazz tradition that was largely unaware of German cabaret until Louis Armstrong recorded "Mack the Knife" in 1955 (see Chapter 14), Bridgewater tackles the post–1935 English-language songs of Weill with flamboyance, adding new, big band arrangements to the mix, including a Latin-flavored, flamenco guitar.[21] She makes one exception in the finale by foraying into Weill's Weimar period with the "Alabama Song," which she almost turns into blues shout, quite the opposite from the manner in which the number was originally conceived by the composer and performed by Lotte Lenya in Germany (despite its title). The international, mixed-race audience cheering the show reflected no allegiance to any particular nationality — they just liked the music. Trying to pigeon-hole multi-dimensional, crossover art such as this is an exercise in futility, and we have little doubt that Weill, Lenya, and Brecht, all political refugees during their own lifetimes, would have loved the whole thing.

This brings us back once again to difficult questions regarding definitions and parameters. What exactly is cabaret music, or more precisely, when does cabaret music stop becoming cabaret music to become something else entirely? In truth, the global spread of cabaret performance art in recent decades demonstrates the near impossibility of doing this because we are in fact dealing with moving target. Most definitions of anything really represent a snapshot in time rather than any attempt to identify certain continuous attributes or moods happening to manifest themselves as a particular zeitgeist during any given moment in history. The best we that we can usually hope for is to pinpoint a certain event at a certain time and then try to catalogue its attributes. A year or two later, things are likely to have changed, and the old definition, even if previously accurate, no longer applies. This was true even during the Weimar era as Berlin literary *Kabarett* evolved into *Kabarett-Revuen* within a matter of months after American jazz shocked and infiltrated German sensibilities (see Chapter 2). As the 21st century progresses, it seems likely that this evolution will continue to accelerate, producing newer, more exotic species of offshoots; nevertheless, distinctive commonalities in form and spirit appear to remain. In attempting to understand the new complex world now taking shape, it might behoove all of us to take a cursory look at how all people, especially intelligent young people, choose to entertain themselves. Then perhaps we will come to better understand the world through a better understanding of ourselves.

Conclusion

"...music unfolds along an unbroken continuum, however dissimilar the sounds on the surface."— Alex Ross[1]

February 24, 2012: closing night at the Fiddlehead, a cabaret-like entertainment venue located on Main Street in Hayward, Wisconsin, about 90 minutes southeast of Duluth. After seven years of offering some of the most eclectic and freewheeling shows in the north woods region, the recently-married owner-operator has decided to move on to less stressful and more profitable endeavors, also motivated in part by a vocal minority of nearby business owners who seemingly object to intelligent nightlife of any kind in their vicinity, no matter how otherwise law-abiding, all ambient noise aside. This same consortium, on the other hand, has never objected to the piping of listless, middle-of-the-road, white bread nostalgia from a P.A. system rigged the entire length of Main Street during normal business hours. There were never any girlie shows at the Fiddlehead (although homely wait staff of either sex were not to be found), and the primary attractions always featured good music, dance, food, drink, and conversation. It was a loss for the community, though probably a gain for the performers. The Fiddlehead has had a good run, as cabarets go, and the excellent house band has booked a series of future shows at other venues, including some exciting ones abroad.[2]

Molly and the Danger Band perform that night from small, elevated wooden stage, perhaps 12 feet long by four feet wide, to a packed house, a happy, revolving audience of approximately 100 people, consisting of every age, gender, and sexual orientation. Molly acts as *conférencier*, telling jokes in between songs, teasing staff and band mates who sometimes kid her back when she is not singing and playing mandolin, guitar or fiddle.[3] Every band member is a multi-instrumentalist, creating a scrappy, improvised feel reminiscent of the original *Threepenny Opera*. Nearly everyone sings and dances. The décor is artsy, cluttered, claustrophobic, and vaguely French, with fleur-de-lis imprints on some of the hardwood floor panels and reproduction *Belle*

193

Époque artwork on the walls, along with antique instruments, collector vinyl LP jackets, and fashionable women's wear for sale. The scene was not unlike one of those described by Christopher Isherwood in Berlin during the early 1930s (see Chapter 7). There were no tangos, but several Irish jigs, which made a good substitute. Country music legends Cleo Bee and Sherwin Linton dropped by and off-the-cuff performed "House of the Risin' Sun," "Me and Bobby McGee," and "America the Beautiful," with the audience joining in patriotically on the last number. In short, the drinking-entertainment concept begun by Rudolphe Salis in Montmartre during the early 1880s continued strong over 130 years later in the north woods of Wisconsin. The next day in Hayward, a 23-year-old Jewish Olympian from Colorado (Tad Elliot) would become talk of the town by winning the 39th annual American Birkebeiner cross-country ski race, finishing the 54-kilometer marathon almost directly in front of the former Fiddlehead, which had closed permanently only a few hours before that same morning. All in all, it seemed a very fitting conclusion for the extensive weekend festivities, one bringing back many ghosts and memories from the not-too-distant German-American past.

History is continuum, like cabaret itself, one could say. One event leads to another in a seemingly inevitable cause-and-effect manner; and yet repetitive cycles manifest themselves from generation to generation. In 1930 Marlene Dietrich made herself world famous by singing Friedrich Hollaender's "Falling in Love Again" on a film set equipped with a sound stage — an innovation unheard of by the general public only three years previous — but to audition successfully for the role she had to sing the inane 1928 American hit "You're the Cream in My Coffee" in a screen test before director Josef von Sternberg.[4] Thirty-four years later (in 1962), Paul McCartney of the yet-to-be-famous Beatles sang lead for "Falling in Love Again" at the Hamburg Star-Club in homage to Dietrich before a mostly German audience; the same Hamburg shows included several Beatles' covers of original songs by American rockabilly star Carl Perkins, probably what the German audience had really paid to hear. A year later in 1963 the group would be standing side-by-side with Dietrich herself for celebrity-seeking photographers in London. Back at the Fiddlehead in 2012, as Molly and the Danger Band performed "Honey Don't" — a Perkins song more associated with the Beatles — a 50-something-year-old Hoosier friend proudly displayed an iPod containing a bootleg recording of the Beatles playing live circa 1964 at the Indianapolis Coliseum, of all places. The mental leaps across time and space by this point had become dizzying. Was the *Kleinkunst* enthusiastically played that night at the Fiddlehead derived from American, English, or German sources? The answer, obviously, is all of the above, however American the context. Putting this all into perspective, cabaret is certainly but one single facet of modern American (and

World) popular music, nonetheless a very important, underappreciated, and under-recognized facet.

Everything, it would seem, is interconnected. The focus of this study has been upon the many strands interweaving the music of Weimar Germany with that of Anglo-American pop culture during the post–World War II era. It is neither the first nor last such chronicle to note this rather obvious link, but perhaps the first one to emphasize it. These separate creative worlds appear to share another characteristic: in both Germany of the 1920s and America of the 1960s, tremendous creativity and innovation seemed to co-exist along side uninhibited freedom and, in many cases, uninhibited vice and decadence. The duality is noteworthy. Can dynamic creativity exist without the freedom to fail or, for that matter, freedom to corrupt? As Alex Ross has eloquently observed: "There is no escaping the interconnectedness of musical experience, even if composers try to barricade themselves against the outer world or to control the reception of their work. Music history is too often treated as a kind of Mercator projection of the globe, a flat image representing a landscape that is in reality borderless and continuous."[5]

There are strong educational implications to this same idea as well. St. John's College (Annapolis, Maryland) President Christopher Nelson, recently awarded an honorary doctorate by Shimer College in Chicago (one of America's great off-the-beaten path institutions of higher learning), has publicly stressed the urgent need for a shift in American educational emphasis: "We need to prepare the young to make their way in a world where boundaries are vanishing.... In other words, we need to help our students become liberated from boundaries rather than defined by them. This is the kind of freedom that a liberal education makes possible.... Liberal education ... seeks to free the learner from the tyrannies of unexamined opinions, current fashions and inherited prejudices...."[6]

This might as well be another way of describing true critical thinking. Quoting from Montaigne's timeless essay "On the Education of Children," Nelson notes that Montaigne touches upon the idea of continuum as well, insisting that all creative activity is nothing more than the transformation of that which already exists. Analogizing with bees creating honey from flowers, Montaigne emphasizes that true education begins with instilling an awareness of this basic quality in all things. Let it be noted here that cabaret music is no exception in this regard.

Let us not overstate the case. To say that all of these American and British artists were simply copying German *Kabarett* or even consciously aware of their original models, or that this was in fact their primary influence would be misleading, if not silly; on the other hand, it would be far worse to completely ignore or deny the debt — which to date has pretty much been the case with most listeners and critical commentary. Cabaret was in truth only one, single thread, albeit a crucially important one, in the complex tapestry that has formed modern American popular music. To understand where this element came from in a previous milieu is to surely have a better appreciation for the music itself, if nothing else. This is not to say that the Beatles, or Bob Dylan, or Bacharach and David, or Kander and Ebb, represent little more than recent, successful upholders of the Weimar tradition. It merely is intended to underscore their utilization of previously existing musical materials to form outstanding creative legacies, not unlike the bees making honey from flowers in Montaigne's analogy. In the final analysis, let it be added that their deep artistic debt to Weimar cabaret may be one more of attitude and temperament than any particular aspect of musical form or style.

Nor has this lengthy process finished playing out. As long as rigid boundaries are defined in music by narrow-minded audiences, critics, or academics, there will surely be creative artists of genius to break these down with previously unimagined syntheses and amalgamations. As previously noted, the artificial 20th century–erected barrier between popular versus classical music spheres has suffered a series of major assaults over the last three generations. While Alex Ross lamented that "Two distinct repertories have formed, one intellectual and one popular," it is also remains true that these same two repertories continue to intermingle at an ever-increasing pace.[7] The two-part organization of this study was chosen in part to further underscore a long-term ongoing and accelerating trend. For example, the coveted Gershwin Prize in music awarded only since 2007, is itself named after a sibling musical partnership ending in 1937 after George Gershwin's untimely death, and a full four years before the United States entered World War II. The life and career of Gershwin, and all American musical barrier-breakers who came in his wake, have spanned the entire history of recorded music. There is no reason to believe that this increasing resistance to musical categorization is about to change anytime soon, especially now that countless non–American talents (led by the Germans) have joined in this artistic voyage of non-conformist discovery as well.

Despite obvious, surface reservations, it is quite appropriate that names like Kurt Weill and Marlene Dietrich have become synonymous with the German cabaret aesthetic. It was they, in hindsight, who broke through to the widest international audience. In fact, these days on FM public classical radio, one rarely hears the music of Weill or Hollaender; on pop station play lists their music is a far more frequent occurrence, typically without listeners or programmers even realizing it. Songs such as "Mack the Knife" and "Falling in Love Again" have taken on a life of their own. In a very real sense, the original *Kabarett* trend had begun to recede by the mid–1920s when its best elements were already being filtered and absorbed into other forms of German popular entertainment. Some of these other forms included the Berlin revues bringing fame to a young Marlene Dietrich, the Weill-Brecht street operas using Lotte Lenya as a *vox populi* mouthpiece, and (often forgotten) the biting political satire of the urban comedy clubs. The Berlin "dives" inhabited by Christopher Isherwood between 1929 and 1933 were more remnants of a peaked trend from several years before, rather than real prototypes or prime exemplars of the genre. Even a semi-authentic venture such as Friedrich Hollaender's Berlin Tingle Tangle club represented more a defiant attempt to capitalize on the cinematic success of *The Blue Angel* in the face of rising fascist hostility, than a prime example of the true literary *Kabarett* dominating the Berlin scene during the early Weimar period. In typical historical fashion, however, Isherwood's "dives" from the late Weimar era were later immortalized by Kander and Ebb (with a major assist from Bob Fosse) into *Cabaret*, becoming the enduring image of the genre that most of us now cling to, even for those of us who should know better. In effect, Isherwood's literary impressions later became cinematic reality for future generations, even though it was, in some respects, a myth itself based on a Berlin scene that ceased to exist after 1924. Most incredible of all, though, was surely Kurt Weill's own career trajectory as one continually successful composer in two separate stylistic worlds, Germany before the war and America afterwards. His achievement in this regard is rare, if not unique.

Are we today living in the Weimar Republic? Once again, this study is not the first place to pose such a provocative question. It may be a question worth asking, however, in relation to our trending musical tastes and preferences. As hallowed, longstanding public and private institutions seem to falter or no longer seem capable of dealing with cascading political and economic crises, we as a people can still, even during the worst of times, retreat to an intimate venue and be happily distracted by entertainers sharing our own particular concerns. Certainly one of the loneliest feelings in life is to see large blocks of society react to external events in ways not personally shared or sympathized with. Feeling alone can be bad enough; to feel completely at odds with one's own fellow citizens is surely one of the worst alienations to be endured. Music, on the other hand, especially "good" music, can help us to overcome this malaise or, in some instances, transcend it, especially if shared with others. Good music, in effect, becomes therapy.

English Glossary of German and French Terminology

Anschluss— Nazi German annexation of Austria in 1938, dramatized in Rodgers and Hammerstein's *The Sound of Music*

Bauhaus, Staatliches— German fine arts school spanning the life of the Weimar Republic (1919–1933), located successively in Weimar, Dessau, and Berlin

Belle Époque—"Beautiful Epoch" in France, spanning roughly from the end of the Franco-Prussian War (1871) to the beginning of World War I (1914); considered golden age for the arts

Der Blaue Engel—"The Blue Angel"; 1930 film by Josef von Sternberg with breakthrough leading performance by Marlene Dietrich

Der Blaue Reiter (later Der Blaue Vier)—("The Blue Rider"/"The Blue Four") Informal school of (mostly) German Expressionist painters from the early 20th century nominally led by Wassily Kandinsky

Cabaret— French word originally meaning "tavern" but during *Belle Epoque* associated with nightclub entertainment; later also associated with strip tease

Chanson réaliste—"Realistic song"; singing style with subject matter less sentimental and more adult in content, popularized in French cabarets

Chanteuse— Female cabaret singer, usually of torch ballads

Le Chat Noir—"The Black Cat"; first French cabaret in Montmartre district of Paris, founded by Rudolphe Salis in 1881

Conférencier—"Emcee" or "Master of Ceremonies"; standard performer in both French and German styles of cabaret

Diseuse— Female cabaret singer-actress-comedienne

Die Driegroschenoper—"The Threepenny Opera"; 1928 music drama by Kurt Weill and Bertolt Brecht, original production starring Lotte Lenya

Entartete Kunst—"Degenerate Art"; Nazi term for proscribed art displayed in 1937 Munich exhibition

Entartete Musik—"Degenerate Music"; Nazi term for proscribed music displayed in 1938 Düsseldorf exhibition

199

Exis— Short for "Existentialists"; nickname for German student friends of the Beatles during their Hamburg days

Expressionism— Early 20th century artistic movement, often associated with German filmmaking of the 1920s, marked by exaggerated, hyper-realism

Gebrauchsmusik—"Utilitarian music"; music written quickly for a specific occasion, often associated with composers such as Kurt Weill and Paul Hindemith

Gesamtkunstwerk—"Art encompassing all of the arts"; Wagnerian term for large scale music drama integrating multiple dramatic, visual, and musical disciplines

Hitlerjugend—"Hitler Youth"; Nazi propaganda program designed to recruit future party members at an early age

Jugendstil— Elaborate "youth style" of arts based in Munich during late 19th century; German equivalent to the French *Art Nouveau* style

Kabarett— Later German version of French cabaret; usually associated with literary style of cabaret flourishing in Berlin during the early 1920s

Kabarett der Komiker—"Cabaret of Comedians" or "Kadeko" for short; famous Berlin venue closed by the Nazis in 1944

Kabarett-Revuen—"Cabaret Revue"; large-scaled song-and-dance productions, usually featuring chorus girls, highly popular in Berlin during the late 1920s

Kabarettoper—"Cabaret Opera"; dramatically unified cabaret revue which appeared briefly during the early 1930s

Die Katacombe—"The Catacombs"; Berlin cabaret closed by Nazis in 1935, closely associated with comedian Werner Finck

Kleinkunst—"Miniature art"; art placing emphasis on small-scale forms and, in the case of music, short time-lengths; antithesis to Gesamtkunstwerk

Kurfürstendamm— Main Berlin entertainment district during the 1920s and 1930s

Mahagonny— Fictional American sin-city invented by Bertolt Brecht during the 1920s and immortalized in musical stage works with Kurt Weill and Lotte Lenya

Le Moulin Rouge—"The Red Mill"; Famous cabaret in Montmartre district of Paris known for popularization of the can-can dance

Nationalsozialist—"National Socialist Party" or "Nazi" for short

Neue Sachlichkeit—"New Objectivity"; German artistic movement of the 1920s emphasizing realism and emotional restraint in reaction to Expressionism

Reeperbahn— Entertainment district of Hamburg

Sadomasochism— Form of perversion, taken from the name of Leopold von Sacher-Masoch, 19th century Viennese author of cult novel *Venus in Furs*

Schlager— German popular song or literally, "hit song"

Shutzstaffel (or "SS" for short)— Nazi paramilitary group often closely associated with atrocities of the Holocaust.

Swingjugend—"Swing youth"; German youth culture admiring American popular music, based in Hamburg, rising in oppositional protest to Hitler Youth

Tingel Tangel— German vaudeville or low-brow cabaret; name probably derived from the clinking sound of dropping coins

Überbrettl—"Superstage"; name of first Berlin cabaret in 1901, name a takeoff on Nietzsche's *Übermensch*

Übermensch—"Superman"; German philosopher Friedrich Nietzsche's term for a new type of ideal, modern man

Wehrmacht— Nazi German armed forces, including army, navy, and air force

Zeitgeist—"Spirit of the times"; coined in late 19th century Germany, usage prevalent by the 1920s

Chapter Notes

Introduction

1. Jelavich, p. vii. In this case, use of the past tense in reference to cabaret is significant. The more narrowly one defines a certain style the more scarce and fleeting become true exemplar.

2. This was in fact far from being the first local production of *Cabaret*, having been last staged by the University of Minnesota–Duluth (UMD) in 2001. Earlier in 2011, Duluth had also seen a successful revival of Kander and Ebb's 1975 musical *Chicago*, a work only slightly less of stature than the same team's *Cabaret* from the previous decade.

3. The German term *Kabarett* is derived from its French equivalent, *cabaret*, originally meaning a smorgasbord-like serving tray, later associated with the Parisian tavern-music halls of Montmartre. See Lareau, p. 2. See also Jelavich, p. 26.

4. Duluth currently boasts no fewer than three synagogues: Temple Israel, Chabad Lubavitch of Northern Minnesota, and Adas Israel Congregation. Bob Dylan is himself, having grown up in nearby Hibbing, MN, of local Jewish descent. It was in Duluth that a teenage Robert Zimmerman reputedly saw Buddy Holly perform shortly before the latter died in a 1959 plane crash.

5. Zeitgeist had first come into usage in Germany during the 19th century Romantic era. During the 20th century, however, partly in thanks to cabaret, the term came to assume a more modern, almost anti–Romantic connotation.

6. The more disreputable aspects of this performance art, which have always co-existed side-by-side with its highbrow dimension (see Chapter 8), may also be witnessed at local venues such as the Centerfold Cabaret, located along the same strip as the more dignified Teratro Zuccone and Greysolon Ballroom.

7. The English translation for the successful 1954 revival of *The Threepenny Opera* was by American composer Marc Blitzstein.

8. Because I am neither a musician nor musically literate, it was immediately realized that my appreciation and understanding of music (such as it is) depends heavily upon both word associations and miniature compositional forms, both hallmarks of cabaret. Ellington and Ebb, of course, excelled at both. Ellington's own thoughts on the subject, with a writing style both florid and reserved, proved to be unhelpful except to pay tribute to his own (mostly) pre-cabaret influences and collaborators. Ebb, though a tremendously entertaining raconteur during published interviews, also tended to be guarded and secretive.

9. Jelavich, p. 2.

10. For example, this shortness of performance length might be viewed as a direct historical precursor to the modern American "hit parade" radio which later hit full stride during the 1950s and 1960s.

11. Professor Jelavich notes that revues were bigger in scope and agitprop more political than most cabaret tended to be in actuality, despite the current public image of the latter. See Jelavich, p. 3.

12. Lareau, p. 2.

13. Jelavich, pp. 1–2.

14. Lareau, p. 106.

15. Lareau, p. 5.

16. For example, Klezmer likely influenced the music of early 20th century Jewish German and Jewish American composers such as Gustav Mahler and George Gershwin. See Ross, pp. 22, 153, 160.

17. Gay, p. xiv.

18. Gay, p. xiii.

19. As Professor Lareau has corrected noted, the political image of cabaret is "largely based on developments after 1945." These topical songs later became "models for many of the new protest singers." He also criticizes Jelavich's portrayal of cabaret as placing too much emphasis on these political themes. See Lareau, pp. 3, 16.

20. This odd tradition could still be wit-

nessed in Germany after World War II as (for example) a young, unheard of Liverpool rock 'n roll group led by art school dropout John Lennon took to the strip joints of Hamburg (see Chapter 17).

21. Lareau, pp. 102–103.

22. Professor Lareau observed that in the cabaret repertoire, male performers tended to do the political acts, while women were often presented as neurotic, hysterical monsters. See Lareau, p. 104. But these stereotypes also run counter to many documented exceptions. What of the great political anthems by Claire Waldoff, Rosa Valetti, and Trude Hesterberg? Perhaps it would be more accurate to say that most cabaret singers and dancers were in fact female while comedians tended to be male.

23. Professor Gay has conveniently categorized this catastrophic phase of German history into three periods, each rapidly cascading into the next: (1) "The Golden Twenties"; (2) "The Beginning of the End": (3) "Descent into Barbarism." See Gay, pp. 155–163.

24. See in particular (with respect to this question) my investigation of religious fanaticism and tolerance in *Perpetua of Carthage: Portrait of a Third Century Martyr* (2009).

Chapter 1

1. Gay, p. 5.

2. The venture was originally known as a French *Cabaret Artistique*. See Jelavich, p. 26. See also Appignanesi, p. 16.

3. Lareau, p. 4.

4. Original French terms for female performers, such as *chanteuse* ("singer") and *diseuse* ("monologist"), often continued to be used by German Weimar cabaret artists.

5. Bierbaum hoped to see the sophisticated principles of the Munich-based *Jugendstil* ("youth style") movement, also known as *Art Nouveau* in France, favorably applied to the coarser stage sensibilities of *Tingel Tangel*. This would also be in keeping with Nietzsche's advocacy for a Dionysian world filled with laughter and dance. See Jelavich, pp. 27–29. Appignanesi notes that in Germany *Tingel Tangel* had become synonymous with artistic freedom. See Appignanesi, p. 31.

6. Lareau, pp. 7–8. See also Jelavich, pp. 36–37. The origins of the phrase *Tingel Tangel* are said to come from the clinking sound of coins hitting collection plates as show girls solicited donations for performances (and sometimes other favors) from customers. As a disgusted German court of law circa 1904 explained to more polite elements of society, *Tingel Tangel* consisted of "commercial presentations at a fixed place of operation, consisting of musicals and similar works, devoid of nay higher artistic or scholarly interest, and which are capable, through either their content or their manner of presentation, of arousing the lower instincts, in particular the sexual lust of the audience." See Jelavich, p. 21; Bierbaum's fictional character Stilpe names *Tingel Tangel* as Germany's artistic hope of the future; See Lareau, p. 180.

7. Lareau writes that "Lola Lola's dive in the 1929 film *The Blue Angel* effectively captures the atmosphere of such locales." See Lareau, p. 5.

8. Jelavich, pp. 39, 56. Nietzsche, who had been seriously ill for many years, passed away in August 1900.

9. Appignanesi, pp. 31–32.

10. In this sense, the non-refreshment serving environment of early German *Kabarett* was not true cabaret and more akin to the theater, as noted by Appignanesi, among others. See Appignanesi, p. 34.

11. Jelavich, pp. 41, 105–106. See also Lareau, p. 106. Oscar Straus (1870–1954) is not to be confused with Richard Strauss (no relation). Metropol-Theater–based Victor Hollaender (1866–1940) was the father of Friedrich Hollaender (see Chapter 6); Victor's music was among that performed on opening night at Überbrettl. Arnold Schoenberg (1874–1951) went on to become one of the most influential composers of the 20th century. Aspects of cabaret art appeared in Schoenberg's music as late as 1919 (long after he had developed a 12-tone compositional technique) in his *Pierrot Lunaire* song cycle. See Ross, p. 50. Only one of Schoenberg's original songs was known to have been performed at Überbrettl. See Jelavich, p. 8.

12. Lareau, p. 4. The Buntes Theater was itself housed in a landmark building at Alexanderstraße 40, the architecture of which was also inspired by the *Jugendstil* movement. See also Jelavich, p. 39.

13. Appignanesi, p. 34.

14. Lareau, p. 8. See also Jelavich, pp. 39, 41.

15. Wolzogen's anti–Semitic remarks with respect to the premature closing of Überbrettl were written late in his life during the 1920s. See Jelavich, pp. 13, 60–61.

16. Jelavich, p. 50,

17. Lareau, p. 181.

18. Jelavich, p. 86.

19. Jelavich, p. 96.

20. Jelavich, p. 99.

21. Appignanesi, pp. 42–43. See also Lareau, p. 8.

22. Jelavich, p. 62.

23. Cabaret Berlin, pp. 3–5, 45. Reinhardt had a head start in his venture. Schall und Rauch (a phrase borrowed from Goethe) really began life as club called Die Brille ("The Spectacles")

at Café Monopol, before officially opening under its new moniker at the Künstlerhaus in the Bellevuestraße of Berlin (Jelavich, p. 64).

24. Lareau, p. 23.

25. Jealousy over the instant success of talented Jewish impresarios such as Reinhardt and Nelson in Berlin may have been the true cause of Wolgozen's later anti–Semitic writings.

26. Jelavich, p. 81. Appignanesi aptly characterized Reinhardt's Kleines Theater as one of Germany's first experimental venues. See Appignanesi, p. 34.

27. Jelavich, p. 65.

28. Jelavich, p. 6.

29. Jelavich, p. 26.

30. Lareau, pp. 9–10.

31. Jelavich, p. 91.

32. Hitler later claimed he was there, although this might be disputed. Ross, pp. 3–4.

33. Ross, p. 10.

34. Ross, p. 21. Only eleven days after the Gratz performance of *Salome*, Mahler premiered his imposing Sixth Symphony at Essen (Ross, pp. 22–23).

35. Curiously, both Strauss and Mahler traveled to America later that same decade and found mixed receptions. *Salome* scandalized audiences in at the Metropolitan Opera New York City, the same institution that had paid Mahler big bucks to become its artistic director in 1907. See Ross, pp. 26, 29. By coincidence, Mahler's last concert with the New York Philharmonic Orchestra (before he returned to Austria) included a piece by Ferruccio Busoni (Ross, p. 33), who would later become the beloved mentor of Kurt Weill.

36. Ross, p. 34.

37. Ross, p. 14. The sinister flip-side of this Wagnerian adulation is also identified by Ross, citing the work of German Expressionist writer Thomas Mann, whose war-time novel *Docktor Fautus* is concerned with similar themes: "The cultish fanaticism of modern art turns out to be not unrelated to the politics of fascism: both attempt to remake the world in utopian forms (Ross, pp. 36–37)."

38. The foundation of any good liberal humanist education includes awareness of what happened to Western civilization before, during, and after the Great War. In my own case, like many others, I am forever indebted to the late Dr. Allen E. Tuttle, former Dean of Valparaiso University, who taught this subject matter with incomparable wisdom and perception.

39. Cabaret Voltaire both opened and closed in 1916. Its participants then moved to other clubs in Zurich and, after the war, to other cities. See Appignanesi, pp. 76, 80.

40. Lareau, p. 11.

41. Appignanesi, pp. 84–85.

42. Appignanesi, p. 87. Jelavich adds that the distinctive politicized and Dada-inspired collage art which later became synonymous with the Weimar Republic (and consequently despised by the Nazis) also had its roots in the pre-war collage experiments of Pablo Picasso and Georges Braque. See Jelavich, p. 19.

Chapter 2

1. Rewald, p. 36

2. Adolf Hitler's admiration for the work of Charlie Chaplin is well documented. This adulation was not returned; Chaplin, even before the U.S. entry into World War II, created a scathing film indictment of Hitler in *The Great Dictator* (1940).

3. Cabaret Berlin, pp. 6, 130. See also Lareau (pp. 24, 52) and Appignanesi (p. 132).

4. Appignanesi, p. 138.

5. Lareau, p. 33. Lareau also wrote that cabaret impresarios such as Reinhardt generally regarded Dada merely as a lure for paying customers: "It was its naughty reputation, its sensationalist and ironically commercialist side..." that drew in audiences (p. 51). See also Jelavich, p. 143.

6. Lareau, pp. 37–38.

7. Tucholsky, as was his frequent custom, wrote the lyrics for "Der alte Motor" under one of several adopted pseudonyms ("Theobald Tiger").

8. Lareau, p. 28.

9. One of Germany's most famous comics of the period, Karl Valentin, was occasionally touted as "Munich's answer to Charlie Chaplin." Valentin became a notable figure in the cabaret scene as well, performing a sketch known as *Tingel Tangel*. According to Lisa Appignanesi, Valentin's "twisted logic" approach had a "formative influence" on his fellow Municher, Bertolt Brecht. See Appignanesi, pp. 141, 150–151. It is fascinating that many cabaret innovators such as Valentin and Brecht came from the same German city in which the Nazis first made huge political gains.

10. Lareau, pp. 12, 15.

11. Gay, p. 131.

12. Jelavich, p. 156. It is interesting that these titles evoke both the Richard Strauss opera from the pre-war era, as well as the horror movie genre being then pioneered in Weimar (see Chapter 9).

13. Jelavich, p. 160.

14. Lareau, p. 13.

15. The discriminating Tucholsky reportedly loved writing songs for Holl. See Lareau, pp. 39–40.

16. *New Orpheus*, p. 42. Alexander Ringer goes on to compare the role of Nelson in *Kabarett* to

that of composer Franz Joseph Haydn with the music scene at 18th century Esterházy. Upon some reflection, this comparison seems less overstated than at first impression (p. 44).

17. Jelavich, pp. 6, 136. See also Appignanesi, p. 138.

18. Two of Valetti's signature songs written by Hollaender included "Wir wollen alle wieder Kinder sein!" ("Oh, How We Wish That We Were Kids Again!") and "Die Rote Melodie" ("The Red Melody"), the latter with lyrics by Tucholsky.

19. Kurt Gerron would also share this distinction (see Chapter 6).

20. Jelavich, p. 6. See also Appignanesi, p. 139.

21. Lareau, pp. 70–71.

22. Jelavich, pp. 150–151.

23. This over seven decades before American TV audiences would look with amazement upon Julia Sweeney's androgynous "Pat" Riley persona on *Saturday Night Live*.

24. Appignanesi, p. 141.

25. Jelavich, pp. 136–137, 153. Wild Stage closed in January 1924, and comedian Wilhelm Bendow soon followed in the same space with TüTü, keeping on staff the creative team of Spoliansky, Schiffer, and Lion, but this venture but did not last long. See Lareau, p. 114.

26. Jelavich, p. 169.

27. The term *couplet* referred to the favored lyric style of early *Kabarett*, becoming synonymous with German cabaret songs during this early time period.

28. Spoto, p. 84.

29. Lareau, p. 110.

30. Jelavich, p. 170. See also Ross, p. 203.

31. Jelavich, p. 170.

32. Jelavich, p. 173.

33. Jelavich, p. 154.

34. Hirsch, p. 18.

35. Ross then added that, in the case Ellington, the most sophisticated jazz composer of his generation, he would proceed to ambitiously incorporate European harmonies into his own original home-grown style. See Ross, pp. 164–165.

36. Ross, p. 287.

37. Marmorstein, p. 29.

38. In this sense, Jolson was a great precursor to Elvis Presley, who came some three decades later.

39. Gay, p. 155.

40. Kleinunst, pp. 54, 165.

41. Alexander Ringer wrote that *Kleinkunst* became "big-time entertainment" for the bourgeois in the form of revues and operettas. See New Orpheus. p. p. 43.

42. The title of "It's in the Air" makes reference to the Berliner joke — taken seriously by many — that their frequently outrageous behav-

ior was caused by the peculiar type of urban air they all inhaled.

43. It was during this same tour that Gershwin first sketched *An American in Paris*. Ross shares the wonderful story of Gershwin asking Stravinsky about the possibility of taking lessons, and Stravinsky replying that he should be taking lessons from Gershwin, based on the latter's tremendous financial success. See Ross, pp. xv, 159.

44. Ross, p. 163.

45. Ross, pp. xv–xvi.

Chapter 3

1. Ross, p. 205. Busoni was also quoted by Weill as telling him that "...fear of triviality is the greatest handicap of the modern artist...." See *New Orpheus*, p. 301.

2. Bach spent the last 27 years of his life in Leipzig as cantor of the school at St. Thomas Church.

3. *New Orpheus*, p. 31.

4. Ross, p. 204.

5. Weill's mother played piano, in addition to his father being a cantor.

6. Bing's wife Edith, who, like her husband, reportedly took a shine to the young Weill, was the sister of noted Expressionist playwright Carl Sternheim, born in Leipzig to a prominent Jewish family but later settling in Munich, where Sternheim's artistic associates would include Frank Wedekind. See www.kwf.org/detailed-chronolgy.

7. www.kwf.org/detailed-chronology.

8. *New Orpheus*, pp. 343–344.

9. Ross, p. 204.

10. Ross, p. 160.

11. Weill's family, like so many others in Germany, experienced financial hardship in the wake of World War I. His father then accepted a director's post for a Jewish orphanage in Leipzig, to where the family relocated in 1920. See www.kwf.org/detailed-chronology.

12. www.kwf.org/detailed-chronology.

13. Hirsch, p. 14.

14. Ross, p. 204.

15. Lenya recalled that "Busoni really loved Kurt, he loved his modesty, he loved his talent. He knew something extraordinary would happen there...." See *Legend*, p. 120.

16. Busoni, unlike Schoenberg, believed that the Romanticism should be updated and built upon, rather than completely disregarded. In a letter to Schoenberg, he wrote that "You are proposing a new value in place of an earlier one, instead of adding the new one to the old." See Ross, p. 63.

17. Kaiser and Busch would also be forced to

leave Germany during the 1930s, even though neither was Jewish, because of their anti–Nazi political stances.

18. Goll's Orpheus theme was chosen by Weill as an express continuum of operatic invention and reform successfully completed in earlier epochs by other composers using the same subject matter, such as Monteverdi and Gluck. See *New Orpheus*, p. xii.

19. *New Orpheus*, p. 47.

20. Prior to taking up with Lenya, Weill had an affair with a married, distant cousin, Nelly Frank, with whom he toured Switzerland and Italy in 1924. See *New Orpheus*, p. 346.

21. *New Orpheus*, pp. 347–348.

22. *Lenya*, p. 66.

23. Ross, p. 206.

24. Ross, p. 208.

25. Appignanesi, p. 131.

26. Appignanesi, p. 130.

27. Appignanesi, p. 131.

28. Brecht moved from Munich to Berlin in 1924 after being hired as a dramaturge for Max Reinhardt's Deutsches Theater.

29. *New Orpheus*, p. 42.

30. *Legend*, p. 51.

31. Hirsch, pp. 18, 35. See also Spoto, p. 84.

32. Ross describes Krenek's opera as part cabaret, part jazz opera, and part *Singspiele*. See Ross, p. 203.

33. *New Orpheus*, pp. 5, 148.

34. *New Orpheus*, p. 149.

35. Weill had accepted an invitation to join the prestigious *Novembergruppe* ("November Group"), an association of path-breaking German artists named after the November 1918 Revolution in Germany which marked the beginning of the end for World War I.

36. *New Orpheus*, p. 64. Brecht would later add a sixth number for the new *Mahagonny Songspiele*. His original source for the word "Mahagonny" is obscure; one good surmise is that Brecht, an avid song collector, lifted it from a now forgotten 1922 novelty tune, "Komm nache Mahagonne (Afrikanischer Shimmy)," by Leopold Krauss-Elka and A.O. Alberts.

37. Donald Spoto also noted the likely influence of Charlie Chaplin's *The Gold Rush* on *Mahagonny Songspiel*, as well as all aspects of American culture, including music and literature, flooding into Europe by this time. See Spoto, p. 74.

38. Ross, p. 223.

39. *New Orpheus*, p. 24.

40. Other famous composers premiering works at the 1927 Baden-Baden festival were Paul Hindemith, Darius Milhaud, and Ernst Toch.

41. *New Orpheus*, pp. 25–26. Weill effectively utilized the German traditions of *sprechgesang und Sprechstimme* ("spoken singing") in *Ma-*

hagonny, and would continue to do so throughout the remaining Berlin phase of his career.

42. Hirsch, p. 28. Alan Lareau noted that Weill's bold departures may have also been influenced by the *Kleinkunst* style of music pioneered in the Berlin literary cabarets of the early 1920s by composers such as Friedrich Hollaender and Mischa Spoliansky (see Chapter 6). See Lareau, p. 112.

43. *New Orpheus*, p. 165.

44. The Theater am Schiffbauerdamm had fewer than 800 seats. See *Lenya*, p. 79.

45. Foster Hirsch described the elusive Elisabeth Hauptmann as "a key player in Brecht's usual entourage of female companions." See Hirsch (p. 33) and *New Orpheus* (p. 165). Lotte Lenya pointedly added that "Brecht absolutely killed one woman after another. He really did." See *Legend*, pp. 66–68.

46. Hirsch, pp. 32–33.

47. Hirsch, p. 35.

48. *New Orpheus*, p. 166.

49. Hirsch, p. 38. For "Mack the Knife" Weill cleverly drew upon the old lower-class German traditions of gruesome ballads (*Moritaten*) and sad songs (*Küchenlied*). See *New Orpheus*, p. 38.

50. Hirsch, p. 41.

51. Hirsch, pp. 40–41.

52. Ross, pp. 209–210.

53. Alex Ross opined that, to Schoenberg, "The most infuriating apostasy was that of Kurt Weill." See Ross, pp. 217–218. See also *New Orpheus*, pp. 104–106.

54. Schoenberg composed his *Brettl-Lieder*, setting poetry from Otto Julius Bierbaum's *Deutsche Chansons*, before moving to Berlin in 1901 to work at Ernst von Wolzogen's Überbrettl (see Chapter 1). See also Bohlman, p. 216–217.

55. *New Orpheus*, pp. 171, 189. According to Lotte Lenya, a reliable insider, Brecht was only unpleasant when he had a public audience. She added that Brecht was very skilled and shrewd at working with actors. See *Legend*, pp. 51, 76. Regarding Brecht's claims to authorship, there is probably a grain of truth since he was known to have musical talent and his own later recording of "Mack the Knife" is wonderfully authoritative. On the other hand, it is now accepted that Brecht also plagiarized other writers and collaborators, particularly Elisabeth Hauptmann. Kate Kühl, an original cast member in *The Threepenny Opera*, later confirmed and made fun of Brecht's well-known propensity for wholesale literary "borrowings." See Lareau, p. 137. One is reminded of Beethoven's famous remark to the effect that good composers borrow and great composers steal.

56. Ross, p. 338.

57. Hirsch, p. 36.

58. *Mahagonny* has sometimes been appro-

priately called the true operatic successor to Berg's *Wozzeck* as a reflection of the modern industrial age. See *New Orpheus*, p. 45.

59. *New Orpheus*, pp. 134, 351.

60. The divorce was finalized on September 18, 1933. See *New Orpheus*, p. 352.

61. *New Orpheus*, p. 206.

62. *New Orpheus*, p. 352.

63. Hirsch, p. 120.

64. *New Orpheus*, p. 220.

65. *New Orpheus*, p. 233.

66. *New Orpheus*, pp. 244, 246.

67. German composer George Frideric Handel (1685–1759), after relocating to London, was famous for his competitive ability to recycle past works (and sometimes those of other composers as well) into new shapes and forms while meeting pressing deadlines inherent in musical theater.

Chapter 4

1. *New Orpheus*, p. 20.

2. Spoto, pp. 18–21.

3. Spoto, pp. 20–25.

4. Spoto, pp. 26, 28. See also *Legend*, p. 233.

5. Spoto, p. 35.

6. Spoto, pp. 34, 36–37, 39.

7. Spoto, p. 41.

8. Spoto, p. 50.

9. Spoto, p. 34. See also *Legend*, p. 235.

10. Spoto, p. 50. See also *Legend*, p. 42. Late in life, Lenya maintained that the greatest compliment she ever received as a singer was to be compared to the operetta star, Fritzi Massary (*Legend*, p. 216).

11. Spoto, p. 56. See also *Legend*, p. 44.

12. Spoto, pp. 52–53.

13. Spoto, p. 54.

14. Spoto, p. 56.

15. According to Lenya's recollections, at their first meeting near the train station Weill was wearing a Borsalino musician's hat, blue bow tie, and something akin to a "bar mitzvah suit." She added: "I could spot him like you spot a fly in a milk bottle." See *Legend*, p. 46.

16. Spoto, p. 66. See also *Legend*, p. 51.

17. Spoto, p. 67.

18. *Legend*, p. 123.

19. Spoto, pp. 68, 70.

20. Spoto, p. 78.

21. According to various accounts, the title of the "Alabama-Song" was randomly chosen because Brecht needed a word to rhyme with "mama" in the preceding verse. Other exotic place names in songs by Weill and Brecht such as Surabaya and Bilboa were often chosen for the same reason. See Spoto (p. 75) and *Legend* (p. 53).

22. Spoto, p. 76.

23. Spoto, p. 79. See also *Legend*, p. 235.

24. *Mahagonny* has sometimes been appropriately called the true operatic successor to Berg's *Wozzeck* as a reflection of the modern industrial age. See *New Orpheus*, p. 45.

25. Spoto, p. 95.

26. Spoto, p. 101. Weill's affairs, unlike Lenya's, were fewer but more serious. Lenya later reminisced that "He [Kurt] was very much in love with the wife of Caspar Neher, Erika. That was a lovely affair. She loved him, but nothing disturbed — that was a wall I didn't touch.... She [Erika] was like a little sexy pony, blonde, sturdy, and witty." See *Legend*, p. 126. Lenya also noted that Caspar Neher always remained his favorite set designer (p. 56).

27. Spoto, p. 104. Many years later, a regretful Lenya disparaged Pasetti and considered the affair a mistake. See *Legend*, p. 78.

28. Spoto, p. 104.

29. Spoto, pp. 109–111.

30. Spoto, p. 108.

31. Spoto, p. 114. See also *Legend*, p. 236.

32. *Legend*, p. 236.

33. *Legend*, p. 78.

34. Spoto, pp. 117, 119–120. See also *Legend*, p. 236.

35. Lenya later recalled Gershwin being heartbroken at *Porgy*'s poor reception. Gershwin, for his part, marveled at the raw, unschooled power of Lenya's vocal delivery. "She sings like a hillbilly" he reputedly exclaimed. See *Legend*, pp. 94, 224.

36. *Legend*, p. 236.

37. Spoto, pp. 237–238. See also *Legend*, p. 97.

38. *Legend*, p. 12.

39. *Legend*, p. 101, 104.

40. *Legend*, pp. 104, 238.

41. *Speak Low*, p. 485.

42. *Legend*, p. 127.

43. *Legend*, pp. 127, 238.

44. Spoto, p. 211.

45. Lenya makes this declaration in a letter to Manfred George, co-producer of the 1943 Hunter College recital in which she sang. See Spoto, p. 182.

46. After this show, many critics long hostile to Weill's music, such as Virgil Thomson, began to change their minds. See *Speak Low*, p. 486.

47. Spoto, pp. 193–194.

48. *Speak Low*, p. 487. Regarding the Brandeis concert in 1952, Lenya was surprised at the reception and later recalled that "I don't think I will ever hear the music played as beautifully as when Lenny did it. It was so magical and effortless." See *Legend*, p. 130.

Today the venue is known as the Lucille Lortel Theatre.

49. Spoto, p. 202. Today the same venue is known as the Lucille Lortel Theatre.

50. Spoto, p. 201.

51. Spoto, p. 205.

52. Spoto, p. 203.

53. As a rough gauge of public sentiment, McCarthy's rapid slide in popular opinion polls coincided with the first run of *The Threepenny Opera* in 1954.

54. Spoto, p. 202.

55. Spoto, p. 207. See also *Speak Low*, p. 487.

56. Spoto, p. 222. Weill had previously won a Tony Award in 1948 for his musical *Street Scene* (see Chapter 11). By that time, Lenya had more or less retired from the stage, or so she thought.

57. Ross, pp. 307–309. See also Spoto, p. 197.

58. www.kwf.org/kurt-weill/chronology. html.

59. Ross, pp. 379, 416.

60. Hirsch, p. 333.

61. Spoto, pp. 213, 217. By this point in time (1955), Brecht had only one year left to live. Between 1956 to 1960, Lenya would periodically return to Hamburg for documentary recordings of *Happy End, Die sieben Todsünden, Aufstig und Fall der Stadt Mahagonny,* and the original German-language version of *Die Dreigroschenoper* (Spoto, p. 240).

62. *Legend*, pp. 217, 219.

63. Spoto, p. 255.

64. The ghost of Lenya's Rosa Klebb is still with us in recent films such as *Indiana Jones and the Kingdom of the Crystal Skull* (2008) and *Austin Powers: International Man of Mystery* (1997), among others. In the latter, the character of Frau Frabissina has a German name more appropriate to Lenya's original portrayal. Interestingly, in *From Russia with Love,* the hidden, real name of the Russian Bond-girl Tatiana is Karoline — Lenya's birth name before she adopted a stage moniker, including the Russian bowdlerization of her Viennese nickname.

65. Hilariously, Lenya did not care much for Jill Hayworth, cast in the role of Sally Bowles, because the young British actress allegedly said she was bored and always complained. Lenya later said that she wanted to tell Hayworth to "get the hell out of the theater." See *Legend*, pp. 186–187.

66. Spoto, p. 288.

67. Spoto, 316.

68. Rather than catalogue these unhappy relationships, it seems more interesting to mention one that apparently got away, Lenya's unrequited crush for Dag Hammarskjöld (1905–1961), Swedish Secretary General of the United Nations. See Spoto, p. 248.

69. *Legend*, p. 230.

70. *Legend*, p. 229.

71. Spoto, p. 343.

Chapter 5

1. *Speak Low*, p. 366.

2. Spoto (*Blue Angel*), p. 7.

3. Spoto (*Blue Angel*), p. 12

4. Bach, p. 28.

5. Spoto (*Blue Angel*), p. 10.

6. Spoto (*Blue Angel*), p. 15

7. Bach, pp. 22–23.

8. Spoto (*Blue Angel*), pp. 24, 27.

9. Bach, p. 49.

10. Spoto (*Blue Angel*), p. 45. See also Bach, p. 50.

11. Spoto (*Blue Angel*), p. 293.

12. Spoto (*Blue Angel*), p. 45.

13. Also featured in *Tragedy of Love* was Dietrich's future co-star in *The Blue Angel*, Emil Jannings. See Bach, pp. 60–61. It was through an unwitting Jannings that Dietrich's name was later mentioned to director Josef von Sternberg. Therefore, in hindsight, Sieber's help given to Dietrich at this very early stage in her career appears crucial, though it took a few years to fully manifest itself.

14. Spoto (*Blue Angel*), p. 33. See also Bach, p. 51.

15. Louise Brooks would later land the coveted title role in Pabst's lauded film version of *Pandora's Box* in 1929 (see Chapter 10). See Bach, p. 86. See also Spoto (*Blue Angel*), p. 35.

16. Spoto (*Blue Angel*), p. 31.

17. Spoto (*Blue Angel*), p. 43–44. See also Bach, pp. 76–78, 485. Some four decades later, George Abbott would prove instrumental in jumpstarting the Broadway careers of John Kander, Fred Ebb, and Liza Minnelli (see Chapter 15).

18. Spoto (*Blue Angel*), p. 45. Sternheim's sister was also married to conductor Albert Bing of Dessau, Kurt Weill's earliest musical mentor (see Chapter 3). As for Rudolf Nelson, one his most famous songs, "Peter, Peter, komm zu mir Zurück" (co-written with Hollaender), after being memorably introduced by in 1929 by Mary Losseff (wife of Richard Tauber), was soon thereafter recorded spectacularly by Dietrich in 1930.

19. Spoto (*Blue Angel*), p. 27.

20. Waldoff arrived in Berlin before the war and quickly established herself at Roland von Berlin and Rudolf Nelson's later venues. By the 1920s, she was one of cabaret's first celebrities. See Jelavich, pp. 101–102. A good sampling of her boisterous art can be heard in Friedrich Hollaender's "Raus mit den Männern!" ("Get Rid of the Men!").

21. Appignanesi, p. 146. Dietrich had was known to have cross-dressed on stage since high school; in Waldoff, however, she may have discovered for the first time a woman with bold

male fashion affectations both in and out of the theater.

22. Bach, pp. 73–74.

23. Dietrich was reportedly fond of tangoing with attractive female performers such as Carola Neher, soon to be a star in Kurt Weill's operas. See Spoto (*Blue Angel*), pp. 38–39.

24. This dramatic account is recalled in Dietrich's own autobiography and retold on Spoliansky's website. See www.mischaspoliansky. com.

25. For this number, Dietrich and Lion pinned violets on themselves, at the time a symbol of same-sex romantic love. See Spoto (*Blue Angel*), pp. 46–47. See also Bach, pp. 84–85.

26. Spoto, pp. 56–57. See also Bach, pp. 96–97.

27. Leni Riefenstahl, Trude Hesterberg, and Lucie Mannheim were said or rumored to be among the formidable competition. See Bach, pp. 106–107.

28. Bach, p. 186.

29. Bach, p. 242.

30. Family photos of the young Dietrich sisters exist in which Elisabeth's image has been intentionally cropped out. See illustrations in Bach.

31. Bach, p. 307. The conduct of Dietrich's sister and brother-in-law at Bergen-Belsen during the war has been defended (including by Dietrich herself on occasion) as resulting from coercion and threats by the Nazis. Therefore, the siblings' mutual denial was allegedly to protect each other. One problem with this explanation is that the behavior in question seemed to continue long after the war was over. Another is that Dietrich's relatives had several opportunities to leave Germany before the war but chose not to.

32. Dietrich was far more successful helping her husband's family trapped in the Russian zone of East Germany. After a personal interview with Marshall Zhukov himself was granted, the Siebers were removed from a detention camp and received favorable treatment. See Spoto (*Blue Angel*), p. 204.

33. Spoto (*Blue Angel*), p. 232.

34. Spoto, for instance, notes that "for six weeks, in the most successful cabaret show in postwar London." See Spoto (*Blue Angel*), p. 251.

35. Bach, p. 400.

36. Bach, pp. 401, 403.

37. Not until 2002 was Dietrich posthumously made an honorary citizen of Berlin.

38. Spoto (*Blue Angel*), p. 292.

39. Spoto (*Blue Angel*), pp. 1–3, 301. See also Bach, pp. 448–449.

40. After this, her only participation in a film project (voice only) was for a documentary on

her own life by Maximilian Schell in 1982–1984. It is not known whether she had any contact with her old Weimar co-performer Margo Lion, who also lived in Paris until her death in 1989.

41. Spoto (*Blue Angel*), pp. 299–300.

Chapter 6

1. Bohlman, p. 201.

2. Ross, p. 362.

3. Hollaender was in fact born in London. He became one of Humperdinck's master students at the Stern Conservatory (see www.fred erickhollandermusic.com); Weill, on the other hand, was later a master student under Ferruccio Busoni after having been one of Humperdinck's students at the Hochschule für Musik (see Chapter 3).

4. Lareau, p. 57.

5. Appignanesi, pp. 135–136.

6. Jelavich, p. 10.

7. Bohlman, pp. 218–219. Much of Hollaender's early film music was written for UFA, Germany's leading film company during the Weimar era.

8. Lareau, p. 112. This praise does not give full credit to Hollaender's influential later work, but his compositions from the early 1920s certainly represent a high-point of sorts.

9. Hollaender also later recorded as director of his Jazz-Symphoniker group, usually with Dietrich singing. See Bohlman, pp. 218–219.

10. Jelavich, p. 190.

11. Jelavich, p. 207. Hollaender often wrote his own lyrics in these late Berlin works, although he also worked with first rate lyricists, including Kurt Tucholsky, Rudolf Nelson, and Marcellus Schiffer. See also *Cabaret Berlin*, p. 111. Other memorable highlights of Hollaender's Weimar songwriting period include the beautiful, poignant tango "Eine kleine Sehnsucht" ("A Little Bit of Yearning"); the outrageous "Gesetzt den Fall" ("Let Us Just Say"); and the free-spirited "Ich weiß nicht, zu wem ich gehöre" ("Don't Know Who I Belong To"), the last written with lyricist Robert Liebmann, who also had teamed with Hollaender on the *Blue Angel* Dietrich anthem, "Ich bin die Fesche Lola" ("They Call Me Naughty Lola").

12. Jelavich, pp. 186, 207. See also *Cabaret Berlin*, p. 111.

13. Hollaender was not being alarmist in his quick exodus from Germany. His relatives in Berlin who had long successfully run the prestigious Stern Conservatory were later murdered during the Holocaust.

14. *Cabaret Berlin*, pp. 116–117. See also www.mischaspolinsky.com.

15. Schiffer's breakthrough at the Wild Stage,

in collaboration with Spoliansky and Lion, was *Die Linie der Mode* ("The Shape of Fashion") in which the exaggerated skinniness and absurd, voguish demeanor of Lion's character anticipates the anorexic, Twiggy-led fashion trends of the 1960s and beyond. This theme would continue to be the Schiffer's forte. Alan Lareau observed that "Schiffer presents Berlin as the breeding ground for endless neurotics — especially pathological women...." See Lareau, pp. 98–99.

16. Other great songs by later written by Spoliansky (with Marcellus Schiffer as lyricist) departing from conventional ideas of human sexuality or, for that matter, conventional images of womanhood, include "Ich bin ein Vamp!" ("I Am a Vamp!") and *Maskulinum — Femininum* ("Masculine-Feminine").

17. See www.mischaspoliansky.com.

18. In early 1935, Weill's anger at Spoliansky for winning a film commission over him in England apparently did not last very long, as the two soon afterwards attended a London musical revue together. See *Speak Low*, pp. 136, 152, 157, 169–170, 176.

19. Lareau, p. 113. The plot concerns a Berlin department store employee ("Mr. Plim") whose sole task is to stage being sacked by store management in order to satisfy customer complaints. Other terrific Spoliansky-Schiffer compositions from the same period dealing with similar themes of commercialism and human vanity include "Alles Schwindel" ("Everything Is a Swindle"); "L'heure bleue" ("The Blue Hour"); and "Das Gesellschaftslied" ("Song of the Trendy Set").

20. Dietrich's male co-stars in these films were Gary Cooper, Melvyn Douglas, James Stewart, and John Wayne. Regarding *Destry Rides Again*, film music historian Gary Marmorstein noted that Hollaender was among the émigré composers who "made up the Western sound as they went along." See Marmorstein, p. 299.

21. Marmorstein, pp. 43, 162.

22. See www.mischaspoliansky.com.

23. Schiffer's two collaborations with Hindemith include the 1929 full-length opera *Neues vom Tage* ("News of the Day") and the 1927 one-act opera *Hin und Zurück* ("There and Back"), the latter first performed at the same Baden-Baden music festival in which Weill & Brecht's *Mahagonny Songspiele* was premiered (see Chapter 3). See Lareau, pp. 74, 97.

24. The Hollaender-Schiffer composition *Sex-Appeal*, originally performed by Lion, is a prototypical cabaret satire that also manages to give a sly, respectful nod towards its subject matter. Schiffer also worked with Hollaender on the composer's second musical revue from 1926, *Hetärengespräche* ("Hetaira-Talk"). See Jelavich, pp. 190–191.

25. Lareau, p. 97.

26. Gay, pp. 128–129.

27. Graetz's passing was noted in moving letter from Kurt Weill to Lotte Lenya dated February 20, 1937. See *Speak Low*, pp. 209–210.

28. Another prominent cabaret victim was Paul Nikolaus, comedian and former *conférencier* at Berlin's Kadeko (see Chapter 8), who committed suicide after fleeing to Switzerland in 1933. See Jelavich, p. 231.

29. A yet-to-be-world-famous Marlene Dietrich, as a protégé of Reinhardt, had earlier played the role of Hippolyta in a German-language production of *A Midsummer Night's Dream* in 1924 (see Chapter 5).

30. Jelavich states that Nelson went into hiding. See Jelavich, pp. 160–163. Other sources maintain that Nelson was an inmate at Westerbork. See www.jewish-theatre.com. Surely the most famous Holocaust victim of this same time and place was the young Anne Frank.

31. Kurt Weill appreciated Nelson's character and talents, urging Lotte Lenya in his letters from Paris to stay on good terms with Nelson for the sake of her career. See *Speak Low*, pp. 140, 144.

32. Gerron also handled the spoken introductions for Lenya's classic 1930 recordings with the Ruth Lewis Band of Weill & Brecht's "Pirate Jenny" and the "Barbara-Song."

33. Jelavich, p. 275. Gerron was not the only *Blue Angel* alumnus-victim of the Holocaust. Charles Puffy (aka Károly Hochstadt) played the owner of the Blue Angel nightclub in the movie. He died in 1943 or 1944 under obscure circumstances reportedly while trying to flee east through the Soviet Union in an attempt to reach the United States.

34. Jelavich, p. 280.

35. In a stupefying coincidence, Gerron's "Carousel" cabaret was conceived and performed around the same time in 1944 that Rodgers and Hammerstein were creating their own musical *Carousel* to premier on Broadway in 1945. There are even some thematic similarities between the two programs.

36. Leo Strauss spelled his last name with a double "s" at the end, like the more famous Strauss family of Vienna, and unlike his father Oscar, who spelled his name "Straus" with one "s."

37. Jelavich, p. 277.

38. Bach, p. 325.

39. Much earlier (in 1941), Hollaender had also penned a semi-autobiographical novel in English titled *Those Torn from Earth*. He was also awarded the *Bundesverdienstkreuz* ("Order of Merit") by the Federal Republic of Germany, among other honors. See www.frederickhollandermusic.com.

40. Jelavich, p. 228.

Chapter 7

1. Isherwood, p. 207.
2. See www.cabaret-berlin.com.
3. *Christopher and His Kind* was later made into a 2011 feature film by the BBC.
4. Isherwood, p. v.
5. Bowles was both an accomplished composer who had studied with Aaron Copland in New York, France, and North Africa. As an author, his most famous work is probably the novel *The Sheltering Sky* (1949), later made into a feature film in 1990.
6. As is well-documented, right up until Hitler declared war on the U.S. in late 1941 (four days after Pearl Harbor), many Americans continued to sympathize with and even admire the Third Reich. Some still do, in fact, while others dare to deny that the Holocaust ever really occurred.
7. Isherwood, p. 206.
8. Both works now typically are published under a single title, *The Berlin Stories* (see Bibliography). The American title for the first installment was *The Last of Mr. Norris*.
9. Isherwood, p. 98.
10. Isherwood, p. 32.
11. Isherwood, p. 22.
12. Isherwood, p. 84.
13. Isherwood, p. 23.
14. Isherwood, p. 21. The second half of the narrative begins with "A Berlin Diary" and is specifically dated by the author as Autumn, 1930 (p. 1).
15. Isherwood, p. 76.
16. Isherwood, p. 25.
17. Ross, pp. 197–198. Lotte Lenya later recalled the same location as a well-known advertising spot for S&M prostitutes (see Chapter 4).
18. Isherwood, pp. 118, 192, 193.
19. Isherwood, pp. 20, 30.
20. Isherwood, p. 34.
21. Sacher-Masoch was also allegedly the great-great-uncle of future English performer Marianne Faithful, a great musical champion of Weimar cabaret tradition.
22. Isherwood, pp. 10, 117. To underscore the prejudices of German society, even some of Isherwood's young student characters in the story are anti–Semitic. See also p. 182.
23. Isherwood, p. 161.
24. Isherwood, p. 158.
25. Isherwood, p. 42.
26. Isherwood, pp. 179, 206–207.
27. Isherwood, p. 199.
28. Isherwood, p. 205.
29. Isherwood, p. 189.
30. The German invasion of Poland took place in 1939, the London Blitz in 1940, and Pearl Harbor in 1941.
31. Isherwood dated his post-war Berlin recollections from his home in Santa Monica, July, 1954. See Isherwood, pp. xiii–ix.
32. Isherwood, p. 10.

Chapter 8

1. Appignanesi, p. 159.
2. Gay, p. 132.
3. William Harrison Hays, Sr. (1879–1954) of Sullivan, Indiana, before accepting a lucrative offer from Hollywood, had been the former campaign manager for President Warren G. Harding, U.S. Postmaster General, National Chairman of the Republican Party, and Presbyterian Church deacon.
4. Black, p. 50.
5. For example, there is the famous anecdote of Sternberg angrily insisting that Dietrich wear underwear on the movie set, an occasional infraction that she was known to commit throughout her career.
6. Jelavich, p. 228. See also Lareau, p. 15. After the Nazi takeover in 1933, the Kadeko was "Aryanized" and continued to operate in watered-down form until it was closed in 1944 by Goebbels, along with most other wartime entertainment venues. After its destruction by Allied bombing in 1945, the site of the Kadeko was appropriately rebuilt as a theatrical facility with the Schaubühne am Lehniner Platz.
7. Jelavich, p. 198.
8. The brilliant Valeska Gert has been sometimes hailed as the "inventor of the social-critical dance pantomime." See Appignanesi, p. 147. See also Lareau, pp. 15, 136, 138.
9. Jelavich, p. 204.
10. Lareau, p. 15.
11. Jelavich, pp. 30–31. Alleged origins of this black-style humor in the Thirty Years War is not surprising, given the absurdities of that conflict as bewildered Catholics and Protestants watched alleged religious strife transform into a prolonged and bloody land grab, with constantly-shifting, multi-denominational alliances on opposing sides.
12. Appignanesi, p. 174. During World War I, Nelson was even known to make unflattering Jewish jokes to his cabaret audiences, despite being Jewish himself (and drawing official complaints in the process). See Jelavich, pp. 123–124. It has been noted that "Jewish humor ... derived in part from the *Purim Spiel*, as distinctive because it was wide-open and could poke fun at almost anything. Most non–Jews were not used to that sort of thing, but it caught on." (interview with Stewart Figa)
13. Jelavich, p. 197.
14. Gay, p. 5.

15. Jelavich, p. 207.
16. See www.cabaret-berlin.com.
17. The Catacombs were located in the basement of Berlin's famed Scala variety theater.
18. Lareau, pp. 152–153, 163.
19. Lareau, p. 165.
20. Finck was briefly portrayed by Jewish comedian Mort Sahl in the ABC television miniseries *Inside the Third Reich* (1982), based on the memoirs of Albert Speer.
21. Thanks to Stewart Figa (during interview) for these observations.
22. Lenya also recalled Berber's enormous drug habit. See *Legend*, p. 215. One surmises that boundary pushing stars like Lenya and Marlene Dietrich, unlike Berber, were able to survive mainly because of their comparative temperance in this regard.
23. One convenient source to get a good feel for the licentious world of Weimar Germany that Nazis and their collaborators later reacted so strongly against is the astonishing coffee-table book by Mel Gordon, *Voluptuous Panic: The Erotic World of Weimar Berlin* (2000).
24. Rewald, p. 11.
25. Jelavich, p. 175. This was possibly a direct insult aimed at the venerated Louis Armstrong (though a trumpeter, not a saxophonist), who wore the Star of David around his neck in homage to New Orleans Jewish family who first showed him kindness as a child.
26. "Degenerate Music," as defined by the Nazis, turned out to comprise a surprisingly eclectic group of composers — more or less anyone whom Hitler was not a fan of. See Ross, pp. 350–351.
27. Ross, p. 362.
28. For example, Weill & Brecht's *Der Jasager* has much in common thematically with the one-act opera *The Second Hurricane* (1936) by Aaron Copland, a quintessentially American New Deal–era composer. See Ross, p. 302.
29. A number of cabaret songs by composers such as Friedrich Hollaender and Mischa Spoliansky from the same late period of the Weimar Republic also have more militantly anti–Nazi overtones (see Chapter 6).

Chapter 9

1. Rewald, p. 20.
2. Statistics cited are from Amos Elon. See Rewald, p. 3.
3. Rewald, p. 3.
4. Rewald, p. 19.
5. Rewald, p. 21.
6. Sabine Rewald, like so many others, judged *neue Sachlichkeit* to be "the most vital of the various post–Expressionist styles that devel-

oped in Germany after the war." See Rewald, p. 4.
7. Gay, p. 4.
8. Ross, p. 61.
9. Spoto (*Blue Angel*), p. 23.
10. Rewald, p. 15.
11. Rewald, p. 5.
12. Rewald, p. 15.
13. Rewald, p. 18.
14. Rewald, p. 19.
15. Rewald, p. 9.
16. Rewald, pp. 29, 31.
17. Rewald, p. 51. Beckmann's *Here Is Intellect* (1921) has a similar biting message.
18. Rewald, p. 53.
19. Rewald, p. 35.
20. Rewald, pp. 33–34, 36, 217.
21. Rewald, p. 143.
22. Rewald, pp. 11, 135. *Cabaret* song lyricist, the late Fred Ebb (see Chapter 16), also amassed a large collection of works from this period, later donated to the Morgan Library and Museum. See Leve, p. 12.
23. Rewald, p. 49.
24. Rewald, pp. 212–213.
25. Rewald, p. 11.
26. Rewald, pp. 11, 23.
27. Rewald, pp. 129, 131.
28. The inherent anti–Semitic themes of *The Golem* prefigured Wegener's later complicity as an artist with the German Nazi regime.
29. The Spoliansky-Schiffer cabaret song "Ich bin ein Vamp!" ("I Am a Vamp!") is one example of this trend, comically combining the image of a vampire with that of a femme fatale narrator.
30. *M* featured a memorable lead performance by future German exile Peter Lorre, as well as a brief appearance by Weimar cabaret star Rosa Valetti, as the murderer's landlady.
31. Gay, p. 6.
32. Some of the most stunning architectural designs produced by the Bauhaus came during its high-water period in Dessau (1925–1932), previous home town of Kurt Weill and (briefly) home to Marlene Dietrich.
33. Spoto (*Blue Angel*), p. 17. Peter Gay remarks that "...some of Feininger's, Klee's, and Kandinsky's most interesting graphic work was done at the Bauhaus." See Gay, p. 99.
34. Striking images of Mendelsohn's Kadeko design can be found at www.cabaret-berlin.com.
35. Lareau, p. 75. Lareau, a German-English professor at University of Wisconsin, prefers the translation for *neue Sachlikeit* as "New Sobriety." See p. 96.
36. Jelavich, p. 191.
37. Bach, pp. 79, 485.
38. Hinton characterizes Weill as himself "a kind of new Orpheus" whose mid–1920s exper-

imental work was "a significant stepping-stone" towards *The Threepenny Opera*—an inevitable move towards *Gebrauchsmusik* ("Utilitarian Music") via *neue Sachlichkeit*. See "*neue Sachlichkeit*, Surrealism, and *Gebrauchsmusik*" by Stephen Hinton, *New Orpheus*, p. 82.

39. Hirsch, p. 56.

Chapter 10

1. BBC interview "The World of Josef von Sternberg" (1966). See Criterion Collection special features for *The Scarlet Empress* (1934).

2. Rewald, p. 17.

3. Sternberg, p. 230. The title of Sternberg's memoir is taken from an early Edison silent film.

4. Appignanesi, pp. 42–43.

5. Berg's creation of *Lulu* had also reputedly been influenced by the recent music of Kurt Weill, especially *The Rise and Fall of the City of Mahagonny*, which he saw performed in Vienna. See Ross, p. 228.

6. Sternberg, p. 230.

7. According to Dietrich's biographer Donald Spoto, Sternberg and Dietrich consciously thought of themselves as Pygmalion and Galatea in their professional relationship. See Spoto (*Blue Angel*), pp. 56–57. Reportedly, at Sternberg's behest, during the filming of *Shanghai Express* Dietrich agreed to do 60 takes of a single scene. See BBC interview "The World of Josef von Sternberg" (1966). See Criterion Collection special features for *The Scarlet Empress* (1934).

8. BBC interview "The World of Josef von Sternberg" (1966). See Criterion Collection special features for *The Scarlet Empress* (1934). The young Sternberg was in fact known to admire the directorial work of his older, fellow Austrian émigré, Erich von Stroheim (1885–1957).

9. *The Salvation Hunters* was favorably noticed by the likes of Charlie Chaplin, Mary Pickford, and Douglas Fairbanks, Jr. *Underworld* has been called the first true gangster movie.

10. Universal Film AG ("UFA") was Germany's largest film studio during the Weimar era and beyond. Because of UFA, as noted by film music historian Gary Marmorstein, "Berlin was the film-making capitol of Europe in the '20s and early '30s, before the Nazis came to power." See Marmorstein, p. 92.

11. Sternberg in his memoir respectfully notes that both Gerron and Puffy later died in the Holocaust. See Sternberg, p. 149.

12. Hollaender was then employed as an accompanist for Lucie Mannheim, considered a frontrunner for the role of Lola Lola. See Sternberg, p. 236.

13. Sternberg, pp. 236–237.

14. Sternberg, p. 230.

15. Sternberg, p. 231.

16. Sternberg, p. 232.

17. Sternberg, p. 236.

18. Spoto (*Blue Angel*), pp. 56–57.

19. Sternberg, p. 238.

20. In these respective films, Sternberg paired Dietrich with young leading men the likes of which included Gary Cooper, Victor McLaglen, Clive Brook, Cary Grant (in his breakthrough role), John Lodge, and Cesar Romero.

21. Dietrich's strictly dramatic roles are sometimes presented by Sternberg as allegories of Dietrich's own rising international fame. For example, in *The Scarlet Express*, her portrayal of a young Catherine the Great is not unlike that of her real-life film career: a talented young German princess going off to a foreign land (Russia-Hollywood) and ruthlessly rising to power by any means necessary.

22. Sternberg noted that he wanted to prove Dietrich had intelligence as well as beauty, since she had often been accused of getting roles solely because of her good looks. Sternberg, p. 247. To promote *Morocco*, Sternberg had her do a similar cross-dressing trailer for Paramount, "Introducing Marlene Dietrich." See Bach, p. 129. Biographer Steven Bach (p. 68), without too much exaggeration, calls Dietrich's performance in *Morocco* "the most memorable enunciation of sexual ambiguity in any picture." For 1930, it certainly must have been a shocker for American audiences.

23. Some of Dietrich's early French persona film roles before her collaboration with Sternberg included *Manon Lescaut* (1926) and *Prinzessin Olala* (1928).

24. *The Blue Angel* was initially censored in Pasadena, California, but this ruling was soon overturned by the newly-enacted Hay's Code (see Chapter 8).

25. BBC interview "The World of Josef von Sternberg" (1966). See Criterion Collection special features for *The Scarlet Empress* (1934). See also Bach, p. 425.

26. Weill & Brecht engaged in a well-known lawsuit to retain artistic control over their original creation. Weill eventually settled, while Brecht fought and lost—a good summation of each artist's character.

27. *Legend*, p. 68.

28. For the French-language version of *The Threepenny Opera*, Pabst wisely cast as Jenny the Weimar chanteuse Margo Lion, also wife and muse of lyricist Marcellus Schiffer (see Chapter 6).

29. Pabst also took advantage of Busch's multiple talents in *Kameraschaft* ("Comradeship") also from 1931, his highly-regarded follow-up to *The Threepenny Opera*.

30. Biographer Donald Spoto noted that

Lenya in this scene alone displays "reservoirs of personal history." See Spoto (*Lenya*), p. 88.

31. *Legend*, p. 215.

Chapter 11

1. *New Orpheus*, p. 217.

2. Hirsch, p. 117. The first American production on Broadway of *The Threepenny Opera* suffered from a hasty English translation by Gifford Cochran and Jerold Krimsky. The show lasted for only 12 performances. See *New Orpheus*, p. 351.

3. Weill and Lenya arrived in New York City on September 10, 1935. See *New Orpheus*, p. 353. Alex Ross wrote that Weill's *Mahagonny* and Gershwin's *Porgy* "both aimed for approximately the same synthesis"—specifically, between the populist, elitist and traditionalist views of music. See Ross (p. 312) and Spoto (*Lenya*), p. 124.

4. Alex Ross observed that Copland and Gershwin had very similar musical backgrounds. See Ross, p. 290.

5. Ross, p. 297.

6. Ross, p. 302.

7. One could go even further and argue that Coplandesque influences on contemporary film music, such as can be found in, say, the distinguished work of Randy Newman (see Chapter 18), partially owe their origins to Weill's early determination in reaching as wide an audience as possible. By contrast, after Weill's death in 1950, Copland seems to have returned to a more esoteric style, resulting in major works such as his opera *The Tender Land* (1954) being rejected by its original television commissioners. Another factor was probably that Copland (unlike Weill) is today remembered primarily as a composer of instrumental, rather than vocal music.

8. Future *Threepenny Opera* English translator Marc Blitzstein was included in this group as well. See Ross, p. 285.

9. Seeger's brief tenure at RA was possibly his finest moment in a long, distinguished career. See Pescatello, pp. 145–146, 158.

10. Pescatello, pp. 136–138, 140, 161. Seeger also had a knack for hiring able subordinates such as the versatile and multi-talented Margaret Valiant (pp. 143–145).

11. Pescatello, p. 163. Sidney Robertson Cowell, wife of composer Henry Cowell (one of Seeger's former students), wrote that Seeger "led the first effective attack on the barriers that separated sophisticated musicians from the music of the American oral tradition." See Pescatello, p. 147.

12. Alex Ross marveled that "Weill's hardbitten Berlin style transferred to the American

stage with remarkable ease...." Perhaps it would be more accurate to say that this style transferred well because of the composer's ability and willingness to evolve. Weill put it best, when he said, "There is only good music and bad music." See Ross, p. 313.

13. Ross, p. 343.

14. Ross, p. 312. See also Spoto (*Lenya*), pp. 126–127.

15. Green's play was loosely based on the Jaroslav Hašek novel *The Good Soldier Schewyk*, a work also admired by Weill. See *Legend*, p. 95.

16. *Legend*, pp. 193–194.

17. Spoto (*Lenya*), p. 127. See also *New Orpheus* (p. 353) and Hirsch (p. 138).

18. *Legend*, pp. 232, 267.

19. Spoto (*Lenya*), p. 129.

20. *Speak Low*, p. 209.

21. Marmorstein, p. 89.

22. Marmorstein, pp. 107, 109.

23. *Speak Low*, pp. 207–208, 226.

24. *Speak Low*, pp. 240, 242.

25. *Legend*, p. 98.

26. Spoto (*Lenya*), p. 134.

27. *New Orpheus*, pp. 291–292.

28. *New Orpheus*, p. 195.

29. *New Orpheus*, p. 9.

30. *New Orpheus*, p. 328.

31. *New Orpheus*, p. 287.

32. *New Orpheus*, p. 355.

33. Spoto (*Lenya*) p. 145.

34. *New Orpheus*. p. 291. See also Spoto (*Lenya*), p. 147. *Lady in the Dark* was also the last Broadway production in a long, distinguished line by Sam Harris.

35. During the production, Weill reportedly forged a close professional relationship with the notoriously difficult Lawrence, becoming, in the words of biographer Foster Hirsch, "in effect her confidant and caretaker." See Hirsch, p. 184.

36. Hirsch, p. 200. See also Spoto (*Lenya*), p. 148.

37. Conductor Maurice Abravanel recalled hearing Aaron Copland praise Weill's economy in composition and ability to achieve great effects with few notes in reference to *Lady in the Dark*. See Hirsch, p. 186. Weill felt that, other than some individual songs, his music to *Lady* was overall superior to that of Gershwin's *Porgy and Bess*, thus fulfilling a personal ambition held since he first arrived in America. See *Speak Low*, p. 287.

38. The George Bernard Shaw 1912 stage version of the Ovid myth would also later yield several famous film and musical treatments, including *Pygmalion* (1938), with which Weill's 1943 creative team was undoubtedly familiar. This British film featured a memorable performance by Leslie Howard as Higgins, plus one of David Lean's first major production credits. From this more serious take on the legend evolved the 1956

hit musical (and 1964 movie) *My Fair Lady* by Lerner & Loewe. Jay Allen Lerner had previously been a Weill protégée and lyricist for the 1948 musical *Love Life*.

39. Hirsch, p. 231.

40. Both of these films mostly dispensed with Weill's music and the original Broadway castings.

41. *New Orpheus*, p. 325. See also Ross, p. 164.

42. *New Orpheus*, p. 325.

43. The Tony Awards began in 1947, named in honor of Antionette Perry (1888–1946), a prominent, multi-talented Broadway figure.

44. *New Orpheus*, p. 293.

45. Frederick Loewe (1901–1988), like Weill, was a German-born émigré to America who had once studied under Ferruccio Busoni. See Hirsch, p. 231.

46. Weill, Lenya, and Lerner all took the trouble to attend the 1948 premier of *Down in the Valley* in Bloomington, Indiana. Interestingly, the program also included a performance of Paul Hindemith's one act opera *Hin und Zurück*, libretto by Marcellus Schiffer (see Chapter 6). This work premiered in 1927 at the same Baden-Baden music festival in Germany which launched Weill and Lenya into international prominence with a featured production of *Mahagonny Songspiele*. See *Legend*, p. 106. Hindemith's *Hin und Zurück*, like Weill's *Down in the Valley*, continues to be a popular work for college student productions in the U.S. For example, a recent 2010 production of *Hin und Zurück* was mounted at Wichita State University in Kansas.

47. *New Orpheus*, pp. 298, 357.

48. For example, one cannot help but note a similarity in the villainous characterizations of Bouche from *Down in the Valley* and Jud from *Oklahoma!*

49. *New Orpheus*, pp. 175–176.

50. Interesting film versions, however, were later made for *Cabin in the Sky* (1943) and *Carmen Jones* (1954), directed by Vincente Minnelli and Otto Preminger, respectively.

51. *New Orpheus*, pp. 10, 357. See also *Legend*, p. 113.

52. *New Orpheus*, p. 12.

53. *New Orpheus*, p. 294.

54. For example, Foster Hirsch has noted that Weill's *Happy End* (1929) had a direct influence on great American musicals following immediately after Weill's death, such as Frank Loesser's *Guys and Dolls* (1950). See Hirsch, pp. 57, 62. Loesser had also worked with Weill's fellow Weimar émigré, Friedrich Hollaender (see Chapter 6).

55. *New Orpheus*, p. 324. Despite their intense rivalry, Weill remained on cordial social terms with both Rodgers and Hammerstein. See *Speak Low*, pp. 303, 308, 333, 460.

56. *Speak Low*, pp. 375–376.

57. Weill recognized these deficiencies in Eisler and consequently did not hold a particularly high opinion of his music. See *Speak Low*, pp. 124, 149.

58. "Eisler on the Go" was later set to music and recorded by Billy Bragg with the group Wilco for their 1998 album, *Mermaid Avenue*.

59. Ross, p. 516.

60. *New Orpheus*, p. 321.

Chapter 12

1. Marais, a veteran actor from Jean Cocteau's films, was introducing Dietrich to a Monte Carlo audience when he made this comment. See Spoto (*Blue Angel*), p. 252.

2. The Marx Brothers were pioneers in popularizing a distinctively "Jewish" style of impudent humor for mass American audiences. To this day, the style is on full display whenever, for example, Billy Crystal hosts the Oscar Awards. It would be fair to say that this no-holds-barred kind of joking "came out" to an even wider public during World War II.

3. Dietrich was lovingly parodied by Brooks in *Blazing Saddles* (1974), as Madeline Kahn portrays the infamous German *chanteuse* Lili Von Shtupp.

4. Jelavich, pp. 188–189.

5. Jelavich, p. 263.

6. *Cabaret Berlin*, pp. 112–113.

7. During this period, Heymann often found himself (as Benatzky later would as well) working with Robert Gilbert, future lyricist behind songs of *The White Horse Inn*.

8. Arguably the best-known of Heymann's American film scores today are from those directed by his fellow German émigré, Ernst Lubitsch, including *Ninotchka* (1939), starring Greta Garbo.

9. *Cabaret Berlin*, pp. 114–115.

10. *New Orpheus*, p. 355. The show was produced by Ernst Aufricht, the same man who had hired Weill and Lenya 15 years earlier for the Berlin premier of *The Threepenny Opera*. See also Hirsch, p. 206.

11. Interestingly, Hanns Eisler had also set this same text to music, more in keeping with Brecht's literary intentions but far less gripping and entertaining than Weill's version. See *New Orpheus*, p. 197.

12. *New Orpheus*, p. 356.

13. *Speak Low*, p. 285. Dietz's musical collaborators on Broadway included Jerome Kern, Vernon Duke, and Arthur Schwartz.

14. Weill tried to interest Robeson in two classically-themed operas (based on the legends of Ulysses and Oedipus). There had also been earlier discussion of an all-black *Threepenny*

Opera. Nothing came of these discussions and correspondence. See *Speak Low*, pp. 287–288, 452, 455, 459, 462. Robeson did find time, however, record a song by Weill's future English librettist, Marc Blitzstein. Blitzstein's "The Purest Kind of Guy" (from his abortive 1939 opera *No for an Answer*) was recorded by Robeson in 1942 around the same time as his famous "Joe Hill" interpretation and other works later included in the collection "Songs of Free Men."

15. Bach (*Blue Angel*), p. 174.
16. *Speak Low*, pp. 82, 99, 103, 115–116.
17. *Speak Low*, pp. 119–120, 122, 127.
18. Weill hoped to work with Dietrich through director Ernst Lubitsch, who directed her in *Angel* (1937). Dietrich, for her part, was supposedly "jealous" that Weill was at one point working with director Fritz Lang. See *Speak Low*, pp. 148, 162, 209, 224, 228, 234–235, 237, 257, 262.
19. *Speak Low*, pp. 364–367.
20. *Speak Low*, p. 369. See also Hirsch, p. 215.
21. Martin had recently made a big hit of Cole Porter's "My Heart Belongs to Daddy," earlier premiering the song on Broadway.
22. Lotte Lenya later remarked that Mary Martin was better in the role of Venus that Marlene Dietrich because of her formally trained voice. Afterwards, Dietrich continued to studiously avoid the Broadway stage throughout most of her career. Her coy withdrawal from Weill's *Venus* project may have been a case of pure nerves. See *Legend*, p. 217.
23. The password assigned to Dietrich by Patton was "Legs." During her tour of duty, Dietrich reportedly had an affair with U.S. General James M. Gavin, who was antagonistic towards Patton but also allowed Dietrich to move about freely in the combat zone. Later Gavin helped Dietrich locate her family in occupied Germany. See Spoto (*Blue Angel*), pp. 197, 200, 203.
24. Two years after the war ended (in 1947), Dietrich starred in the film *Golden Earings*, in which she portrays a singing gypsy who covertly assists the Allied war effort in Europe.
25. Spoto (*Blue Angel*), p. 232. Dietrich was Awarded the Medal of Freedom in 1947 and the Legion of Honor in 1950.
26. Jelavich, p. 233.
27. For an impressive list of Allied combatant testimonials regarding Dietrich's widespread positive effect on troop morale, as well as images including the one cited here, see www.marlene dietrich.or.uk/id3.html.

Chapter 13

1. Spoto (*Blue Angel*), p. 269.
2. Hirsch, pp. 85–86.

3. Bach (*Blue Angel*), pp. 367–368.
4. Spoto (*Blue Angel*), p. 245. See also Bach, p. 368.
5. Spoto (*Blue Angel*), p. 253.
6. Louis' creation had been inspired by Rita Hayworth's costume in the film *Salome* (1953). See Spoto (*Blue Angel*), pp. 246–247.
7. Spoto (*Blue Angel*), p. 251.
8. Bach, pp. 367–368.
9. It is important to recall that Dietrich triumphed in Las Vegas after other talented performers had been far less successful there. For example, Frank Sinatra had made his Las Vegas debut in 1951, but this failed to revive his then-sagging career. Only later, particularly, during the 1960s, did Sinatra's name become synonymous with Vegas.
10. Bach, p. 394.
11. Brocken, p. 66.
12. Brocken, pp. 71–72.
13. Spoto, p. 281. The suggestion was originally made by Dietrich's daughter Maria, then strongly endorsed by the professional judgment of Bacharach. See Bach, p. 415.
14. Brocken, p. 70.
15. Brocken, p. 38.
16. Bacharach was later awarded an honorary degree by McGill University in 1972. See Brock, p. 51.
17. Brocken, pp. 42–43. Members of Les Six included Milhaud, Francis Poulenc, Georges Auric, Louis Durey, Arthur Honegger, and Germaine Tailleferre.
18. Milhaud also encouraged Bacharach's fascination with the music of Satie, who had died in 1925, as well as the Dadaist Movement of the Great War. See Brocken, pp. 44–45.
19. It should be added that Bacharach's first wife, singer Paula Stewart (who also had a theatrical and cabaret background), became a cast member for the successful off-Broadway revival of Weill & Brecht's *Threepenny Opera* in 1956. Bacharach and Stewart were a married couple between 1953 and 1959. See Brocken, p. 45.
20. At the Casa Carioca, Bacharach worked with (among others) Italian-American crooner Vito Farnola, later known to the industry as Vic Damone. See Brocken, p. 61.
21. This was Dietrich's first stage appearance in Germany since 1929. See Brocken, p. 70.
22. Excellent biographical information on Bacharach can be found at www.bacharachon line.com; an eagerly-anticipated memoir is due to be published in late 2012 as well.
23. Stevie Wonder remarked on this quality in Bacharach's music to a White House audience in 2012 before launching into an amazing performance of "Alfie"—complete with extended coda and harmonica fantasia. Bacharach, along with lyricist Hal David, was presented with the

prestigious Gershwin Prize at this ceremony (see Chapter 15).

24. Marmorstein, p. 392.

25. A magnificent cover version of Bacharach & David's "Any Day Now" was recorded by Presley during this same period. The song had originally been recorded by Chuck Jackson in 1962.

26. Marcus, p. 127.

27. Marcus, p. 122.

28. One is reminded of the famous anecdote of Dietrich's notorious infatuation for Yul Brenner, with whom she was involved after her Vegas triumph and before meeting Bacharach. While filming the Italian comedy *The Monte Carlo Story* (1957), a story set in the nearest European equivalent to Las Vegas, Dietrich reportedly lied to the production team about needing to take a weekend off in Paris so as to record songs from *Mahagonny*; she in fact had a liaison in Paris with Brenner. See Bach, pp. 378–380.

29. Curiously, Weill & Brecht's *The Rise and Fall of the City of Mahagonny* did not see an American revival on a major stage (New York City's Metropolitan Opera) until 1979, both after Presley's death and Dietrich's retirement.

Chapter 14

1. Riccardi, p. 113.

2. Perhaps the nearest, most comparable instance of a similar phenomenon would be the 1940 Billie Holiday recording of Friedrich Hollaender's "Falling in Love Again."

3. Recording for *Satch Plays Fats* was finished May 1955. George Avakian wrote to Joe Glaser on September 9, 1955 (nine days before the sessions) that he would like to see Louis Armstrong record "the Kurt Weill 'Moritat' ('Ballad of Mack the Knife'...)." Avakian emphasized the song's hit potential in Europe, and mentioned that they already had the score and parts in hand. See Riccardi, p. 112. This letter may have been written after Armstrong agreed to make the recording, and obviously after Turk Murphy had written the arrangement.

4. An instrumental version in France of "Mack the Knife" had been recorded in 1954 by Sidney Bechet, a New Orleans touring veteran of Weimar Germany (see Chapter 2), but it never took off commercially as did Turk Murphy's swing arrangement for Armstrong's All-Stars.

5. *Legend*, p. 159.

6. Riccardi, p. 113. After Armstrong's endorsement, Dick Hyman also agreed to record an instrumental version of the song on harpsichord, but one that is largely forgotten today.

7. Both Ellington and Benny Goodman had played Carnegie Hall before the end of World War II.

8. Modern American composers Steve Reich and Philip Glass also counted among Milhaud's many students.

9. Probably the best known example is Milhaud's *La creation du monde* ("The Creation of the World").

10. Riccardi, pp. 112–113.

11. *Legend*, p. 149.

12. Regarding Lenya's difficulty with swing tempo, Avakian later exclaimed, "I couldn't believe it." See Riccardi, p. 113.

13. Riccardi, pp. 112–113.

14. *Legend*, p. 150.

15. Hirsch, p. 333.

16. Darin's upbeat version can be heard during the opening of the same film.

17. For a very good summary of "Mack the Knife: recordings to date, both vocal and instrumental, see www.jazzstandards.com.

18. Prima performed the song as a medley which included Williams & Graham's "I Ain't Got Nobody." He had recorded it as early as 1945 but the song did not really take off for him until the mid–1950s when it became a regular part of his Las Vegas act.

19. Another memorable versions of "Is That All There Is?" was also been recorded by Tony Bennett (1969) around the same time.

20. Lotte Lenya was known to have praised Leonard Bernstein's *West Side Story* as being in the same spirit as Kurt Weill's music.

21. Riccardi, p. 251.

22. Riccardi, p. 252. Armstrong later rerecorded "Cabaret" in 1967, which today tends to be his better known version (see p. 340, note 20).

23. The electric guitar had first appeared during the 1920s and soon afterwards was put to good use by some very fine jazz musicians (i.e., Charlie Christian, Django Reinhardt), but did not hit its full stride until the post–World War II era, particularly in America and Great Britain.

Chapter 15

1. Brocken, p. 58.

2. Prior recipients include Paul Simon, Stevie Wonder, and Paul McCartney.

3. The performances were aired by PBS on May 21, 2012.

4. Brocken, p. 19.

5. Spoto (*Blue Angel*), p. 289. See also Bach, p. 416.

6. Dietrich also sang Pete Seeger's "Where Have All the Flowers Gone?" in German. See Brocken, p. 69.

7. Brocken, p. 84.

8. Warwick took it upon herself to change

"Martha" to "Michael" over the objections of Hal David, which the lyricist later retracted upon the new version's commercial success. "Kentucky Bluebird" was first recorded as "Message to Martha" by Jerry Butler in 1962.

9. The famously critical Dietrich reportedly took a big liking to Warwick, and the admiration was mutual. See Brocken, p. 72.

10. The song was rumored to have in fact been written specifically for Bob Dylan, whom Bacharach admired (see Chapter 18). See Brocken, p. 72. Brocken also notes that Thomas' 1970 recording of Bacharach's "Everybody's Out of Town" is reminiscent of Kurt Weill's "Alabama-Song" (p. 209).

11. Strictly speaking, Bacharach's first solo album was *Burt Bacharach Plays His Hits*, released on Kapp Records in 1965. Joel Grey and Tony Middleton make guest vocal appearances in this recording.

12. Brocken, p. 14.

13. Bacharach & David's "Kentucky Bluebird" (aka "Message to Martha/Michael") should not be confused with the similar-titled and themed country song by Cook & Wilson.

14. Another good example of this technique is the Bacharach & David composition "Blue on Blue," first recorded by Bobby Vinton in 1963, and the album title of which contains a good overview of diverse uses for the word "blue" in contemporary American pop music.

15. "Tin Pan Alley" originally referred to an actual physical location in Manhattan near Times Square, but later came to signify the entire Broadway musical business establishment. The Brill Building is located north of Times Square.

16. In retrospect, Bacharach and David were both happy with their musical work for the film, which (as usual) was stellar, but the rest of the project was a failure on multiple levels, dragging down the musical soundtrack as part of the same fiasco.

17. Bacharach has since publicly accepted part of the blame for the monumental, but temporary falling out. See NPR *Fresh Air* interview with Terry Gross, May 5, 2010.

18. See www.bacharachonline.com/bacharach_articles, citing "Props for Burt Bacharach" by Skip Heller, *Pulse Magazine*, October 1995.

19. In 2007, however, a fascinating CD of live material, *Marlene Dietrich with the Burt Bacharach Orchestra*, was released on the Bureau B label.

20. Brocken, p. 157.

Chapter 16

1. Garebian, p. x.
2. Kander & Ebb, p. 5.
3. Kander & Ebb, p 7.

4. Kander & Ebb, p. 8.
5. Kander & Ebb, p. 10.
6. The advice was given in specific reference to Frank Sinatra. Late in life, Ebb held up Loesser's *Guys and Dolls* as an inspirational model, comparing favorably to more recent Broadway hits such as *The Lion King* and *Mama Mia*. See Kander & Ebb, pp. 15, 41–42, 105, 223, 226. Loesser's wife in turn was an admirer of Lotte Lenya. See Spoto (*Lenya*), p. 325.

7. Kand & Ebb, p. 32.
8. Leve, p. 15.
9. Leve, p. 259.
10. Leve, p. 16.
11. Leve, p. 17. Streisand recorded two Kander & Ebb songs on her second album in 1963, "My Coloring Book" and "I Don't Care Much."

12. Leve, p. 1.
13. For *Golden Gate*, a story dealing with the aftermath of the great San Francisco earthquake, the songwriters were initially approached with the idea by Fred Ebb's friend, the playwright Richard Morris. The yet-to-be-produced musical has since been rewritten twice, in 1970 and 1982, in hopes that it might one day be staged. See Leve, pp. 38, 239, 243.

14. The musical was based on the 1963 novel by Lester Atwell, *Love Is Just Around the Corner*, set in New York City during the Depression. *Flora, the Red Menace* was the first Broadway musical that dared to deal with Communism, albeit, in a humorous manner. James Leve opined that Kander's music reflects the influence of both Kurt Weill and Marc Blitzstein. See Leve, pp. 171, 175, 180, 183.

15. Liza Minnelli had received good notices for her first off–Broadway show, *Best Foot Forward*, auditioned for *Flora* without telling her agent after hearing two of the songs at Fred Ebb's apartment. She credited Ebb with giving her more confidence as a singer, always having considered herself more of a singing-actress in the cabaret tradition. See Kander & Ebb, pp. x–xi, 43–44. Ebb, with Kay Ballard, first saw Minnelli perform in *Best Foot Forward*. See, p. 305. It obviously helped that her mother Judy Garland had previously recorded one of Ebb's songs ("Heartbroken").

16. Garebian, p. 15.
17. Garebian, pp. 36–37.
18. Garebian here quotes Norman Nandel. See Garebian, p. 15.
19. Garebian, p. 28.
20. Leve, p. 22. See also Garebian, p. 16. Masteroff's Tony nomination had come for his book work on the 1963 musical by Bock & Harnick, *She Loves Me*.
21. Leve, pp. 5, 40.
22. Leve, pp. 37, 39, 68.
23. Garebian, p. 112.

24. Kander & Ebb, p. 60.

25. Hirsch, p. 338. Kander had also found work in 1954 in a production John Gay's *Beggar's Opera*, the original English model for *Threepenny Opera*. See Leve, p. 14. Kander later remarked, "I deliberately stayed away from listening to Kurt Weill." He was reassured by Lenya that his music evoked Weimar Berlin more than Weill. The main similarity, she added jokingly, was that both composers sweated. See Kander & Ebb, p. 69. Kander, while attending Oberlin College, had also worked on an operatic version of *Winterset* by Maxwell Anderson, the same playwright who often collaborated with Weill (p. 127).

26. Kander & Ebb, p. 63. See also Leve (p. 49) and Garebian (p. 68).

27. Leve, pp. 42, 53.

28. Leve, p. 23.

29. Leve, p. 41.

30. Garebian, pp. 40, 44.

31. Garebian, pp. 107, 110.

32. Garebian, pp. 57–58.

33. Garebian, pp. 86, 89.

34. Garebian, p. 96.

35. Spoto (*Lenya*), pp. 285–286. Lenya, though nominated, was denied her second Tony Award, given instead to Barbara Harris in Bock & Harnick's *The Apple Tree*.

36. Kander & Ebb, pp. 64–68.

37. Hirsch, p. 339.

38. Kander & Ebb, pp. 100–101.

39. Billy Wilder was offered the job initially but rejected it because the story hit too close to home for him as a German émigré. Joel Grey later recalled that Fosse worked "as if his career was on the line"—which it probably was at the time. See Garebian, pp. 134, 149.

40. Garebian, p. 135.

41. York amazed onlookers first by convincing Fosse to rewrite parts of the script, then by winning over a very skeptical Liza Minnelli with his resourcefulness on costuming. Prince had recently worked with York on the 1970 British black comedy *Something for Everyone*. See Garebian, pp. 133, 145–146. John Kander's first film soundtrack was written for the same movie as well. See Leve, p. 140.

42. Garebian, p. 150.

43. *Glitter and Doom*, p. 13.

44. Leve, pp. 37, 71.

45. Kael, p. 430.

46. Kael perceptively notes that in the movie the pro-Nazi "Tomorrow Belongs to Me" is the only number filmed outside the cabaret itself. See Kael, p. 433.

47. Kael, p. 431.

48. In terms of mood, Kael writes that "Though it [*Cabaret*] uses camp material, it carries camp to its ultimate vileness — in the m.c.'s mockery of all things human, including himself." See Kael, p. 431.

49. Kael, p. 433.

50. Kael, p. 431.

51. The songwriters were grateful for Sinatra's recording, but slightly put off by his changing the lyrics. Ebb personally preferred Minnelli's recording from the film. See Kander & Ebb, pp. 109–110.

52. As James Leve wrote, "Ebb helped to manufacture the Liza Minnelli persona, in effect transferring his own diva worship of Judy Garland onto her daughter." See Leve, p. 231.

53. Lenya added that she had seen *Chicago* three times. This was long before it became a smash revival during the 1990s. See *Legend*, pp. 223–224. Kander and Ebb, for their part, attended Lenya's last public singing appearance on November 12, 1978, at Avery Fisher Hall, a fundraiser for the American Musical and Dramatic Academy.

54. Leve, pp. 77, 79.

55. Hilariously, in *Colored Lights*, raconteur Fred Ebb heaps nearly 10 pages of abuse on the memory of Bob Fosse, but concludes with deep gratitude by calling him a great genius who played an important role in the phenomenal successes of both *Cabaret* and *Chicago*. See Kander & Ebb, p. 140.

56. Leve, p. 101.

57. Kander & Ebb, p. 171.

58. Kander & Ebb, p. 122. This criticism was probably influenced at least in part by Prince's combative relationship with Fosse, the Prince-Sondheim rivalry with Kander & Ebb during the 1970s, and a protective attitude towards his own considerable accomplishments in *Cabaret*.

59. Kander & Ebb, p. xx. *Kiss of the Spider Woman* also harks back to cabaret's old fascination with Latin America, particularly the Argentine tango. Manuel Puig, the novelist, was known as a tango enthusiast. See Kander & Ebb, p. 179. Kander & Ebb's successful 2007 musical *Curtains* utilized material from an earlier abandoned project titled *Tango Mogador*. See Leve, p. 260.

60. Rivera had earlier won a Tony Award for her performance in Kander & Ebb's *The Rink* in 1984. She was also nominated for her 1975 Velma Kelly role opposite Gwen Verdon's Roxie Hart in *Chicago*.

61. Kander & Ebb, p. 158.

62. Leve, pp. 226–227. See also Kander & Ebb, p. 202.

63. Leve, p. 283. Unfortunately, *The Visit* was being performed at Chicago's Goodman Theatre (starring Chita Rivera) when the 9/11 attacks occurred. Its limited production history has not recovered to date, despite having many artistic merits.

64. Leve, pp. 291, 293. *The Scottsboro Boys* received 12 Tony nominations, but did not win any. Its jarring material may have been too far ahead of the curve for popular taste, not unlike *Chicago* before it.

65. James Leve notes that Kander & Ebb both came of age when Rodgers & Hammerstein dominated musical theater; these works, however, were incapable of responding to the uncertainties and anxieties faced by society from the 1960s going forward. See Leve, p. 3.

Chapter 17

1. *Beatles*, p. 51.

2. Existentialist writers are often credited with placing a newfound emphasis on individual, subjective experiences in life, seemingly in direct opposition to the emotional detachment of "New Objectivity" which had played such a central role in the 1920s *Kabarett* scene of Weimar Berlin. Within the sphere of music, perhaps it would be more accurate to say that the two often complimented one another. Rock and roll, unlike more adult popular music, by its very nature always tended more towards subjective points of view.

3. Coleman, p. 202.

4. There was also a Liverpool group at that time called the Blue Angels. See *Beatles*, pp. 41, 44, 68. See also Coleman, pp. 196, 199.

5. *Beatles*, p. 45. See also Coleman, p. 204.

6. *Beatles*, p. 48. According to anecdotal accounts, during late 1960, members of the Hurricanes and Beatles (including Lennon, McCartney, Starr, and possibly Harrison) combined to make three (now lost) demo recordings, one of which was Kurt Weill's "September Song." This would have been the first time that this number was recorded by rock and roll artists. See www.beatlessource.com/bs/ao-smrtime.html.

7. Lennon later praised the theatrics of Ringo's group: "They really knew how to put on a show." See *Beatles*, pp. 48–49. Undoubtedly, the Beatles learned from the Hurricanes in this regard as they went along.

8. *Beatles*, p. 50. Biographer Ray Coleman credits Lennon with coining the nickname "Exis." See Coleman, p. 215.

9. George Harrison later remarked that "Astrid was the one, really, who influenced our image more than anybody. She made us look good." See *Beatles*, p. 52. Vollmer, however, was an outstanding photographer as well, and many of the early images are credited to him.

10. *Beatles*, p. 47. Ray Coleman notes the claustrophobic, cabaret-like atmosphere (read: alcohol served) of the Beatles' Hamburg playing venues. See Coleman, pp. 205–207.

11. *Beatles*, p. 46.

12. McCartney also noted that "It was a very rich period for experience because we were kids let off the leash." See *Beatles*, pp. 45–46.

13. *Beatles*, p. 68.

14. *Beatles*, p. 73.

15. Lennon, leading the group trend as usual, purchased his first Rickenbacker guitar during the group's initial stint in Germany. See *Beatles*, p. 81.

16. *Beatles*, p. 49.

17. The most famous Beatles recording with Sheridan ("My Bonnie"), in one version, includes a German language lead-in.

18. Best friends Lennon and Sutcliffe were both admirers of Buddy Holly & the Crickets, hence the name "Beatles" with a pun on the word "beat."

19. According to Lennon, the group was still quite rowdy in performance at this point in time, often appearing alongside Little Richard and the Beatles' Liverpudlian cohorts, Gerry & the Pacemakers. See *Beatles*, p. 78. Lennon admired and was influenced by the singing of Gerry Marsden.

20. The slang refers to an aspiring musician traveling to a remote "crossroads" area, where a deal is made with the devil to grant extraordinary abilities in return for possession of the musician's soul. The phrase is thought to have been popularized in relation to the life and art of American bluesman Robert Johnson (1911–1938), whose songs frequently suggest that such a bargain had been made.

21. Coleman, p. 219.

22. *Beatles*, p. 56.

23. Over four decades later, both Bacharach and McCartney would be awarded the prestigious Gershwin Prize for their lifetime achievements in popular music (see Chapter 15). The creative paths of these two artists perhaps first crossed when, under Martin's direction, the Beatles recorded Bacharach's "Baby It's You" in 1963, although they had been performing it since 1961.

24. Spoto (*Blue Angel*), p. 281. See also Bach, p. 412.

25. After Epstein's untimely death from a drug overdose in 1967, the group (and Lennon in particular) began to drift apart. For a good overview of the Beatles' recorded in legacy in German, see www.German.about.com/library/blmus_beatles.htm.

26. By that time, Voorman had established himself as a well-known session player and former bassist for Manfred Mann's group.

27. The lyric phrase "falling in love again" appeared soon afterwards in Lennon's hit song "(Just Like) Starting Over" from *Double Fantasy*, Lennon's last LP in 1980.

28. Songs about substance abuse became part

of the late-1960s music culture, and many of the pioneers in this regard can be found in Weimar *Kabarett* of the 1920s (see Chapter 2).

29. After a long period of unavailability and rumored greatness, a reconstructed and restored version of *The Rolling Stones Rock and Roll Circus* finally became available on DVD in 1996.

30. Filming of the show lasted 15 hours over the course of two days, and the Rolling Stones, along with the audience, were reportedly exhausted by the end. The visual evidence supports this claim.

31. One of the group's earliest and greatest non-conformist anthems was "I'm Not Like Everybody Else," written by Ray Davies and sung by brother Dave.

32. After enjoying a string of influential Top-40 hits beginning with "You Really Got Me" in 1964, the Kinks were banned from touring in the U.S. between 1965 and 1969, reputedly for on-stage rowdiness, a remarkable accusation given the mood of the times.

33. Marcus, p. 111.

Chapter 18

1. Dylan, p. 287. Dylan recalls hearing "Pirate Jenny" at the Theatre de Lys where Lotte Lenya performed in memorable productions of *The Threepenny Opera* and *Brecht on Brecht* between 1954 and 1962. This is possible, but Dylan does not mention Lenya by name; moreover, his girlfriend Suze Rotolo wrote that Dylan in fact saw Micki Grant sing "Pirate Jenny" in rehearsal at the Sheridan Square Playhouse in early 1963. This would have been a new production of *Brecht on Brecht* following the original one starring Lenya in 1961–1962. See Note 10 below. If a conflation by Dylan, then a perfectly understandable one, given the amount of time he has spent in various performing venues over the years.

2. The Beatles and Dylan first met in New York on August 28, 1964.

3. Lisa Appignanesi directly links the German cabaret tradition Bob Dylan's development of the early 1960s "satirical-protest song." See Appignanesi, p. 171.

4. After Dylan played his first Carnegie Hall concert in 1961, Pete Seeger phoned Rotolo and told her that she "...was a muse to an exceptional songwriter and artist." Seeger compared her to his wife Toshi. Rotolo felt honored by the appellation and comparison. See Rotolo, pp. 260–261.

5. Rotolo, pp. 202–203. Rotolo did the artwork for the 1962 issue of *Broadside*, in which Dylan's lyrics for "Blowin' in the Wind" first were printed.

6. Rotolo wrote that "My fascination with Brecht had begun with the cast album of the *Threepenny Opera* that my parents owned." She remembered as a child looking at the LP cover art and the exaggerated makeup of Lotte Lenya and other cast original members: "They certainly didn't look like the women I saw walking around the streets in Queens. The music was raw and raucous and had nothing to do with opera as far as I could tell." See Rotolo, p. 238.

7. Rotolo, pp. 205–206.

8. Rotolo, p. 240.

9. Rotolo, p. 239.

10. Rotolo, p. 236.

11. Rotolo: "I wanted to share with Bob my interest in Brecht.... There was no doubt Bob had heard of Brecht ... but he might not have read anything by him or seen his plays." She noted that Grant's performance as an African-American Pirate Jenny "took on another dimension" with respect to Civil Rights era, adding that "The hour of her ship had come in." See Rotolo, p. 237. Alex Ross mistakenly refers to Dylan witnessing Lenya herself perform "Pirate Jenny," although it is possible this may have occurred at a later date. See Ross, pp. 210–211.

12. Dylan aptly described *Brecht on Brecht* as "...a presentation of songs written by Bertolt Brecht, the antifascist Marxist German poet-playwright whose works were banned in Germany, and Kurt Weill, whose melodies were like a combination of both opera and jazz." Like many of his generation, Dylan's first unknowing exposure to German cabaret, by his own admission, had been with Bobby Darin's 1959 hit recording of "Mack the Knife." See Dylan, pp. 272–273.

13. Dylan, p. 275.

14. For Dylan, the waterfront foghorn image in Weill & Brecht's "Pirate Jenny" resonated, reminding him of his childhood not far from Duluth, Minnesota, located on Lake Superior. Critic Alex Ross also noticed this connection. See Ross, pp. 210–211. To this day, travel to and from Duluth, either by boat or plane, can easily be disrupted by recurring heavy fog.

15. Dylan, p. 276.

16. Dylan's girlfriend Suze Rotolo was also uneasy with the term "singer-songwriter." She later wrote that the categorization probably encouraged a lot of mediocre songwriting: "This was time when the appellation *singer-songwriter* and the term *protest singer* were coined. Both labels seemed confining to me.... It was unfortunate that it became de rigueur for all singers to write songs instead of interpreting the work of other, better songwriters." See Rotolo, p. 248.

17. Ross, pp. 210–211.

18. Prominent figures in the Beat movement included William S. Burroughs, Allen Ginsberg,

and Jack Kerouac. Burroughs would later read Brecht's "What Keeps Mankind Alive?" on the Kurt Weill tribute album *September Songs* (1997).

19. Dylan has written that the basic building blocks for his own early songwriting style consisted of Woody Guthrie, Robert Johnson (recordings courtesy of John Hammond), French Symbolist poet Arthur Rimbaud and the cabaret revue he heard in Greenwich Village (both courtesy of Suze Rotolo).

20. Kaufman, p. 3. A politically radical personality by nature, Guthrie was born on Bastille Day, July 14, 1912, and proudly never shied away from controversy (p. 10).

21. Guthrie's singing partner Maxine Crissman was also known to have "personal politics of standing up for the underdog." See Kaufman, pp. 2–5, 9.

22. Kaufman, pp. 9, 12, 14, 16–17, 22–23.

23. Kaufman, pp. 19, 34–35.

24. Kaufman, p. 136.

25. Seeger later recalled that musically, "My father was the one person I really related to..." See Dunaway, p. 39.

26. Dunaway, pp. 39–40.

27. Ross, pp. 296, 309. See also Dunaway, pp. 48–50.

28. Seeger's own political radicalism had been nurtured from an early age by family ties with the intelligentsia of the New Deal. Even before his birth, an uncle had died during World War I while fighting in the French Foreign Legion.

29. Both numbers are from the LP *Burnt Weeny Sandwich*, released in 1970 but recorded earlier before the (first) breakup of the group.

30. Marcus, p. 99. Randy Newman's uncle Alfred Newman was a pupil of Arnold Schoenberg who wrote, among many other well-known scores for Hollywood, the famous 20th Century–Fox fanfare theme. See also Marmorstein, p. 83.

31. Marcus, p. 99.

32. Unlike say, Weill & Brecht, who used an imagined place setting of Louisiana in *The Seven Deadly Sins* (see Chapter 3), Newman writes everyman songs about the same geographic place ("Louisiana" and "Kingfish") with a tone of authority, having spent part of his childhood there.

33. After the beginning of the second Iraqi War, Texas-native Dixie Chicks lead singer Natalie Maines told a London audience: "...we're ashamed that the President of the United States is from Texas."

34. Ross gives the music of Duke Ellington as an example. See Ross, p. 165.

35. The later tragedy of Robeson's is especially thought-provoking, given that it was he who was forced to repeatedly use the "N" word in the original 1927 production of Kern & Hammerstein's *Show Boat*. Lead Belly's 1937 song

"The Hindenburg Disaster" reflects widespread fascination with early Nazi-era events in America. A more irreverent take on the same tragedy can be found in the Captain Beefheart-Frank Zappa collaboration "The Blimp" (from the 1969 LP *Trout Mask Replica*). Lastly (and perhaps most famously), the image of the Hindenburg disaster became a multiple album logo for British group Led Zeppelin during the late 1960s.

36. Dylan, pp. 82–83.

37. Perhaps the outstanding example in this regard was Edwin Starr's (anti–Vietnam War) mega-hit "War" for Motown in 1969, written by Barrett & Strong. See Marcus, p. 22.

38. Hendrix and the Family Stone performed at the 1969 Woodstock festival and received tremendous mass exposure because of it. Hendrix was essentially a virtuoso bluesman who also happened to admire Dylan. Sly Stone (aka Sylvester Stewart) began his unusual, barrier-crossing career (as noted by Greil Marcus) by playing to the children of transplanted Oklahoma natives in the San Francisco Bay area, the same demographic celebrated by Woody Guthrie in his early work. See Marcus, pp. 69–70. The brash, tumultuous sound of Brown's late 1960s work proved to be the great precursor to hip-hop and, accordingly, the most musically influential over the long term (see Chapter 19).

39. Marcus, pp. 74–77. The self-parody and self-deprecation dominating Sly Stone's *There's a Riot Goin' On* calls to mind similar qualities in cabaret music pioneered by the Dadaist movement (see Chapter 1).

40. Oftentimes these songs were written by professional teams such as Gamble & Huff or Whitfield & Strong, then performed by the recording artist; other artists such as Stevie Wonder or Curtis Mayfield were outstanding exceptions in this regard, performing mostly their own material.

41. Marcus, p. 223.

Chapter 19

1. Smith, p. 178.

2. By the mid–1970s, Bob Dylan had re-established his popular and critical importance as a recording artist with three striking albums, *Planet Waves* (1973), *Before the Flood* (1974), and *Blood on the Tracks* (1974).

3. Smith, pp. 82, 94.

4. Smith, pp. 114, 176.

5. Smith told Mapplethorpe: "...I like this stuff." See Smith, p. 154. The photo is reproduced in the book.

6. Smith, p. 178.

7. Smith, pp. 180–181, 232.

8. Smith also mentions Ava Gardner's film performance in *One Touch of Venus*, from which Weill's song was taken. See Smith, p. 232.

9. Smith, p. 219.

10. Costello had recorded Bacharach songs as early as 1978, with "I Just Don't Know What to Do with Myself" and later in 1999 with "I'll Never Fall in Love Again."

11. During this same era, Hansa by the Wall would also be the recording studio for the German band Tangerine Dream, whose soundtrack work for American movies later received wide exposure. Some of these films included *Sorcerer* (1977), *Thief* (1981), and *Risky Business* (1983). See Marmorstein, p. 400.

12. Eno also worked with the American group Devo in 1978, whose absurdist stage image was a direct throwback to the Dadaist movement.

13. "Rapper's Delight" by the Sugarhill Gang, generally considered the first full-fledged rap hit single, appeared in 1979; the technical innovations leading up to its production, however, had been in the works for some time before that, but with little public exposure outside of New York City.

14. The group's name stands for co-founders Joseph "Run" Simmons and Darryl "DMC" McDaniels, along with Jason "Jam-Master Jay" Mizell.

15. A secondary source for this "gangster" sensibility came from 1960s Jamaican music, later marvelously diversified and brought to a wider audience by Bob Marley & the Wailers. Reggae music proved to be a big influence of many English groups of the 1970s, especially the Clash. The main source, however, came from American soul music of the late 1960s and early 1970s, including James Brown, which to this day is sampled on a regular basis by hip-hop artists.

16. Lauper also covered the Prince-written hit song "When You Were Mine."

17. Vega's album including "Marlene on the Wall" was co-produced by Patti Smith guitarist Lenny Kaye.

18. U2, like its nearest American rival R.E.M., admitted being heavily influenced, despite political differences, by the driving Marxist agit-prop of English new wave band Gang of Four.

19. R.E.M. attempted to reinvent itself with a similar pilgrimage to Berlin for its recent final album, *Collapse into Now* (2011), resulting in some fine recorded music ("Überlin"), but this did not preserve the group, which disbanded shortly afterwards.

20. U2's *Achtung Baby* LP was followed in short order by their worldwide Zoo TV Tour of 1992–1993, a multi-media extravaganza incorporating new ironic and irreverent elements that seemed to hark back to Dadaism and Weimar cabaret revue.

Chapter 20

1. Gay, p. xiii.

2. Lareau, p. 180.

3. Gay, p. xiv, note 2.

4. The poet Kurt Tucholsky agreed with Herrmann-Neiße that audience demands were a big problem; the latter cited Trude Hesterberg's Wild Stage as an ideal model that tried to educate these same audiences by providing them something better. See Lareau, pp. 182–183.

5. The small-scaled literary cabarets of Berlin, with their (at best) small profit-margins, were unable to survive hyperinflation of the German mark during the early 1920s. See Lareau, p. 188.

6. Lareau, p. 188.

7. Lareau, p. 17.

8. Ross, p. 590.

9. Ross gives many contemporary examples of formally trained composers who have enjoyed success in both the classical and popular spheres, similar to George Gershwin before them. See Ross, p. 590.

10. One sees a parallel in the quick evolution of literary *Kabarett* to *Kabarett-revuen* and *Kabarettoper* in Weimar Berlin (to find wider audiences and profits) to artistic and financial struggles of today's alternative artists. For example, the American alternative group Green Day (led by Billie Joe Armstrong) recorded the Grammy-winning *American Idiot* (2004), an outstanding album of politically tinged, Existential angst; not satisfied with its exposure, the group converted the album into a Broadway musical (2010), and now there are rumors of an upcoming film version as well.

11. Sting later starred in a 1989 Broadway production of *The Threepenny Opera*.

12. *LoveMusik* has reportedly been translated into Spanish, German, Hungarian, Hebrew and Japanese.

13. The first Broadway musical revue of this kind was *A Kurt Weill Cabaret* in 1963, recorded by MGM Records and revived in 1979.

14. A German biopic, *Marlene*, was made in 2000, starring Katja Flint and directed by Joseph Vilsmaier.

15. A London West End musical review had also been produced (and recorded) in 1997, titled *Marlene: A Tribute to Dietrich*, starring Siân Phillips.

16. See "Art of cabaret has a visionary in Ute Lemper," by Howard Reich, *Chicago Tribune*, April 15, 2003. This writer witnessed a similar performance by the same artist at the same venue in 1997.

17. Thanks to Stewart Figa for these observations.

18. Garebian, p. 196.

19. Vidal's 1984 novel *Duluth*, an outrageous

send-up of "Morning in America," recalls (among many other things) the Dadaist movement of World War I (see Chapter 1), itself playing a central role in the development of German *Kabarett* during the 1920s.

20. The performance is available on DVD. Bridgewater's stage name is appropriate, as she has made a stellar career of crossing over boundaries and making unlikely but rewarding musical connections.

21. Bridgewater recorded "Mack the Knife" for her 1997 LP *Dear Ella.*

Conclusion

1. Ross, pp. xvii–xviii.

2. The decision of the house band to continue their shows on the road calls to mind Rosa Valetti's decision in Berlin during the early 1920s to close her cabaret Megalomania while keeping its performers active on a rotating basis at other venues.

3. Molly plays a violin that is literally colored red.

4. See DVD, *The Blue Angel* (Criterion Collection), Special Features. A bemused Friedrich Hollaender plays piano for Dietrich during the screen test.

5. Ross, p. 589.

6. See "Learning for Learning's Sake: The Foundation for A Liberal Education" by Christopher B. Nelson, American Council on Education's Magazine *The Presidency* (August 1, 2011).

7. Ross, p. xvii.

Select Bibliography

The existing body of literature on German *Kabarett* culture is rich and extensive, needing little further elaboration. Studies making connections between past and present, however, are surprisingly few. The basic premise is that by studying the influential performing art styles of Weimar Germany, one can then have a better understanding of today's popular culture both in America and across the globe. As Shakespeare wrote, what's past is prologue. To repeat, however, scholarly groundwork has already been laid. In addition to Alex Ross' terrific overview of 20th century music, anyone doubting the moral decay of Weimar Germany rivaling that of our own times need only consult the provocative coffee table picture book *Voluptuous Panic: The Erotic World of Weimar Berlin* by Professor Mel Gordon of Berkeley. The purpose of citing such works is not to appeal to reader prurience, but rather to emphasize the close connection between the breakdown of conventional mores in a particular society and the art forms produced by that society, as British Weimar eyewitness Christopher Isherwood noted perceptively at the time. Books about contemporary artists working within various shades of the cabaret tradition are also plentiful. Once again, however, the emphases of these more recent works tend to be focused away from obvious links to an earlier time and place. This scholarly reticence is perhaps due in part to concern that contemporary artists somehow might be accused of plagiarizing or aping works by earlier predecessors. Lotte Lenya herself personally assured Kander and Ebb at the time of *Cabaret*'s production that this concern was unjustified. I say, why apologize or try to deny the obvious? No one is ever going to accuse Kander and Ebb of being mere imitators of Weill and Brecht any more than the seminal work of Bacharach and David is going to be dismissed simply because they admired the art of Marlene Dietrich. All in all, this aspect of modern popular music, one so often downplayed by its chroniclers, should be played up and highlighted rather than denied, since, thus far at least, many seem too embarrassed or timid to do so. In short, the time has come.

Appignanesi, Lisa. *The Cabaret*. New York: Universe Books, 1976.
Bach, Steven. *Marlene Dietrich: Life and Legend*. New York: William Morrow, 1992.
The Beatles Anthology. San Francisco: Chronicle Books, 2000.
Black, Gregory D. *Hollywood Censored: Morality Codes, Catholics, and the Movies*. New York: Cambridge University Press, 1994.
Bohlman, Philip V. *Jewish Music and Modernity*. New York: Oxford University Press, 2008.
Brocken, Michael. *Bacharach: Maestro! The Life of a Pop Genius*. New Malden, Surrey: Chrome Dreams, 2003.

Cabaret Berlin: Revue, Kabarett and Film Music Between the Wars, Lori Münz, Editor. Hamburg: EarBooks/edel CLASSICS GmbH, 2005.

Coleman, Ray. *Lennon: The Definitive Biography.* New York: McGraw-Hill, 1985.

Dunaway, David King. *How Can I Keep from Singing: Pete Seeger.* New York: McGraw-Hill, 1981.

Dylan, Bob. *Chronicles: Volume One.* New York: Simon & Schuster, 2004.

Farneth, David, ed. *Lenya: The Legend—A Pictorial Autobiography.* Woodstock, NY: Overlook Press, 2009.

Garebian, Keith. *The Making of Cabaret*, second edition. New York: Oxford University Press, 211.

Gay, Peter. *Weimar Culture: The Outsider as Insider.* New York: Harper & Row, 1968.

Gordon, Mel. *The Seven Addictions and Five Professions of Anita Berber: Weimar Berlin's Priestess of Debauchery.* Los Angeles: Feral House, 2006.

_____. *Voluptuous Panic: The Erotic World of Weimar Berlin.* Los Angeles: Feral House, 2000.

Hirsch, Foster. *Kurt Weill on Stage: From Berlin to Broadway.* New York: Knopf, 2002.

Isherwood, Christopher. *The Berlin Stories.* New York: A New Directions Paperback, 1935/1963.

Jelavich, Peter. *Berlin Cabaret.* Cambridge, MA: Harvard University Press, 1993.

Kael, Pauline. *For Keeps: 30 Years at the Movies.* New York: Dutton, 1994.

Kander, John, and Fred Ebb. as told to Greg Lawrence, *Colored Lights: Forty Years of Words and Music, Show Biz, Collaboration, and All That Jazz.* New York: Faber and Faber, 2003.

Kaufman, Will. *Woody Guthrie: American Radical.* Urbana: University of Illinois Press, 2011.

Kowalke, Kim, ed. *A New Orpheus: Essays on Kurt Weill.* New Haven: Yale University Press, 1986.

Lareau, Alan. *The Wild Stage: Literary Cabarets of the Weimar Republic.* Columbia, SC: Camden House, 1995.

Leve, James. *Kander and Ebb.* New Haven: Yale University Press, 2009.

Marcus, Greil. *Mystery Train: Images of America in Rock 'n Roll Music*, Third Revised Edition. New York: Plume/Penguin, 1975/1990.

Marmorstein, Gary. *Hollywood Rhapsody: Movie Music and Its Makers 1900 to 1975.* New York: Schirmer Books, 1997.

Metzger, Rainer, and Christian Brandstätter. *Berlin: The Twenties.* New York: Harry N. Abrams, 2007.

Pescatello, Ann M. *Charles Seeger: A Life in American Music.* Pittsburgh: University of Pittsburgh Press, 1992.

Rewald, Sabine, Ian Buruma, and Matthias Eberle. *Glitter and Doom: German Portraits from the 1920s.* New Haven: Yale University Press, 2006.

Riccardi, Ricky. *What a Wonderful World: The Magic of Louis Armstrong's Later Years.* New York: Pantheon Books, 2011.

Ross, Alex. *The Rest Is Noise: Listening to the Twentieth Century.* Picador, 2007.

Rotolo, Suze. *A Freewheelin' Time: A Memoir of Greenwich Village in the Sixties.* New York: Broadway Books, 2008.

Smith, Patti. *Just Kids.* New York: Harpercollins, 2010.

Spoto, Donald. *Blue Angel: The Life of Marlene Dietrich.* New York: Doubleday, 1992.

_____. *Lenya: A Life.* Boston: Little Brown, 1989.

Sternberg, Josef von. *Fun in a Chinese Laundry.* New York: Macmillan, 1965.

Symonette, Lys, and Kim H. Kowalke, ed. and trans. *Speak Low (When You Speak Love): The Letters of Kurt Weill and Lotte Lenya.* Berkeley: University of California Press, 1996.

Index

227